D0212974

33
66
96

Pressure to learn english + christianity

AMERICANS

Status

Competition

in an

Ethnic Community

PRENTICE-HALL, INC., ENGLEWOOD CLIFFS, NEW JERSEY

GARDNER WEBB COLLEGE LIBRARY

Library of Congress Cataloging in Publication Data

LOPATA, HELENA ZNANIECKI, (date)
  Polish Americans.

  (Ethnic groups in American life)
  Bibliography: p.
  Includes index.
  1. Polish Americans.   I. Title.
E184.P7L66   301.45'19'185073   75–41401
ISBN   0–13–686444–9
ISBN   0–13–686436–8   pbk.

© 1976 by Prentice-Hall, Inc., Englewood Cliffs, New Jersey

*All rights reserved. No part of this book may be
reproduced in any form or by any means without
permission in writing from the publisher.*

10   9   8   7   6   5   4   3   2   1

Printed in the United States of America

PRENTICE-HALL INTERNATIONAL, INC., *London*
PRENTICE-HALL OF AUSTRALIA PTY. LIMITED, *Sydney*
PRENTICE-HALL OF CANADA, LTD., *Toronto*
PRENTICE-HALL OF INDIA PRIVATE LIMITED, *New Delhi*
PRENTICE-HALL OF JAPAN, INC., *Tokyo*
PRENTICE-HALL OF SOUTHEAST ASIA PTE. LTD., *Singapore*

E
184
P7
L66

To Eileen Markley Znaniecki
and the other
Poles
Americans
Polish Americans
Americans of Polish heritage
in my family

Contents

Foreword

As the United States, with its racially and ethnically variegated population, moves through the 1970s, the myths of the melting pot and complete assimilation recede farther and farther into the distance both in this country and abroad. Contrary to the expectations and pronouncements of many social scientists, industrialization and urbanization have not reduced the salience of ethnicity in the modern world, nor is there substantial evidence that ethnicity as a critical issue subsides because it happens to exist within the borders of a particular social system: capitalist, socialist, communist, or some mixture in between. The stubborn persistence of the racial and ethnic factor as a source of ethnic communality, and the conflict of ethnic collectives as interest groups seeking by various means their (frequently previously withheld) fair share of material and status rewards make it all the more imperative that the resources of the sociologist, the political scientist, the historian, the psychologist, the anthropologist, and other practitioners of the art and science of understanding human behavior be brought to bear on the problem. Such application should produce both the theoretical knowledge and the practical measures that would help create a state of affairs where the positive potentialities of ethnic pluralism can be effectively realized while the negative results of unlimited ethnic conflict can be minimized and kept within tolerable bounds.

Thus, the ethnic problem before the American people today is what shape the new pluralism shall take. Is it to be cultural pluralism, with its emphasis on a broad kaleidoscope of ethnic patterns and peoples reaching to the point of conscious promotion of sustained bilingualism? Or is structural pluralism, with its social separation in primary group relationships, to be the dominant mode, with differing cultural heritages to be recognized and maintained by symbolic appropriations and reinterpretations of one's ethnic past? What form and resolution will the political contests take brought on by the black revolt and newly-emphasized ethnic consciousness and sense of pride among Mexican Americans, Puerto Rican Americans, American Indians, and Oriental Americans, together with the probably consequent revival of collective consciousness among the traditional white ethnic groups of European ancestral origin?

The issues around which this new pluralism will form have such names as affirmative action, de jure and de facto segregation, school busing to achieve racial integration, cultural nationalism, community control of local institutions, and breakdown of racial and ethnic barriers to housing, ethnic voting, and confrontation politics; and they are all intimately related to the overriding question of how present-day America deals with the problems of inflation, unemployment, and recession, which fall with particularly heavy impact on its racial minorities.

In order to make the best decisions on these issues, the American of the 1970s needs to be well informed on the history, contributions, and current problems of the racial and ethnic groups that make up the American people, and how the issues highlighted above are affected by, and in turn affect, the nature of the emerging pluralism. The books in this series are designed to provide this information in a scholarly, yet highly accessible, manner. Each book on a particular ethnic group (and we include the white Protestants as such a sociologically definable entity) is written by an expert in the field of intergroup relations and the social life of the group about which he writes. In many cases the author derives ethnically himself or herself from that group. I hope that the publication of this series will aid substantially in the process of enabling Americans to understand more fully what it means to live in a multiethnic society and, concomitantly, what we must do in the future to eliminate the corrosive and devastating phenomena of prejudice and discrimination and to ensure that a pluralistic society can at the same time fulfill its promised destiny of being truly "one nation indivisible."

MILTON M. GORDON

Preface

I find it impossible to write a personal preface within the normal space allotted for such presentations. After all, it took years of several lives to collect all the data and, hopefully, insights.

Much of the literature on the immigrants to America, ethnic communities, assimilation, the hyphenated-Americans, and so forth, has been simplistic and biased. This applies to the writings of early sociologists just as much as to the various commissions appointed to investigate the situation early in the twentieth century (*see* Jones, 1960). A major source of the bias among sociologists was an idealization of the stable village or small community, of Gemeinschaft or primary relations, and of total cooperation involving good, happy, and passively adapted people. From such a vantage point, what was happening in the centers of American cities as they were filling with millions of former villagers was bewildering, even repugnant, warranting predictions of disaster and doom. The sociologists who studied the newly forming ethnic communities in America came from other backgrounds; Park from a small town and a newspaperman's interest in deviancy and dramatic evidences of disorganization, Wirth as a refugee from intelligentsian Germany far removed from the Russian-Jewish *Ghetto*, Thomas with a concern for dramatically maladjusted people, Znaniecki accustomed to relatively stabilized cities and villages, and Zorbaugh, Thrasher, and the many other urbanologists with attention focused on problems and the contrasts between the *Gold Coast and the Slum* (Zorbaugh, 1929).

The observers of immigrant communities in the early years of this century were not looking for a social structure or a gradually emerging fabric, but for indices of a lack of organization and even of disorganization of prior social systems (Thomas and Znaniecki's major theme of 1918–1920 revolved around this point, but so did the works of the other men). Sociologists who followed were really more concerned with life in the *Street Corner Society* (Whyte, 1943) and the processes of assimilation (Drachsler, *Democracy and Assimilation*, 1920; Smith, *Americans in the Making*, 1939, etc.) than in the over-all social system the groups had created. Wirth's *The Ghetto* (1928) is a partial exception to this generalization in that it concentrated on the community. Of course the sociologists were not the only ones concerned with the problems of the immigrants and the ability of the American society to absorb numbers of people whose behavior diverged dramatically from accepted middle class or at least formal Protestant norms. The sociologists, however, certainly helped create a strong and consistent picture of disorganization. Society's concern over immigrants was so strong, and its justification so well documented in the writings of our fellow social scientists, that the flood doors were closed by the quota laws of the twenties and everyone breathed a little easier with the optimistic hope that these *"barbarians"* would settle down and assimilate, *soon*, without untold problems. There were some social scientists like Hourwich (1912) who tried to convince the American public that the immigrants were not the cause of economic problems, and that the industrialization process itself resulted in numerous dislocations (see the discussion in Chapter 4); or Taft (1936) who examined criminal statistics in an effort to calm fears about the crime ridden immigrants, but their voices were not sufficiently strong. Over the years, besides surrounding the ethnic communities with "benign neglect" and telling each other that it was good for "those people" to be in there, sharing warm primary relations along with the good and smelly foods, Americans of non-ethnic identity, or at least of forgotten or allegedly superior ethnic identity tried occasionally and sporadically to "assist" the immigration process. Park (1922) recommended ways of controlling the foreign press, judged dysfunctional to assimilation, and Edith Bowler (1931) advised the National Commission on Law Observance and Enforcement on methods of controlling the foreign-stock crime and juvenile delinquency; but other sociologists turned their attention elsewhere as the depression and World War II emerged on the scene.

The "black is beautiful" and "black power" movements, followed by the "white backlash" in *The Rise of the Unmeltable Ethnics* (Novak, 1972) have brought forth another tendency in the sociological perception of American ethnic communities, the tendency to lump them together. The process by which ethnics are seen as a single mass of people with equal status (see even Kramer, *The Minority Community*, 1970) has several forms. Seen from the perspective of *The Sociological Eye*, but in a simplistic manner that Hughes (1971) would never employ, the ethnic-minority-status communities are presented as internally homogenous, except for generational and some social class differences due to the fact that not everyone moved the same distance and at the same rate up the traditional American status ladder. In addition, several ethnic communities are combined along two lines of demarcation, social class and religion. Novak's (1972) work equates the "unmeltable ethnics" with working class people and norms as does much of the literature concentrating on the working class in general. The third form of combining ethnic groups is a consequence of the continuing concern with the "melting pot," somewhat more diversified than in its original version, thanks to Kennedy (1952), Herberg (1955), and Glazer and Moynihan (1970) in a *Triple Melting Pot*. In spite of Gordon's (1964) insistence on the importance of studying the social structure of each ethnic group, much of the current literature slides into discussions of this supposed triple-melting-pot, without testing its applicability for many groups. The ease with which this theory was accepted is due to two factors. One is the use of individual behavior, particularly of intermarriage, as an index of assimilation; the other is the fact that much of the literature generalizes from the Jewish case where peoples of different ethnic flavor, that was acquired through centuries of life in various national culture societies, melted into a single "Jewish" ethnic community. The other immigrant groups are then combined by the writers into one of the two remaining religious classifications, thus denying their ethnicity entirely.

The Catholic Americans have been attracting more attention in recent years, and some of it has not only a lumping together but also a class-biased flavor. The ethnic communities are seen as problem-ridden, teeming with criminals victimizing ignorant and passive ethnics. This class-biased view of the ethnic community is similar to the one illustrated by Davis, Gardner, and Gardner (1941) about the class perceptions in a community in the *Deep South*. From the vantage point of the intellectual or at least professionally competent sociologist, the ethnic enclave with a Catholic base and its second or third generation "minority" community is thus seen as homogeneous, and mainly concerned with its position *vis-a-vis* similar groups in American society. It is not seen as having a life of its own or a social structure weaving members together.

Much of the recent attention given ethnicity in America uses a theoretical framework dating back to Park's days. Assimilation is being examined from the standpoint of what items of past ethnic culture individuals or family units preserve, without reference to the web of social relations or new cultural items being developed. Seeing change as nothing more than a loss of prior items oversimplifies the ethnic scene.

Other approaches to the ethnic community emanate from other biases. In the case of Polonia, for example, the members of the Polish national culture society who come from Poland, immediately react to Polonia's lack of Polishness by their definition (Nowakowski, 1964, and many others over the years) and predict its demise for this reason. Other intellectuals, visiting or in refugee settlements (Janta, 1957; Symmons-Symonolewicz, 1966a, 1966b, and others of the new emigration) decry

Polonia as a representation of Polish culture because they regard it primarily as a folk community with only traces of national culture. People who were brought up in this community often view the changes within it from individual assimilationistic vantage points, they predict assimilation because of generational or class deviations from the basic folk culture they knew, that was limited to the food, dance, costume, and religious ritual combination (Janta, 1957). The Roman Catholic Church sees Polonia as being a problem from the beginning, while other observers look for future sources of political power as in *The White Ethnic Movement and Ethnic Politics* (Weed, 1973).

Thus, ethnic communities including Polonia, have in the past, and with variations in the present, been examined as social problems, breeding places for social problems, ghettos with all the negative connotations that term elicits, masses of people with the same status position, having identity from their minority position only, having identity from their religion only, centers of primary relations of village-style harmony only, containing rapidly assimilating—or too slowly assimilating—people, and so on, but usually not as social structures with a life of their own. The "hyphenated-Americans" have been treated individually or, rarely, in family units, and examined through census and other surveys for unique characteristics or patterns of change. In such studies they are not examined as members of a social structure, let alone of complex social structures. They are seen as objects of curiosity, as objects of discrimination and prejudice, or as containers of future behavior emanating from current attitudes. Above all, in spite of and even as contained within Novak's (1973) claim of *The Rise of the Unmeltable Ethnics*, they are seen as passive and undifferentiated, except for some variations in Christmas customs. The trait of passivity permeates the very image of the immigrant, valiantly but passively adapting to the problems of his environment (unless he is a rebel), holding back the flood of disorganization with temporary measures only if pushed by necessity, gradually but inevitably being acculturated with the hope of eventual assimilation just to be slapped with prejudice and, now lacking a distinctive culture, turning with his children and grandchildren to others of the same background to create a minority community of psychologically scarred people. The ideal end to this process is seen as a relatively happy adjustment of still passive people, within a "pluralistic" society, living in harmony and peace with fellow ethnics (or at least fellow Catholics, Protestants or Jews).

It is this image (drawn perhaps a bit dramatically since this is the preface in which such an excess is permissible) which I hope to at least partially dispel, taking literally Gordon's (1964:30–31) admonition to study the social structure, not just "the social-psychological sense of peoplehood" of the ethnic group. "By the structure of a society I mean the set of crystallized social relationships which its members have with each other which places them in groups, large or small, permanent or temporary, formally organized or unorganized, and which relates them to the major institutional activities of the society, such as economic and occupational life, religion, marriage and the family, education, government and recreation." We will study the structure of the patterned relations over time, within the community and in its relations to the two broader national culture societies of Poland and America (*see also* Znaniecki, 1952 and 1965). In this work, we can benefit from some of the recent contributions to the study of ethnic communities. Gordon's (1964) analysis of *Assimilation in American Life* provides many theoretical guides to understanding the complexities of the process of integration and internal differentiation of the ethnic groups. The concept of ethclass, by which the ethnic community is divided into social classes within which primary relations and interaction are maintained, is a very useful sociological tool (see definition of concept p. 118, Chapter VI). Suttles' (1968) *Social Construction of the Slum* also provides insights into the ways different groups organize life within adjoining, and even overlapping territories. Also of help are the studies of other ethnic groups, particularly those in this Prentice-Hall series.

Many different methods and techniques were used to research and prepare this study of Polish Americans. These methods involved immersion in the community's activities at several local levels and the superterritorial level at two, or really three, different periods of time. The documents contained within Thomas and Znanecki's (1918–1920) *The Polish Peasant in Europe and America* serves as the first immersion, since the letters, diary, and commentary present detailed pictures of daily personal and group life in the years before 1918. I became immersed in the life of the community on two occasions, between 1950 and 1954, and 1972 through 1974. Primary sources that were used include verbal and written communications by community members and groups, as well as newspaper and other periodical accounts, with participant observation supplying much data on ways in which events are carried forth by different companionate circles. Much of the data contained in this volume come from secondary sources, in which other authors have analyzed primary data and organized their presentation (*see* bibliography).

Any author trying to summarize Polonia in America is bound to be accused of relying too heavily upon Chicago's Polonia. This dependence is partly because it is the largest local community and the headquarters of so many organizations. A major library containing materials on Polonia, records of various organizations, and a "morgue" for periodicals spanning many years is located in this city. One of the few remaining dailies in the Polish language is published here, and Chicago has been the residence of the researchers connected with the Znaniecki family. Attempts were made, however, to cover events and maintain contacts with the local Polonias in other locations, and there are several studies of communities in other parts of the country.

What remains to be stated are the thanks, to the American, Polish, Polish-American, American of Polish descent, American of Polish heritage, and Americans of other heritage families with whom I have discussed at great length the intricacies of ethnicity including the Lopatas, Owsiaks, Burns, Kents, McClures, Benoliels, Jacksons, Kellehers, Hankes, Gutnayers, Blocks, Shures, St. Clair Drakes, Gidynskis, Goldsteins, Schwartzs, Brehms, Petersens, Petersons, Winchs, Greers, Wayne Wheeler, and, naturally, my multiple-identity mother.

There have been several other sociologists, in addition to those mentioned above, to whom I owe thanks. Of special importance are Everett Hughes, Louis Wirth, and Herbert Blumer, forming the dissertation committee which sent me out into Polonia after taking one look at my name, and all the faculty from whom I learned sociology at the Universities of Illinois and Chicago. Professor Abel, Felix Cross, Eugene Kleban, Richard Kolm, Danuta Mostwin, Stanley Piwowarski, The Terleckis, Mr. Alexander Janta and others of the Polish Institute of Arts and Sciences in America with whom I have met on several occasions in conferences and with whom I hope to work in an extended study of Polonian communities, have also been of great help, as have the Polish sociologists Nowakowski, Szczepanski, Piotrowski, and Kurzynowski. Thanks also go to Andrew Greeley and his associates for the work they are doing from which I have been able to learn much about the Polish Americans. I am grateful to Hobby (Robert Habenstein) and Charles Mindel for forcing me to do a chapter on the "Polish Family" thus pushing me back into contact with Polonia, and to Milton Gordon for enlightenment, encouragement, and editing.

Of course, this study could not have been started many years ago or completed now without the help of many individuals and groups of Polonia. My information for the dissertation was collected in the years between 1950 and 1954 with the help of Sabina Logish and George Walter of the Polish Roman Catholic Union Library, and data obtained in recent years with the help of Father Bilinski and his staff. Fathers Ziemba and Chrobot, and Robert Geryk of St. Mary's College and Orchard Lake Center for Polish Studies and Culture, Jan Librach and Franciszek Puslowski of the Polish Institute of Arts and Sciences in America helped me find materials on the Polish Americans. The Polish American leaders who have been specially cooperative include Alojzy Mazewski, Roman Pucinski, Judge Adesko, Mitchell Kobelinski, Adela Lagodzinska, Kazimierz Leonard, Robert Lewandowski, the Drs. Rytel, Father Madaj, and Eugene Kusielewicz. Also helpful were the members of the Legion Mlodych Polek (Legion of Young Polish Women), particularly Anna Migon who assisted on several occasions, the members of the Polish American Congress, the Polish Arts Club, the Council of Polish Arts Clubs, the Polish American Historical Society, the Stowarzyszenie Samopomocu Nowej Emigracji, the Polish American Commercial Club, the Polish Army Veterans Association, the Club Mielec, the Polish Roman Catholic Union, the Polish National Alliance, the Polish Women's Alliance, the Queen Kinga group, Spojnia, the Polish American Club, the Polish Falcons and the Polish Institute of Arts and Sciences in America.

Eileen Markley Znaniecki helped me in many ways during the early stages of the research, including corrections of my English and spelling, after Everett Hughes OKed my dissertation with the comment, "Please find someone who knows English; you do not spell of course—off course." Milton Gordon, Ed Stanford of Prentice-Hall, and three anonymous readers helped with their comments on an earlier draft, and Richard Lopata with the painful process of cutting 130 pages from the "final" draft. Lucille McGill and Carla Christianson helped get it on the printed page in final form and Monica Velasco has earned undying gratitude by the fantastic job she consistently does in juggling everything and meeting deadlines (in spite of the fact that I had promised her she would not have to be involved in this venture so that she could manage the Center for the Comparative Study of Social Roles' other projects).

HELENA ZNANIECKI LOPATA

This book analyzes the life styles of Polish Americans and the history and current life styles of Polonia, the structurally complex ethnic community maintained by them for over a century with the help of changing ideologies and a highly developed status competition. Several basic sociological concepts form the framework for this analysis: Polish Americans, national culture society, political state, ethnic community, life style, and status competition.

POLISH AMERICANS

Identification

A major problem of writing about Polish Americans is identifying the people. There are two main sources of identification: self- and other-imposed labels, and participation in Polonia as an ethnic community. The complexity of the ethnic situation in America and of Polonia as an ethnic community makes the *identifying label* "Polish American" only partially meaningful, but we need it to begin our analysis. Besides, identifying labels have greater significance than just establishing a demographic base in that they form part of self-identity, indicate a sharing of culture with others of the same label, and influence interaction. Being

Background to the Study of Polish Americans

labeled a "Polish Americtan" may affect how a person acts, the traits he or she calls forth in the self and the behavior offered to or received from others.[1] We are concerned here with identifying Polish Americans in order to study them. The content and consequences of ethnic identity upon life styles are discussed in chapter five.

In order to simplify self- and other-identification, let us first examine the duality of identification—as a Pole or as an American—available to someone who migrated from Poland to America. This person can be called a Pole, a Polish American, an American of Polish descent, or an

---

[1] In recent years a number of sociologists have become convinced of the need to de-sex the English language, which has consistently neglected the female half of the human species. Although techniques for de-sexing it have not been fully worked out in mutual consensus, I consider it of sufficient importance to use one of the suggested versions in my own publications.

American of Polish heritage. An added complication is that other Poles, Polish Americans, or Americans may have different labels for that person than he or she has for the self, and different labels may be used at different times by each of these groups. The continuum of identification and labeling made possible by the processes of acculturation and assimilation into American culture and society is given additional depth by the presence of American Polonia as a third unit.

When speaking of Polish Americans we could include all of the estimated 12 million "Americans of Polish descent" quoted by community leaders, including everyone who had at least one ancestor who came from Poland (Mazewski, quoted in Zmurkiewicz, 1972:10). However, there is no way of meaningfully dealing with millions of people who never demonstrate identification as Poles or Polish Americans. We cannot include them in our study if there is no way of locating them and distinguishing between them and people of other ethnic identity. In addition, we cannot use definite population figures because of inadequate methods of gathering initial data about Poles entering as immigrants or going through the generations in this country (see chapter 3).

Descriptions of Polish Americans are made additionally difficult because the prior method of census classification by country or birth neglects religious identity. Thus, there is no way of distinguishing between Jewish and Catholic Poles. The Polish Catholics and the Polish Jews of rural or small town areas, particularly in the land occupied by Russia, had very different cultures and values with divergent consequences for life style, status competition in American settlements, and status mobility. The two groups went in separate directions in life style in America but mathematical medians drawn for the Polish foreign stock population camouflage these.

However, there is a wealth of information available in the historical and current descriptions of the life style of Polonia as an ethnic community. This information is a combination of two sources, demographic facts contained in surveys of the American population and community life descriptions in a variety of Polonian publications which form the base of this book.

Comparison to Other Ethnic Groups

The Poles who immigrated to the United States resembled other migrant groups in that most came from lower-class rural and agricultural areas in the mother country, had little formal education, were confronted with a very foreign country, lacked familiarity with the cosmopolitan world, and had no "calling cards" guaranteeing positive social contact and interaction with the dominant society. They had an advantage over black and oriental immigrants in that they were able to blend in with the general population through the acculturation process (Gordon, 1964). Like other immigrants, they tended to huddle together in urban subcommunities that had clear physical or social boundaries isolating them from the rest of society. And, like other immigrants, they were unable to reproduce the social structure and way of life of their homeland. Gradually, they built marginal local communities of varying degrees of complexity.

The Poles in America are different from other minority groups in several ways. First, they did not plan to settle here, to remain and become "Americanized."[2] They came to earn money, invest in property, and wait for the right opportunity to return to Poland and buy land there which would assure them a desirable social status within the familiar world of a limited reference group. Of course, other migrants had dreamt of returning to the homeland but the Poles displayed an unusual lack of interest in American society and in acquiring traits which could gain them a higher social status here. Since all the ills of life in Poland could be blamed on foreign occupation, the immigrants did not even resent the Polish upper classes as much as the immigrants of other European countries detested the top layers of their home countries. Their relation with the mother country was, in fact, unique and it strongly influenced Polonia's life.

Second, the culture of the Polish immigrants was internally heterogeneous but very divergent from the dominant American culture, so that they were able to build a complex ethnic community while they were unsuited to immediate involvement in the society and easy interaction with its members. The culture was heterogeneous in its social class, regional, and "emigration" wave variations.[3] The pre-World War I "old emigration" immigrants were very different from the World War II induced "new emigration" Poles. An example of the divergence between these complexities of Polish culture and the dominant American culture can be seen in religion. Although their religion was Catholic, they had their own saints, spoke Polish during ceremonies and confessionals, and had special ways of celebrating important events. In America, they immediately entered into conflict with the Roman Catholic church which

---

[2] Although other immigrant groups such as the Italians also felt some reluctance to declare permanent settlement in America, observers of the Polish peasant in America report a firmness of their original commitment to return to Poland (Thomas and Znaniecki, 1958: vol 2: p. 1496).

[3] The Polish Americans definitely distinguish the "old emigration" which came to America prior to World War II (which means mainly around World War I) from the "new emigration" which arrived here during and after World War II. Note the term "emigration" which accentuates the process of leaving the home country rather than of entrance into a new country.

was so strong that part of the community broke away to form a Polish National Catholic church.

Third, the great numbers of Polish immigrants contributed to their social isolation from the rest of the society. Because they were so many, they were able to create relatively self-sufficient local ethnic communities and the combination of their size and community isolation increased the prejudice and discrimination from other groups. They were also the last of the Europeans to enter in such large waves (with the exception of Italians in some areas of the country).

Finally, the complexity of the Polish American ethnic community is unique. The impetus for such a complex structure, founded upon the original heterogeneity of the immigrant and temporary resident population, came from what may be the major characteristic of Polonia: the highly individualistic and competitive status competition. Polonia has not only developed a complex status competitive structure, it has also been able to motivate even second and third generation Polish Americans to concentrate their energies and concerns in this direction. This competition reinforces other community-binding characteristics, feelings of "peoplehood," of minority status, of foreignness, and of sharing a difficult life in the country of settlement (Gordon, 1964).

NATIONAL CULTURE SOCIETIES AND POLITICAL STATES

Polonia, as the Polish American ethnic community is called, is involved in the life of several types of societies. Florian Znaniecki (1952:10-21) developed a four-fold classification of societies which is of special relevance here:

First, *the tribal society*, designated by a distinct name, united by a belief in common ancestors from which its culture was orginally derived, and possessing some degree of social integration. Its culture is traditional and non-literate. A tribe occupies a given territory, although it can change it by migration.

Second, *the political society* or state, which has a common legal system and an organized, independent government controlling all the people who inhabit a definite territory.

Third, *the ecclesiastical society*, which has á common and distinct literary, religious culture and an independent, organized church.

Fourth, *the national culture society*, which has a common and distinct secular, literary culture and an independent organization functioning for the preservation, growth, and expansion of this culture.

Polonia is an ethnic community located in the American national culture society and the American political state, but it was founded on the Polish national culture society. In fact, it was considered by Poles in Poland and by its own nationalistic leaders to be part of the Polish national culture society for many years. Poland existed for a period of 125 years prior to World War I as a national culture society without its own political state because three other states, Russia, Prussia, and Austria partitioned it and occupied its territory, dominating the people. The people of these three territories considered themselves in three provinces of the Polish nation, labeling Polonia in America as the fourth province. Poland also functioned as a national culture society in spite of not having a local government in World War II, the government in exile being located in London and its armies being attached to the armed forces of other political states. The identification of Polonia as the "fourth province of Poland," during many years prior, during, and after World War I had an important influence on this community, illustrating the importance of distinguishing the different types of societies. Its level of Polish patriotism was very high at this period of its history.

Nationalism is the term usually applied to identification with a national culture, to feelings of solidarity with others who share the same national culture and to awareness of having such a common bond (Znaniecki, 1952). It is accompanied by a resistance to denationalization, that is, to being acculturated into other cultures or assimilated into other societies (Gordon, 1964). Societies with a strong national consciousness wish to transmit the shared culture to new generations and sometimes even to people originally from other cultures. This wish is particularly strong among nationalism-developing countries whose leaders try to discourage identification on the tribal, folk, or religious levels and encourage identification on a broader national culture level. Nationalism creates a "common ancestry" for the members of the society (even in the face of inevitable and known biological mixture), and a "national character." Nationalism idealizes the language, customs and total institutions, history, land, and other geographical features of the territory occupied and worked by generations of ancestors. It selects and symbolizes objects of art, science, literature, architecture, and other tangible or ideational cultural traits created by "our people." It tends to increase in threatening times; for example, it was intensified in Poland by the partitions and the wars.

Identification with the political state is being referred to in this volume as "patriotism." Political states are usually controlled by a political party or another group which centralizes power through organized agencies (such as the army, the police, the courts, etc.), and which demands loyalty of citizens. The combination of patriotism and nationalism can be a powerful source of social organization, especially when assisted by mass education. National culture societies often try to obtain control over or create a political state, and then solidify this control by increasing the number of members and by developing intensive education in the national culture. Political states gain support by convincing their members that patriotism is the best means of maintaining the national consciousness. Thus, both political state and national culture society expansion in recent centuries has used psychological pressures as well as political force to change the identification of conquered populations.

Modern national culture societies and political states are so complex that the common cultural overlap may be only a minor part of any subgroup's life. In pre-World War I Poland, for example, the national culture was just beginning to bridge the wide gap between the upper classes and the peasants. Peoples not sharing all of the dominant culture of a national culture society or political state acquire a minority status. According to Wirth:

> We may define a minority as a group of people who because of their physical or cultural characteristics, are singled out from the others in the society in which they live for differential and unequal treatment, and who therefore regard themselves as objects of collective discriminations (1945: 348).

In spite of the divergence of definitions of ethnicity it is possible to combine the characteristics discussed by various authors (Ware, 1937; Gordon, 1964; Kramer, 1970; Breton, 1964; Etzioni, 1959). An ethnic community consists of:

> 1. A group of people, rather than a demographic collectivity, in that they share a culture and a web of relations;
> 2. Sharing an ethnic culture distinctive from the dominant culture, independently developed and limited to this community only, based on a national culture or parts of it of a society living elsewhere, thus evolved as a marginal product combining two or more cultures, as modified by adaptation to a new environment and changing over times;
> 3. Identifying with this culture and with each other through various forms of solidarity;
> 4. Living in a society dominated by a different national culture, or several different cultures;
> 5. Relatively concentrated in residentially distinctive communities, although not necessarily in a single location or set of locations, some members even scattered outside of community centers;
> 6. Containing a network of organizations and informal social relations of varying degrees of institutional completeness so that members *can*, but do not necessarily need to, limit their significant and important interactions to its confines.

The point about the independence, or at least relative independence, of the ethnic community from local territoriality requiring member concentration and institutional centralization and control is an important one in terms of the American society (Etzioni, 1959).

In the case of the ethnic community of Polonia, our discussion can distinguish the following ranges of residential and organizational sub-units. In the first place, there is the local *neighborhood* having a more or less strong concentration of Polish Americans, with some form of institutional network tying together the parish, the local clubs, the social services, etc. People living in the same neighborhood often come into daily contact with each other. The next type of ethnic concentration is the *settlement* which is generally made up of more than one neighborhood and usually has greater institutional completeness. Several such settlements form a *local ethnic community*. A local ethnic community can never operate on the basis of face-to-face contact alone and must develop more complex forms of communication. Between it and the total *ethnic community* there may be *regional* groupings of several local communities and of isolated settlements which are not part of a local community.

American Polonia is united by ties of organization, mass communication, and personal relations and interaction. This ethnic community is differentiated from the Canadian or Australian Polonias in that the society in which it is located adds special flavor to it because of its national structure and culture. Poles in Poland talk of Polonia in general when referring to all the Poles settled outside of the territory occupied centrally by this national culture society. However, the Polonias in different parts of the world have developed different relations with the mother country, depending on mutual interests and its definition of how far they have drifted in culture and identity away from the national ideal.

Polonia in America does not have cultural or structural completeness of the type typical of a national or religious culture society. Nor does it have the political power of a political state, being dependent upon the American dominant society and state. However, it has a life and vitality of its own and it is possible to study those Polish Americans who have and are contributing to this life. As stated before, the only way we can refer to Polish Americans who are not and never have been active in Polonia is through population surveys in which individual ethnic identity, rather than involvement in the ethnic community is elicited.

LIFE STYLE

Each family unit and each independent person weave the aspects of daily life into a fabric sociologists define as life style. A life style is exactly that, the "style" with which individuals or families go through life, which places them into one of several, sometimes overlapping, societal strata and companionate circles of association. As Form and Stone (1970) have pointed out, people and groups vary considerably in the symbols they use to build and identify life styles, but alternate patterns of styles emerge within communities of more than a few families. These patterns are known to inhabitants, and are used as criteria for judgment and association. Components of life styles include place and type of work; the sources and amounts of income; objects such as homes, furniture, cars, or boats, recreational activities; community involvement and relationships to others; rituals connected with eating, loving, and playing; ways of rearing children; deference and demeanor *vis-a-vis* other people, etc.

Local Polonias have evolved a variety of types of life style, packaged in general around social class norms of behavior which are, in current times, not really very different from those of the dominant society. These life styles are reflected in the associations and activities of the various companionate circles (see chapter six).

STATUS COMPETITION

Sociologists have long recognized the presence of status hierarchies and status competition among different social units, individuals, families, organizations, and even nations. However, they have been mainly interested in the effects of such competition upon individuals and social structure.[4]

American literature dealing with status competition is often negatively oriented, contending that it is "undemocratic" or dysfunctional to human happiness and the social system (see Packard, 1959, 1962). In fact, however, such competition can hold a community together and give life meaning to its members. This appears to be the situation in Polonia. Status competition serves as a useful organizing concept in analyzing Polonia because the activity is so fully developed as a system and because it forms an important part of the community life, with both positive and negative consequences.

Social status may be defined as a location assigned to an individual, a social group, or other social object by a larger social unit in a more or less complicated prestige hierarchy. In order to have a status system we need the following conditions:

> 1. A set of criteria of prestige characteristics, i.e., it is more prestigious to own bigger and more expensive things than to own things which are small and inexpensive;

---

[4] There is an extensive literature on status decrystallization, summarized by Burton (1972) in an unpublished dissertation on *Status Consistency and Secondary Stratification Characteristics in an Urban Metropolis*. The concept of identity decrystallization follows the same line of conceptualization.

2. A set of items, i.e., cars, homes, pay checks, etc., which can be measured by the degree to which they have the prestigious characteristics;

3. A hierarchial ladder with defined rungs;

4. A sufficiently precise method of measuring the degree to which a given item possesses the measured characteristic to determine its location on a particular rung in the hierarchical ladder;

5. A method of communicating such locations to relevant persons, who can then combine this knowledge with information on how that item fares in other status hierarchies based on other sets of criteria.

A person is located in a particular status position from his or her location in a combination of the following hierarchies: the prestige of the family into which he or she is born, education, occupation, income, residence, age, sex, race, organizational membership, prestige of associates, family behavior, ownership and use of material objects, and general life style.

In all societies and their subunits, even villages—in spite of the simplistic view of peasant communities so typical of modern sociology—the various sources of status available to any individual or family within a single social class are sufficiently complex and flexible to enable a competition for what may be called "status points" *vis-a-vis* other individuals, families or larger social groups within the community, nation, or cosmopolitan world. Even when the personal status is dependent upon the status of the family unit through generations, an individual may acquire status points or insure the loss of some by others against whom he or she is competing, through the use of the established sources. Often the competition is facilitated by cooperation from close associates who benefit from the rise of the principal status achiever. Families, employees, friends and neighbors may combine efforts to help an individual raise his social position *vis-a-vis* others within the group in which the competition is significant, permissible, or possible, usually because the behavior of people who are identified with them is used by others as a criterion of their own reputation.

The "products" of status ascription or achievement include: a personal and unit "reputation," that is, an overall status as a community-known crystallization of ranks in several status hierarchies; specific advantages (or disadvantages) in daily life and within each social role which come from the overall position; influence or power in interactional scenes which is not based on role-related authority; and access to certain roles, objects, and experiences which are status related.

The process by which a person is placed into a more or less crystallized location is dependent on several social variables. In the first place, there must be a community within which his "reputation" is known, that is, a community of people who share status hierarchies and know him or her well enough to undertake the process of ranking and of communicating the ranks to each other. This is one of the major functions of gossip, the better known one being social control. The dissemination of knowledge about a person, accompanied by weighing of criteria and gradual crystallization of personal status, always in comparison with other persons is accomplished through gossip. The basic unit of status may be a family or group or a town, but there has to be a broader unit which is able to compare the universe of sub-units which are going through the ranking procedures. If we stick to the criterion of "reputation," we see that there is no need to limit status competition to territorially bound communities. Another prerequisite for the status competition is the willingness to enter it and to go through the process of classifying other members of the community.

We should keep in mind that people use only those sources of status which are developed and acknowledged within the community. The fact that other sources of status are available in the broader society, or that the sources used internally are not acceptable to other groups (and can even become sources of prejudice against the community) is evident in any study of intergroup relations. The dominant group establishes its status hierarchies by selecting some aspects of life for positive and others for negative evaluation. What is prestigious among the people of India's Brahmin caste, for example, may not be a source of high status in America. Many an immigrant has been dismayed when the new society found his or her status symbols meaningless or, worse still, repulsive.

Polish Americans are very much interested and involved in status competition on all levels. The complexity, breadth, and decrystallization of traditional status roles has made it possible for most members of the community to compete at different levels. Participation is possible for the immigrant woman who does not speak English or literary Polish, and whose whole life is restricted to her neighborhood. She has many sources for accumulating status points, competing not against men or upper-class women, but against her "almost" peers. The presence of Polonia as a superterritorial ethnic community enables people to obtain reputations within it and even venture out to gain reputations in the Polish and/or American societies directly or as representatives of the community.

Having defined our basic concepts and given a brief background of Polish Americans, we can now examine the socialization processes of Poland and the relations that Polish immigrants developed, maintained, and modified with that national culture society after arriving in America. We then will analyze the life and social organization they developed in their own community, Polonia, and their relationship with American society. Ethnic communities which arose out of a migration from a national culture society into another national or political society must somehow work out all three sets of relations, with the mother country, among themselves internally, and with the host society and its other subunits.

CHAPTER TWO

The relationship of national culture society and political state in Polish history makes Poland a sociologically interesting country. The two types of societies—national and political—do not necessarily exist at the same time and in the same place (Znaniecki, 1952). The Polish political state has extended over many different tribal, folk, and later national culture groups. Its national society has survived without any political state on several occasions. People scattered among many nations and political states have identified with Poland's national society and have interacted with each other across borders and oceans. This phenomenon strongly affected what happened in Polonia.

LIFE IN POLAND

Poland
and Polonia

A Brief History

Szczepanski (1970:6–13) identifies four major periods in Polish history prior to 1772: the *Kingdom Period* (960 to 1138), during which Poland became organized as an independent nation; the *Duchy Period* (1138 to 1320), during which the kingdom dissolved into smaller units lacking a central power; the *Empire Period* (1320–1572), known as Poland's "Golden Age," when the kingdom was unified beginning with the reign of Casimir the Great and became the third largest in Europe (see also Tschan, Grimm, and Squires, 1942:664); and the *Period of Elective Kings* (1572 to 1772) when Poland experienced the first partition. The country was weakened in the years prior to the partition by the introduction of the *liberum veto* in the Sejm (Parliament), allowing any deputy to stop the passage of any bill.

The first partition of Poland between Russia, Prussia and Austria took place in 1772 and the second in 1792. The final partition in 1795 wiped it from the map of Europe as an independent political state. During the period of foreign occupation both Prussia and Russia made efforts to de-Polonize the Polish people by forbidding the use of Polish language in schools, restricting education and, in the case of the Germans, devising various means of getting the Poles off the land. Austria was more lenient with its Polish sector, but the area suffered from a great deal of poverty. As a result of the oppression and poverty, extensive emigration of political refugees, peasants, and landless laborers took place in the years prior to World War I.

During the period of foreign occupation, the national culture society was maintained with the help of the nationalistically conscious intelligentsia and a flexible social organization tying together the Poles in the three provinces and those living as political or economic émigrés abroad. Uprising against the occupying powers led to a great deal of political emigration and the formation of two competing governments-in-exile. Each side defined one of the two major enemies, Russia or Prussia, as the lesser evil with whom cooperation was possible in the struggle for independence.

Poland did not regain this independence until after World War I in 1918. It then immediately plunged into war with Russia to regain lands it considered Polish, settling down to rebuilding the country in 1920. In the interwar years between 1920 and 1939 the Polish government made gains in education, industrialization, and land reform, but the country was not militarily strong enough to stop the invasion by the Nazis in 1939.

World War II tore Poland apart in several ways.

> Poland paid the highest price of all the belligerent nations: of the 35 million prewar citizens of Poland, over 6 million perished; that is 220 out of every 1,000 were killed . . . Only about 66,000 Poles, however, were killed in active battle. The rest died in bombed cities, in prisons, and, above all, in concentration camps" (Szczepanski, 1970:34).

The Nazis considered "untermenschen" all "non-Aryans," in which category they placed both Catholic and Jewish Poles. They organized a complex system of extermination of two categories of Poles: the intelligentsia and approximately 3,000,000 Polish Jews. In addition, they used Poles for labor in several camps in Germany, while "political prisoners" were held in prisons and concentration camps.

Zubrzycki (1956:51–61) lists two main forms of population movements affecting both military personnel and civilians during the war years; the voluntary movement of refugees and forced expulsions and transfers of people by the conquerors; "To the first category there belongs, to begin with, a mass flight of the Polish population before the rapid advance of the German army in September, 1939" (p. 51).

Many of these refugees crossed into Rumania, Hungary and Latvia. Using figures of the International Labour Office and one of the main histories of World War II in Poland, Zubrzycki estimates that there were 32,000 Polish civilians and 70,000 soldiers interned in these countries by the end of 1939. The voluntary movement also included many young Poles who escaped in following years to join the Polish armed forces fighting in other parts of the world.

The mass expulsions and forced transfers included those carried out by the Germans, which "until the end of 1940 affected about 1,500,000 persons (1,200,000 Poles and 300,000 Jews" [p. 52]). "The second mass transfer of this sort was organized by the Soviet Union in the Eastern Areas of Poland between October, 1939 and June, 1941" (p. 52). "The Polish government in exile estimated the number at one and a half million, while the Institute of Jewish Affairs in the U.S.A. put it at two million, of whom 600,000 were Jews." . . . Finally, an estimated 3,500,000 Poles were deported to work in Germany.

Much of the country was destroyed during the World War II invasions and the movement of the Germans across Poland in their attack on the Soviet Union and subsequent retreat. According to Szczepanski (1970: 34) 800,000 Poles died in Warsaw alone, comprising two-thirds of its prewar population, during the battle at the beginning of the war, and the two uprisings. In spite of their losses, the Poles, accustomed to fighting the occupying forces, organized an underground army of 380,000 which was reputedly one of the most efficient in Europe (see Jan Karski, 1944, *Story of a Secret State*). The émigrés formed a government-in-exile, located first in Paris, then in London.

After the war, Poland was taken over by a communist (socialist) government, organized with the help of the Soviet Union and opposed to the government-in-exile. As a result of this political move, many of the refugees, displaced persons, and ex-combatants refused to return to Poland, having very strong feelings against the Soviet Union for its action early in World War II and nationalistic dislike for Russia dating back to the Czarist period. The purposeful extermination of peoples and the refusal of the émigrés to return, left Poland lacking young people, particularly young men, and the top social classes, particularly the intelligentsia.

Since World War II Poland has undergone two political subperiods, the first under a harsh and highly restrictive Stalinistic atmosphere behind the "iron curtain." Poles were not allowed to emigrate or even to travel outside the communist countries, and the society had many characteristics of a police state. Uprisings of workers plus changes in the Soviet and Polish political scenes resulted in a "thawing" of the political control over the society, starting in 1956.[1] Contact with the West resumed, facilitated by the traditional Polish orientation in that direction. Thus, the history of Poland is tied to the history of Europe and to its being a buffer state in a militarily and politically expansionistic world.

Composition of the Population: Minorities

The inhabitants of Poland are not all of Polish extraction:

---

[1] Although Stalin died in 1953, it was not until 1956 and the Poznan riots that the "thaw" was actually felt in Poland (Bethell, 1972:194, 202).

... In round figures, as of January 1, 1939, Poland had 35,500,000 inhabitants, which included approximately 5,000,000 Ukrainians, 1,900,000
White Russians, 800,000 Germans and 3,400,000 Jews (about 400,000 of the
latter listed themselves in the census as being of the Hebrew religion, but
of Polish nationality) (Ehrenpreis and Kridl, 1946:391).

Generally speaking, the changing political boundaries of that part of
Europe, and the strength of political, religious, and national loyalties on
the part of most of the population resulted in an uneasy relation in Poland between the dominant segment composing two-thirds of the population and the different minority groups. The Jews "were granted an
asylum in the more tolerant Polish principalities under charters such as
that conferred by Boleslaw the Pius of Greater Poland in 1264" (Boswell,
1950:105). A large number of Jews immigrated to Poland in the ensuing
centuries, with a variety of backgrounds and manner of settlement, resulting in a highly diversified minority. Their relations with the dominant
group and other minorities went through vicissitudes of cooperation and
hostility, depending on historical events and on their location in rural or
urban areas, within the social class hierarchy, and in the different regions
of Poland. Hostility against the Jews was particularly strong in the eastern part of Poland when under Russian rule. Scattered in villages or the
shtetls of small towns, they were visibly different and retained the posture
of strangers because of the functions they performed for the non-Jewish
community.[2] Jews often undertook commercial and other money exchang-
ing activities forbidden to the Poles and marginal to the Polish peasant
culture, as did the Chinese (Fallers, 1967) and other groups entering a
society to become its middle-men and merchants, operating between the

---

[2] And yet, the nonurban Pole and the nonurban Jew lived very similar lives,
particularly in the Russian occupied part of Poland. *Fiddler on the Roof*, as a play and
movie, captured this feeling of life, and the Europeans who flocked to it and sat with
tears in their eyes were not just Jews. "The shtetl was a collection of ramshackle houses
and mud streets in which several hundred or several thousand people huddled together, excluded, prevented by law from engaging in all normal occupations, yet rub-
bing elbows with the local peasants, who might be huddled in their own ramshackle
houses just a street or two away" (Yaffe, 1969:16). Going through the daily routine of a
harsh life, the two groups crossed paths, sometimes with genuine respect, but more
often with disdain and even open hostility. They shared many values—disapproval of
education for women, patriarchal emphasis on the importance of man's work, strong
negative attitudes toward the *prosty zyd* (plain Jew) or landless peasant, internal status
competition that excluded each other's community, poverty, and insularity (the Pole
was surrounded by fields and a larger structured society outside his range of identification; the Jew was surrounded by the Poles.) They differed in several ways: in their
attitude toward religion and its representatives, in their method of socializing children,
in their value of analytical and literary knowledge, in the value placed on physical
labor and family norms. The Polish peasant at the turn of the twentieth century had
no tools for freeing himself from the class position and subsistence economy into which
he was born. The Jewish child could gain high status within the community regardless
of family background by proving his ability to learn and think. Both had an avenue of
escape from the grinding and anxiety-ridden life—emigration—and both used it.

upper and lower classes. Fictional and sociological descriptions of village life in Poland (Reymont, 1925; Thomas and Znaniecki, 1918–1920) often make reference to the marginal position and function of the Jew. The Polish peasant usually distrusted and feared the person upon whom he was or could be economically dependent. Political officials and the gentry often used the Jews to impose their taxes or enforce the purchase of their products. Both the *Slavonic Encyclopedia* (Roucek, 1949) and *The Cambridge History of Poland* (Reddaway et al., 1950) state that the poverty of the peasants in eastern Poland became so severe at one time that the "results of such a situation were the disastrous happenings after 1658, when the peasants of Eastern provinces joined the Cossacks, who were better off, being armed, and a part of them receiving government pay. Together they started a massacre of the gentry, the Jesuits and the Jews" (Bruckner, 1950:566–567). A second factor which made the relations between the Poles and the Jews especially difficult in eastern Poland was the action of the Russian Czars. Starting in 1881 with the reign of Alexander III, "physical assaults," and "expulsions and limitation of rights of Jews became the order of the day and led to great expulsion from Moscow, 1891 . . . and strict segregation within the limits of the Pale of Settlement," (*Slavonic Encyclopedia*, 1949:553). A third factor contributing to the hostility of the Poles toward the Jews, according to the *Slavonic Encyclopedia*, was the activity of the Catholic Church which, through its councils and parishes, pushed for restrictive legislation.

The Jews living in partitioned Poland under Austrian rule had more rights than did Jews elsewhere. Gradually, more and more Jews moved into cities, contributing to the expanding middle classes and those Poles who had been freed from the medieval restrictions on their occupations. As late as 1939, only "about 10 percent of the Polish Jews, however, regarded themselves as part of the Polish nation and used the Polish language in everyday life" (Ehrenpreis and Kridl, 1946:392). Thus, the vast majority of the Jews was not well assimilated.[3]

---

[3] According to Celia Stopnicka Heller (1973:221–37) studying "Assimilation: A Deviant Pattern Among Jews of Inter-war Poland," there was a group of assimilationists in Poland: "No exact figures exist but one can attempt an estimate on the basis of census data. Thus, I have arrived at the estimate that the assimilationists constituted one-ninth to one-tenth of the Jewish population, which numbered over three million (270,000–300,00 assimilationists). However, this figure has been considered too high by a few historians whom I have consulted; they think that it was between 150,000 and 200,000 but emphasize that there is no way of arriving at an exact figure.

The estimates of what proportion the assimilationists constituted in the various strata of the Jewish population are even looser than the above, for no census or other figures exist as a base. Assimilationists were especially prominent among artists and the top Jewish intellectuals; the latter were among the most prominent intellectuals of Poland. On the basis of the interviews I conducted, I should estimate that as many as 90 percent of the top Jewish intellectuals were assimilationists. Another stratum in

The hostility between the Christian and Jewish Poles is apparent from their failure to form joint ethnic communities in America. The Jews tended to settle with other Jews, regardless of their country of prior settlement. The other minorities in Poland (the Ruthenians, Ukrainians, and Germans) were also alienated from the Poles in America. Only among the intelligentsia in America did the lines of difference and hostility between the Jew and the non-Jew from Poland lessen (Gordon, 1964).

Social Class Structure
in the Twentieth Century

Prior to World War I, there were two separate class systems in Poland, one in the country and one in the city (Thomas and Znaniecki (1918–1920; 1958:128–140).[4] The country hierarchy was still the more important because Poland was an agrarian society. It was made up of:

1. *"A few families of great nobility."* Some had royal or aristocratic titles, but these were obtained from political or religious sources outside of Poland, which operated as a democracy of the nobility and the clergy;
2. *"Numerous middle nobility."*
3. *"Peasant nobility,"* a class found only in Poland, characterized by coats of arms and some political rights, but lacking the financial resources such as serfs or extended lands of the regular nobility.
   a) "village nobility."
   b) "bed nobility" (referring to their small beds of land).
   c) "grey nobility."
4. *"Peasant farmers,"* including:
   a) "crown peasants" (almost completely free but having no political rights).
   b) "church peasants" (under control of the church).
   c) "private serfs" (of landowners, mainly nobility).
5. *Landless peasants,* called "komocniki," who hired themselves out to work on the land of others; regarded as highly inferior since they lacked economic independence.

---

which they were proportionally over-represented was that of the very rich Jews. I should guess that about half of them were assimilationists. But assimilationists were virtually non-existent among the workers, the small traders, and the poor, who were minimally acculturated. Thus, the great distance between the assimilationists and the bulk of the Jewish people was both a class and a cultural distance."

[4] Throughout this book I will use both the date of the original publication of a work which is being referred to and the date of the copy I have available for indicating page numbers. The purpose in using the original date is to remind the reader of the time when the work was initially written, since circumstances, theoretical frameworks, concepts and methods in the social sciences vary considerably in their history. It is important for the reader to realize that a quotation was written in 1921, for example, rather than in 1972 when it was reprinted. Unfortunately, this reference style has not permeated sociological literature.

Szczepanski (1970:23–26) shows how the country hierarchy was woven into a national society hierarchy with the city strata in the interwar years:

1. *Estate owning nobility*, were "highly conscious of their long-held historical role as the leading class of the nation," which includes the first two classes of the country nobility.
2. *Owners of large and medium sized enterprises*, industrial, commercial, and financial; members of this lower-upper class had arrived in this urban strata relatively recently.
3. *The intelligentsia*, "was a highly differentiated and stratified class composed of all kinds of white-collar people and intellectuals."
4. *The middle and lower middle class* (petite bourgeosie), "were the owners of small enterprises—handicrafts, commercial shops, and all kinds of service establishments (11 percent of the population)."
5. *The peasantry*, was "the most numerous class in Polish society during the interwar years;" included owners of all farms up to 50 hectares" (52 percent of the population).
6. "*The working class*, in the Marxist sense of the term—that is, gainfully employed manual workers possessing none of their own tools of work and getting their living from selling their labor" included 20 percent of the population, counting families.
    a) skilled workers, (few in number)
    b) semiskilled, (the most numerous)
    c) unskilled, (mostly domestic servants)
    d) farm laborers on farms and estates, (9 percent of the population)
7. *Various marginal elements*, beggars, vagrants, the permanently unemployed, the mentally retarded who were not under treatment in medical establishments, and the like. Their numbers have never been accurately ascertained.

Special mention must be made again of the intelligentsia and the peasantry and the relation between them. The intelligentsia, different from the American intellectual class, played an important function in the formation of the Polish national culture society through the selection, creation, and integration of cultural items and complexes, through dissemination of this culture to other classes of society, and through the building of national consciousness and solidarity (Znaniecki, 1952). The national culture so developed contained two images of national character, one for the intelligentsia, the other for the peasantry, which influenced the relations between these groups not only in Poland but in America. The intelligentsia's image focused on "the cultured man, participating widely in the nation's cultural heritage, a man with knowledge of history, literature, the arts and good manners" (Szczepanski, 1962:408). Other qualities included individualism, a highly developed feeling of honor and personal dignity, "intransigence to subordination," and inability to organize collectively for any long-term efforts. The image also included a strong emphasis on status competition, patriotism, and national pride, with an overlaying romanticism of the tragic hero who cannot save his country from defeat.

Although these traits define the Polish national character in upper class terms, the peasant image also contains an emphasis on individualism, intransigence, and status competition. The similarity did not help bridge the strong gulf and social distance between the peasant and the intelligentsia (Benet, no date:33). The peasant classes were generally anti-intellectual; education and knowledge were the province of the upper classes.

Status Competition

Movement between the two main Polish social classes was a rare phenomenon. However, the internal structure of a village was socially complex. The Poles developed a set of interwoven relations knit into overlapping networks (Bott, 1957) which were very different from the popular image of a simple village life. The usual portrayal of peasant life in "gemeisschaft terms" of "warmth, intimacy and closeness" (Greeley, 1969:5) ignores the status competition within what Thomas and Znaniecki (1918–1920; see also Reymont, 1925) called the *okolica*.[5] The *okolica* is the area within which a person's reputation is contained, the social area in which the person lives and interacts, the social life space which contains his identities. The *okolica* of the peasant includes the family, home, lands, the village of families, and sometimes other villages. This *okolica* also contains a relatively complicated set of social hierarchies of status sources enabling individual and family competition. Each person is born into a family with a certain position *vis-a-vis* other families within this social area. This status is cumulative and competitive; points are won by the acquisition of new prestige items and lost by the dissipation of such items. Each competitive family member depends upon his or her family to provide him or her with a suitable background, to help acquire objects needed for status competition, and to continue working for the acquisition of new points. Thus, to the extent that each member was locked into the village and could not "make it on his own" and the extent to which daily life and exceptional events were made public through gossip, family soli-

---

[5] Diaz and Potter (1967) do not make such assumptions. "Life in most villages is certainly not a rustic communal paradise. Communities frequently are rent by bitter factional disputes, whether they are between political parties, different lineages, different castes, or merely different clique groups around strong men" (p. 163). But they ignore the possibility that status competition leads to such conflict and alliances.

darity was a necessity, and strong measures of family social control were used to prevent deviations which might shame the family.

The Polish peasant had several means of acquiring status. The most prestigious material object was land, which could be obtained only at a loss to other people, since all that was available for cultivation was already owned by others. Next were the more durable goods—houses, barns, and major tools of work. Third came the less durable possessions such as stock, smaller tools, and clothing. Finally came "income" goods, such as eggs and milk, or home-crafted products which could be sold at market or exchanged for durable goods (Thomas and Znaniecki, 1918–1920; 1958 edition: 156–157).

Marriage was a major means of uniting economic units. It created a new family linked bilaterally with both families of orientation. This new unit was expected to start at the economic status level which the marital partners enjoyed prior to its formation. This was accomplished with the help of both families of orientation through dowries and gifts for daughters and land for sons, if possible. Marriage was not a matter of love, but an arrangement guaranteeing the best status and economic position for the unit.

The final source of status was personal reputation in terms of efficiency, specialization in an admired craft, personality, looks, and behavior within the village, which reinforced the individuality and independence of each person, who was aware of his or her importance as contributor to the family's status. The importance of the personal reputation made the function of shame and continued self- and other-control very important in village life. As Finestone (1964) emphasized, a member of a Polish family had to continually earn his or her right to belong to a family.

This, then, was Poland as a national culture society. Feudal in social organization until very recently, partly as a result of policies of the occupying forces, but partly because of the political strength of the relatively numerous landed nobility or gentry, its class system was polarized between the various strata of peasants and the szlachta or gentry. Its village life was complex and individualistic, containing a family cooperative system of status competition within a geographically circumscribed *okolica*. In the years prior to World War I the situation within which the peasantry and the nobility were living, particularly under the Russian and Prussian occupation, and the poverty problems of both the Russian and Austrian provinces led to a mass and heterogeneous emigration. The political exiles tended first to go to European countries, while the peasants and other emigres went to America. However, as Polonia in America became more established, more and more migration was directed toward it by Poles living elsewhere.

RELATIONS BETWEEN POLAND
AND AMERICA'S POLONIA

A major function of an ethnic community, in addition to organizing itself and developing an internal structure, is to establish, maintain, and modify relations with its country of origin and its country of settlement. Organized, patterned relations require an ideology explaining the position of the community in both societies, the initiation and maintenance of selected types of relations, and their assimilation into the life style of the society of settlement.

Both the formal and the informal relations of an ethnic community with its country of origin and country of settlement are affected by a number of factors. Immigration and emigration laws influence the size and composition of the ethnic community, as evidenced by the contrast in the proportion of orientals in Hawaii and Australia. The comparative forms of economic and political development in both societies also affect the segments of the population who migrate and how they are able to adjust to the new environment. Had Poland not been under foreign occupation at different times during its recent life, the Polonian communities throughout the world would not have been as strongly influenced by the presence of a heterogeneous and numerous, temporary, or even permanent group of nationalistically oriented people who helped build the complex and patriotically oriented social structure. Finally, either one of the two societies may try to influence the other through manipulation of the ethnic community. Poland's interest in American Polonia has been strongly affected by its location in a powerful state.

The amount of influence exerted by Poland upon Polonia as an ethnic community, Polonia's ideology concerning this influence, and the changes in relations are due to several factors. Early in Polonia's life Poland was idealized by individual Polish Americans as the land of their birth, or of the birth of their parents or grandparents. It was the source of a shared culture, and Polish Americans were able to identify with a village in Poland without learning a new language and culture, both requirements of identification with America. Concentrated ethnic settlement made access to the Polish Americans easy for political leaders from Poland. The complexity of Polonia as a community increased the ability of the leaders to influence their small parish or mutual aid societies. Poland needed Polonia several times in its history and set out purposely to influence its members into active involvement in its problems. The drama and worldwide aspects of its political situation added excitement to life and new sources of internal status competition. The communication and movement back and forth across the ocean, and the size of the group maintaining contact insured that what happened in Poland was part of the daily life of Polonia.

Creation of the Fourth
Province of Poland

As the efforts by its nationalistic and political leaders to free Poland from occupation by Russia, Prussia, and Austria intensified prior to World War I, these leaders turned their attention to Polonia in America. They needed three things from Polonia: money, military forces, and political pressure on political states, mainly America. Awareness that concerted effort to involve Polonia could bring these benefits came from three facts about Polonia. First, the Polish Americans had been working hard in the expanding economic system and had been amassing funds that could be used in the fight for independence. Second, the emigration had been drawing young men away from Poland, thereby depleting the reservoir of men for the armed services when the expected war actually broke out. Third, the Polish Americans had already influenced President Wilson by forcing him to apologize for the very negative statement about them in his *History of the American People* (1902) written prior to his political involvement. The nationalistic and politically oriented Poles wanted the Polish Americans to continue exerting pressure on President Wilson so that he would force the European powers to return Poland as a political state.

A major problem facing the political leaders of Poland, living in that country or as exiles elsewhere, in their efforts to influence Polonia to help them with money, men, and political pressure was the absence of nationalism or even patriotism among the majority of peasant immigrants in America. Their identification with Poland was very personal and not nationalistic; they did not know much of the national culture or feel solidarity with other Poles, particularly of other social classes. Their identification with Poland was restricted to a very small segment of its land and people. This does not mean that nationalism was completely absent in Polonia, only that it was limited to the upper classes and educated members.

The political leaders of Poland capitalized on four characteristics of Polish American identification in their efforts to convince Polonia to make serious commitments to the fight for independence: identity with the people back home, their plans on returning to Poland once it became established, the ability to blame all past ills in the mother country on the foreign oppressors instead of the upper classes, and concern with status competition. Representatives of the social classes who had completely ignored the peasant as a conational in the home country and in Polonia's past now offered many symbols of attention and forms of status. Paderewski, an internationally famous pianist, played for Polish American audiences after having visited President Wilson in the White House. Polish immigrants and their children were easily convinced that their status in the mother land would be improved by their known sacrifices during the struggle for political independence, and that they would have a free state to return to when they collected their new wealth. Improvement of the status of Polonia in America was promised with the reestablishment of Poland as an independent European power. The emotional fervor aroused in Polonia by these arguments is documented in reports of meetings, the Polish language press, and constitutions and congresses of new groups. And so the peasants, most of whom entered America with less than 50 dollars in their possession, contributed millions of dollars both personally, by sending relief to friends and relatives, and through organized action of political groups. Jan Smulski, president of the Polish National Department, created just before World War I, estimated that American Poles "altogether had channelled over $20,000,000 into all aspects of the Polish cause." This figure did not include the $67,000,000 they bought in American Liberty Bonds during the war (Renkiewicz, 1973:21). The money went to support the governments-in-exile and the fighting when war broke out. Not only money, but military men were contributed by Polonia to Poland's fight for freedom. Thanks to the cooperation of the United States and France, recruitment for the Polish Army in France started in America in 1917 and resulted in the formation of a division of 28,000 volunteers. Finally the political pressure, whether applied more effectively by the Polish Americans or by the friendship which developed between Paderewski and American political leaders, resulted in President Wilson's decision that Poland should regain its political independence after the war (see *The Cambridge History of Poland* and Gerson's *Woodrow Wilson and the Rebirth of Poland*, 1914–1920). The thirteenth of Wilson's fourteen points establishing the political world after the war read:

> An independent Polish state should be erected, which should include the territories inhabited by indisputably Polish populations, which should be assured a free and secure access to the sea, and whose political and economic independence and territorial integrity should be guaranteed by international covenant (Gerson, 1953:84).

Thus, from *okolica*-bound peasants, parish and mutual aid club members, the Polish Americans expanded their horizons in two decades to become identified as the "fourth province of Poland." They contributed to Poland's political rebirth through intensive effort and a willingness to part with money that was being saved for their most important status symbols—land and durable property. Their action was a reflection of political patriotism and an emotional response to dynamic leadership, despite the fact that they did not identify with the parties, ideologies, or internal struggle in Poland. They were simply interested in restoring Poland as a nation protected by a political state, in helping victims of the war, and in gaining status rewards in the process.

Withdrawal of Identification
as the Fourth Province
of Poland

The Polish Americans continued to send relief money to help Poland rebuild itself after World War I, investing $18,472,800 in government bonds and millions more in new businesses (Wachtl, 1944). However, in the years following 1918, Polonia gradually became disenchanted with the Polish state and began to withdraw its identification and its economic contributions (Lopata, 1954). A major factor in this disenchantment was disappointment in the response to its efforts. Members who felt they had been sacrificing their own life styles and delaying their hopes for a better life continued to be inundated with requests for funds, visitors or repatriates to Poland found themselves still treated as peasants even if they could buy status symbols, and former members of the Polish armed forces were disappointed in their rewards. Poland lost interest in Polonia, turning to its internal problems. From the point of view of social psychology, this disenchantment was inevitable, but it was accompanied by much anger and bitterness.

A last major factor in the separation of the fourth province of Poland from the rest of the nation was the impossibility of maintaining a similar life style and culture. The Polish Americans had been gradually, and often unconsciously, Americanizing and creating their own ethnic culture. Poland also changed, becoming very different from the Poland of the immigrant's memories. The withdrawal of identification with Poland was so complete that, during a 1934 convention of the World Alliance of Poles from Abroad, the demand that representatives of organizations in other countries swear allegiance to Poland was met with indignation by the Polish Americans. The delegation refused to sign such a pledge, declaring that Polonia was an "inseparable, harmonious part of the American nation, however tied to Poland by feeling, traditions and cultural ties" (Haiman, 1948:427).

During the 1930s, Polonia maintained contact with Poland in three different ways. The first was personal interaction, correspondence, and, less frequently, visits back and forth of families and friends. Immigration fell below the Polish quota because most of the close relatives of earlier immigrants had already gone to America before the quota system was put into effect and because of the American depression. The second method of contact was through organized excursions aimed at familiarizing people with nationally significant symbols of Poland, allowing for personal contact, and obtaining official recognition. Third, various groups sponsored events involving both countries. The Polish Americans who returned to Poland after it regained political independence formed organizations to maintain contact and encourage participation in celebrations involving groups on both continents.

World War II
and Its Aftermath

World War II revived Polonia's interest in Poland as a national culture society, a political state, and a victim of Nazi persecution. However, there was much less direct involvement in helping Poland than there was during World War I, reflecting Polonia's Americanization and concern with America's war problems. Arrangements were again made by the Polish government-in-exile with the United States government to recruit Americans of Polish descent to join Polish divisions attached to the French armed services. General Sikorski, chief of staff, who fled Poland during the invasion, and even the aging Paderewski (who died June 29, 1941) came to America, touring Polonia and urging men to enlist. A training camp was opened to use for the planned Kosciuszko Legion in Canada, but the recruitment was not successful and only a handful of Polish Americans ended up in Europe as part of the Polish forces. This situation produced mutual recriminations and the strong attack on Polonia simply angered the community. *Dziennik Zwiazkowy*, the Polish National Alliance daily newspaper, summarized the atmosphere by stating "We have our own problems" (Wachtl, 1944:421). It is probable that the Americanization process had been so extensive in Polonia that few young men were motivated to join what was to them a "foreign army," speaking Polish, and sharing a cultural background different from that of the descendants of the immigrants.

However, the humanitarian interest of Polonias all over the world in helping their relatives, friends, and even unknown Poles resulted in intensive relief work during the war years. Millions of dollars of medicines and other medical equipment, food, and clothing were sent through all available channels.

With the establishment of a communist government under the influence of the Soviet Union after World War II, official contact between

Poland and Polonia practically ceased. Even the Polish governmental representatives in America were shunned, partly because of anticommunism, and partly because of fear of political reprisals on relatives in Poland if anticommunist activities became known to the political powers in that country. Humanitarian efforts continued to be directed toward Poland, particularly after the political thaw of 1956. Many of Poland's families were dependent upon the food and clothing they received for many years after the war. In addition, Polonia organized a variety of other efforts. Some clubs and local groups "adopted" a Polish village or orphanage and sent money, tools, supplies, and equipment to it. Other organizations bought hospital equipment, school furnishings, and any other items needed to reestablish the basic activities of a society. Books were collected to replace volumes burned by the Nazis or destroyed in the war. The rebuilding of Warsaw and other cities and towns was accomplished partly with funds from America.

In the political arena, Polonia concentrated on three sets of activities: protests against the Yalta treaty which gave lands considered by the Poles to be historically theirs to the Russians, efforts at pressuring American political figures to demand the "freeing" of Poland from the communist rule, and an arrangement for screening and processing Polish displaced persons, ex-combatants, and families who were allowed to enter the United States by special presidential or congressional acts. Feelings in Polonia during the years following World War II ran high and were heavily anticommunist; the community organized numerous activities in its attempts to get America to change its commitment to the Yalta treaty and to somehow rid Poland of its government. The efforts were not successful, in terms of their effect on governmental policy, but they unified the community on that issue, within its continued competition among groups. It brought information as to the mistreatment of Poles under the system to the society's attention.

One of the situations which resulted in an increase of Polonia's orientation toward the Polish national culture society in the 1940s and 1950s was the presence all over the world of a very large number of displaced persons and ex-combatants who refused to go back to Poland. Help to the displaced persons released from concentration and labor camps by the allied forces and to the ex-combatants and their families now living primarily in England and France operated on many levels. The most immediate was provision of food, clothing and medicine. Secondly, the newly formed (1944) Polish-American Congress put extensive pressure on the American government, aided by the humanitarian appeal of the cause, to permit those people who were uprooted and who did not wish to return to Poland to enter this country. The government did respond with several specific acts, on the condition that an elaborate set of procedures were developed to screen out undesirable immigrants, those having dangerous or dependency producing illnesses, and those known as communist sympathizers or activists. The entrants, who were not only Poles but other Europeans, needed guarantees from American residents. This condition created some problems, because many Polish Americans were afraid to sign such guarantees, and relief organizations had to take over the process.[6]

The presence of the newly arrived refugees, displaced persons, and ex-combatants changed Polonia's orientation toward Poland and the internal life of the community in many ways. The new emigration was very different from the old, having been brought up in an independent Poland, with a more urban and better educated population, having undergone the uprooting experiences of the war, labor and concentration camps, and often knowing English from years of residence in Great Britain. The members of this emigration considered the members of the established Polonia as of peasant background, lacking knowledge of Polish culture and using archaic, folk, and Americanized language and social skills. They made the old emigration and its descendants realize how much they had already acculturated and also made them very angry. The term "DP," applied to the new emigration, acquired a derogatory flavor, implying brutalization by the war and a lack of sophistication in American ways. The common concerns of both emigrations was anticommunism and an interest in Poland. The intelligentsia of the new emigration, shocked at the lack of knowledge of the Polish national culture, began a process of "educating" Polonia through the development of new activities and through the press. Although the new emigration created conflict and competition within Polonia, it influenced the orientation and continued interest in Poland, laying foundations for current attitudes.

Relations with Poland Today

As the Polish society resumed its functioning in rebuilt or newly created structures, the requests for help from Polonia began to shift from the basics of life to luxury items. Used clothing became redefined as less prestigious than new, doubleknit polyesters replaced nylon as desired gifts, and American "Levis" have recently become so popular that no other blue jeans are desired.

---

[6] Most of these displaced persons were sponsored by voluntary associations within different nationality communities. Most of Polonia's work was channeled through the Polish American Immigration and Relief Committee, headquartered in New York but with an active branch in Chicago.

Some of the requests from Poland (expressed through private correspondence, asked of visitors, and solicited through organizations) are met with bitterness and anger by some Polish Americans. Newspaper editorials occasionally complain about the demands, and personal interviews with Polish Americans document many instances of irritation. Puacz (1972) explains that Poles still see America as a wealthy uncle, as demonstrated in their reaction to Nixon's visit in 1972. The Poles in Poland, long deprived of luxury items, feel that their rich relatives should not begrudge them. But the Polonians are irritated by the continuation of demands for such an extensive period of time after having sacrificed much of their income to help in emergencies.

In addition to obtaining luxury items, Poland is now concentrating on re-creating items of national culture. In recent years, Poland rebuilt a famous palace in Warsaw with funds obtained from America and work volunteered by many Polish groups. The "thawed" communist government is even encouraging and contributing to the rebuilding of churches —not as symbols of Catholicism but as tourist attractions and symbols of the national culture. With the gradual lifting of the iron curtain, contact with Poland in other than humanitarian ways has become reestablished. By the 1970s, a brisk intercontinental traffic has developed. Voluntary organizations arrange for "excursions" to Poland and numerous travel agencies have sprung up in the various settlements. Tourism is becoming a major industry in Poland, most of the visitors still being the emigrants and their descendants. The government is encouraging this movement by removing the obstacles to travel, arranging for international scientific conferences, building additional housing and eating facilities, and re-building historical and cultural attractions. Summer is becoming a season of completely booked hotels and congestion in restaurants.

Thus, contact with Poland has increased considerably in recent years. An organization now exists within Poland (the "Polonia" Society) which unites Polonias around the world. It has held four congresses to date in Poland, with representatives from many organizations in the United States, Australia, Brazil, Canada, and France. Within the last few years the Polonia Society has gained 2,000 individual memberships from "civic leaders in 76 countries of the West" and it keeps in contact with schools and the press (*Dziennik Zwiazkowy*, June 25, 1973:3). Other contacts with Poland include tours for special purposes. For example, the Association of Doctors of Polonia of Detroit visited medical facilities in 1973, particularly those built and equipped with Polish American funds. Cooperative activity between Poland and the Association of Doctors of American Polonia has included comparative research with the help of funds provided by the American Public Law 480 (*Dziennik Zwiazkowy*, June 30, 1973:3).

In addition to increased travel to Poland, Poles are more frequently coming to America. Of great interest to many Polish Americans are the performances of Polish sports teams in international competition or as they tour the United States in local competition. Concerts by leading musicians, operas, and theatrical performances draw large audiences in Polonia's local communities. The "temporary emigrants," who are also increasing in number, enter as students or guests of relatives or other Americans. The American government has been charging that these visitors often come for extended times and work for money, although legally forbidden to do so.[7]

Travel restrictions have lessened, but they still exist. Visitors to America are required to have officially documented invitations and there is still a screening process by American embassies to prevent the entrance of "undesirables." Travel agencies and authorized dealers assist in making the necessary arrangements, such as invitations in proper form to relatives or friends for temporary or permanent stays. They usually provide such services as translation of documents, settlement of matters requiring knowledge of Polish laws, prolongation of passports and visas, and even arrangement for adoption of Polish children. They assist retired people in organizing their settlement in Poland with a guaranteed receipt of American Social Security payments. All these services reflect the dramatic changes in the relations between Polonia and Poland since the early postwar years (see Chicago *Sun-Times Midwest Magazine*, 1973, for interviews with Polish American retirees in Poland).

Polish Americans are affected by the contact with visitors from Poland, in personal, official, or scientific exchanges. Such visits sometimes strain relations and produce ambivalent reactions. Criticism of America brings out the Americanized identity of Polonians and negative comments by Americans bring forth the Polish identity in the Poles. Polish Americans feel that the Poles do not understand them or America, while Poles view Polonia as a limited community with little remaining Polishness. Nowakowski, a Polish sociologist who spent several months in America, concluded that people on both sides of the ocean have mistaken pictures of each other, in spite of the expanded contact (1964:34–35). Many Polish

---

[7] Polonian leaders have recently accused the American government of discriminating against the Poles by refusing them visas in the embassy in Warsaw. Congressman John Dingell (1974) wrote to Secretary of State Henry Kissinger claiming that in 1969 only 865 visas were refused while in 1973 there were 6,853 such refusals (unfortunately no mention is made of the total number of applications). The State Department of the United States government had "alleged that a growing number of Poles on visitor visas have been apprehended working illegally in the United States, as well as attempting to change their status from visitor to immigrant," and referred to the situation as the "Polish problem." The letter did not deny the practice, but insisted that the visa refusals were discriminatory.

Americans still visualize Poland as a poor and backward country with a nineteenth century social structure. The Poles, on the other hand, according to Nowakowski, see Polish Americans as Polish patriots who are interested in constantly coming to Poland's aid. Finding an absence of knowledge of even the Polish language, Nowakowski concluded that any help that Polonia gave to Poland was not a result of patriotism growing out of nationalism (see also Tryfan, 1973). The Polish Americans are aware of the judgment by Polish visitors concerning their lack of Polishness. Personal contacts with the visitors, interaction at public events, and stories in the ethnic press provide such data. Usually, the judgments are met with anger (Lopata, 1954), but they may also assist the leaders in their efforts to turn to community toward the Polish national culture.

The expanded contact between Poles and Polish Americans has resulted in a double-bind effect when carried out in conjunction with Polonia's official anticommunist stand. In the 1970s, the Polish American Congress still organizes official protests, sends memorandums, and applies political pressure on America and the United Nations to change the Polish government (see details of activities in chapter four). The motto of the newspaper which advertizes all forms of interaction with Poland still reads, "Remember that since the Polish nation is forced into silence, the *Alliance Daily* is its Free Voice." Anticommunist sentiment is still prevalent in Polonia and one of the most damning judgments of a member is that he is "pink."

The presence of this double-bind position in Polonia is acknowledged by its leaders.[8] Stypulkowski (1970:1) reiterates the Polish American Congress' stance against communism, distinguishing between the "ultimate goal" and the "practical propositions within the framework of the present international situation." The *"ultimate goal* for the overwhelming majority of the Polish community and for the whole Polish nation, consists in the recovery of external political independence and internal freedom. . . ."* A decision to separate the Polish nation and the "alien government imposed on it by force," was made at a conference of "practitioners and theorists of politics," called together by the

---

[8] The president of the Polish American Congress, (Dziennik Zwiazkowy, Sept. 19, 1973:2), explained the continued anticommunistic stances as helpful to Poles. "Some say that they are hurting our country by criticizing its government. This is a lie, thrown up by the communistic propaganda. Our sisters and brothers in Poland want us to tell the truth to the world of their lot . . ." (p. 2). This Polonian leader feels that "pressure on the regime in Warsaw to meet its obligations to the people" is productive and has resulted in such achievements as an agreement to build more churches in new communities, relaxing of censorship of the press and publications, noninterference with the religious education of the youth, conservation of historical monuments and artistic objects, lifting of censorship of letters, reduction of the tax on packages entering Poland, and return "to the Polish nation of the beautiful Panorama by Raclawski."

president of the Polish American Congress in Washington in 1970. These experts concluded that "it would be wrong to overlook and deny the existence of the Polish state, which is the home of almost 33 million Poles and which, however circumscribed in its domestic and international activities, offers basic conditions for the nation's survival and for the protection of national interests." Yet, the "PAC must continue to withhold its moral recognition and support of this regime," by implication advising readers to refrain from political involvement (*Polish American Congress Newsletter*, July 20, 1970:7–8).

SUMMARY

Poland has been a buffer state between two political states, that have become increasingly centralized and expansionistic since at least the 17th century. Having gone through a successful expansion during its "Golden Age," the Polish state weakened through the inaction forced by the complete democratization of the upper classes' participation in the Sejm, or parliament. Each member of the nobility and clergy could stop any official action through the use of the *libertum veto*. Partitioned by Russia, Prussia, and Austria, it remained under foreign occupation for 125 years until after World War I. The national culture society was maintained during this time by the political leaders and the nationalistically oriented nobility. Life in the villages, where a high proportion of Poles were living, involved a complex system of status competition, with multiple sources of status and individualistic personal reputation assisted by strong family solidarity. However, poverty and oppression by the occupying powers led increasing numbers of peasants to economic emigration, first to other parts of Europe and then, before the turn of the century, to America. Simultaneously, the szchlata, or gentry, and some of the urban dwellers were pushed out of the country because of their political activity, so that the emigrants and temporary émigrés who came to America were a heterogeneous lot.

For over a century Polonia has been involved in the life of Poland as a national culture society and as a political state. This involvement has been modified over time by Poland's efforts to influence Polonia toward nationalistic identification with the Poles in the three provinces under occupation, or at least to assist in the struggle for independence. Capitalizing on the Polish American identification with the *okolica* back home and the people within it, with some aspects of Polish folk culture, and the desire for status, these leaders were able to obtain from Polonia large sums of money, a division of men, and the use of political pressure on American government officials in the Polish cause, prior to and during World War I. These accomplishments were made in spite of the fact

that the peasant members of the old emigration never became nationalists, familiar and idealistically identified with the Polish national culture.
Theirs, and their descendants' "Polishness" remained that of local, folk
level.

The peak of identification with Poland occurred in the years surrounding World War I. During this time Polonia called itself "the fourth
province" of Poland. This was followed by disenchantment and a withdrawal from involvement in Polish affairs, accompanied by bitterness and
resentment. World War II produced humanitarian efforts at relief, continued in the rebuilding period in spite of the formation of a communist
government in Poland, while Polonia became highly anticommunist.
Recent years have brought an increase in personal contact with Poles in
Poland through correspondence, the sending of help and gifts, and travel.
In spite of these contacts, there remains an anticommunist sentiment in
Polonia, and an ignorance of each other and of the culture in which Polonia and Poland are embedded. There is, simultaneously, an increasing
awareness that the two cultures are different and a movement in Polonia,
with the help of the new emigration and the third generation of the old
emigration, to make its culture more like that of the Polish national
culture.

In the meantime, of course, Polonia has developed, maintained, and
modified its own structure and way of life. We now turn to the history
and current composition of American Polonia.

IMMIGRATION OF POLES
TO AMERICA

A major factor in the successful establishment of American Polonia was the sheer number of people who could become its members; however, the population base is difficult, if not impossible, to establish precisely for several reasons. First, Poland was under foreign political domination during most of the periods of immigration to America. Second, the American Immigration and Naturalization Service changed its procedures for recording Polish immigrants several times. Third, there was a heavy back and forth traffic between Poland and America, even though "immigrants" were technically people who declared their intention of staying permanently in America. The tendency of Poles who entered as temporary residents or as nonimmigrants to change their status also confused the picture. Fourth, Poland's minority groups, upon arriving in America, inconsistently identified themselves, or were wrongly identified by the immigration officials. Finally, the problems of enumeration facing all ethnic communities in America also confront Polonia. As new generations appear on the scene, who is to be included under the classification of Polish American? Should only the foreign stock, i.e. those born in Poland and their immediate descendants, be included, or can one count anyone with an ancestor from that country, or is it necessary to ask people how they identify?

At the turn of the twentieth century, immigration to America was extensive, the Immigration Bureau's working conditions were far from adequate, and the policies of identity assignment shifted frequently.[1] Millions of immigrants streamed through the entry ports. Few of them

Developing and Maintaining an Ethnic Community

---

[1] The situation at the ports of entry to the United States was subject to many investigations during the years of the heavy influx. This was particularly true of Ellis Island where "the annual number was over three quarters of a million" and "the number passing through within a single day was five thousand or more, an average of two per minute" (Heaps, 1967).

spoke English and their village-bound pronunciations and intonations facilitated misunderstanding even by agents speaking their national language. Some immigrants could not identify the political or national society from which they had come. In addition, the American government changed the identification base by which it classified all immigrants several times, the immigration recording and reporting agency was moved through the years from one department of the government to another, and the data selected for reporting and the method of presentation were modified by new personnel who rejected prior methods. These problems were complicated in the case of Polish immigrants by events occurring in Poland and the American government's reactions to them.

Methods of Recording

Over time, three bases for classifying all immigrants have been used by the American Immigration Bureau (unfortunately providing unmatched data, unsystematically applied): "country of birth," "races or peoples," and "country of last (and future, in cases of emigration) permanent residence." Country of birth did not mean national culture society but political state. Feeling that this information was insufficient during the height of the immigration the Bureau introduced a new classification of "races or peoples."[2] Both methods were used in recording immigrants from around the turn of the century till 1932. After 1932, the Department of Labor (which was then housing the Bureau), seemed to lose interest in many of the more detailed figures on immigration. It dropped the reporting of nonimmigrants and all references to "races or peoples," or reported them only sporadically. Country of last permanent residence has been used occasionally, particularly in recent years, possibly because of quotas and restrictions by country of origin. During some of America's history the outflow of emigrants was of interest to the Bureau which recorded and occasionally reported the country of future permanent residence.

Poland did not appear as a major country of immigration in the American Immigration Bureau's *Annual Report* until 1885, undoubtedly because there were so few Polish immigrants. The changing recording and reporting policies since then provide us with a very mixed set of data

---

2 Jones (1960) identified the Immigration and Naturalization Commission's reports on the new immigrants and the classification of the entrants by "races or peoples" as highly questionable and reflective of the members' biases, but there is no clear-cut definition of procedures by which people were so classified. The concept of "race" was popular at the time since careful anthropological analyses had not yet dispelled the myth that a people such as Poles or Jews formed a biologically homogeneous separate species of mankind.

on Polish immigration. From 1885 until 1898 Polish immigrants were listed by country of birth. Realizing that Poland did not officially exist as a country, the Bureau changed its mind. "Beginning in 1899 Polish immigrants have been included in the country to which they belong," which means the country which was occupying their part of Poland (United States Department of Justice, *Annual Report*, 1902:Table X). It is quite probable that instructions to so reclassify Poles went out to port officials even earlier than 1899, in view of the otherwise unexplainable reverse in the immigration trends of the prior time. Even the Census Bureau was instructed for two decades not to record Poland as a country of birth of American population.

Luckily for students of Polish immigration, the classification of "races or peoples" was added about the time that Poland as a country of birth was dropped, so there is some data now available as to the numbers who entered, as well as for those who left. By 1920, Poland officially reemerged as a political state and the Immigration and Naturalization Bureau reported both "country of birth" and "races or peoples" figures for Polish immigrants. In fact, the immigration figures for the years between 1920 to 1932 are extensive. However, the dropping of the second method of classification in 1932 leaves us with only "country of birth" or, in some years "country of last permanent address" to fall back on in estimating the number of Polish immigrants from that year to the present. The main complication in comparing "races or peoples" and "country of birth" figures is that many people leaving Poland as a political state did not identify themselves as Polish in national identity and did not join Polonian communities.

Many of the people who gave the Russian, Austro-Hungarian, or German Empires, or later, Poland as country of birth were Jews, Ruthenians, Bohemians, Germans, etc. The number who identified as Jews when given the opportunity of doing so is very large, but the proportion they, rather than non-Jewish Poles, form of the total emigration varies by year and by country. This problem of not being able to separate peoples who would identify as Poles and who were potential members of Polonia is a major one for the student of this ethnic community.[3]

---

[3] In only a few years of the immigration history we can separate those who identified themselves as Polish (See the Lopata's *International Migration Review* article, 1975) from those who identified themselves as Hebrew. Emmons (1971:54) quotes Saul Kaplan, Director of Research at the Jewish Welfare Federation of Chicago, who "estimated that at least 80 percent and perhaps 90 percent of the Russians in Chicago are Jewish, although no reliable data are available." Emmons found in a University of Illinois, Circle Campus, survey of the population of Chicago that 10 percent of the Poles gave Judaism as their religious preference.

Immigration Policies
of the United States

The total number of immigrants from Poland who were likely to become involved in Polonia has been affected by America's policies as well as by world conditions. Anti-immigration sentiment had been active in America for decades (see chapter 5) but it became so intensified by the 1920s that the federal legislature finally passed a number of immigration acts, all of which considerably restricted the number of persons admitted from Poland. The initial quota act of 1921 restricted immigration to only three percent of the "foreign born persons of such nationality resident in the United States as recorded in the 1910 Census" (Hutchinson, 1949:16). The act also called for the establishment of tests to determine if the applicant met standards of admissibility. In 1924 the law was revised to be even more restrictive of Poles: 1890 was made the base year, and only two percent was the proportion allowed for each nationality. This would have resulted in only a trickle of Polish immigrants since the number of people giving Poland as their country of birth in 1890 was so small. The next revision of the quota acts, which went into effect in 1929, was based on the 1920 census, but the proportions were dropped. The quotas it established formed a "flat one-sixth of one percent of the population of that nationality present in the United States in the 1920 census" (Bogue, 1969: 806). According to this quota system, Poland was allowed 6,488 of its nationals per year. The discriminatory and prejudicial features of the quota act were a sore point for many Americans who attempted to change it over the years.

Finally, in 1968, the quota act was replaced by a uniform limit of 20,000 people per year for each independent country in the eastern hemisphere. Close relatives of people already settled in America have been favored, 75 percent of the quota being reserved for them until 1972, when it was dropped to 50 percent (Cross, 1973:22).[4]

The American government made exceptions to its immigration policies, even prior to rescinding the quota system, by allowing entrance to many specially classified Poles and other nationals following World War II. The displacement of the Polish population during the war was extensive (see chapter 2) and subject to sympathetic humanitarian action. According to one Polish author (Wicislo, 1959:86), "There were 12,000,000 displaced persons liberated from extermination and concentration camps by

---

[4] President John Kennedy (1964) was instrumental in changing the quota system. See the preface (written by Robert Kennedy) in *A Nation of Immigrants* (published posthumously).

allied armies in 1945 . . . 3,201,000 of them were Poles." The American government passed eight special acts resulting in entrance of 162,462 Poles between 1945 and June 30, 1969 (Department of Justice, 1969:45).

Immigration Figures

There are several ways people can enter the United States legally. First, they can come as immigrants, which means as persons intending to settle permanently. Since 1929, Polish immigrants have been classified either in the quota or nonquota categories. Nonquota immigrants include relatives of Poles already settled here, or persons admitted under special provisions, such as displaced persons and refugees. Second, people can enter the United States as nonimmigrants if they are representatives of governments or other official bodies, students, travelers, visitors, or in transit. In recent years (since 1952), people with temporary visas have been listed separately by the Immigration and Naturalization Service in its *Annual Report* (United States Department of Justice). Both immigrants and nonimmigrants can also, of course, leave this country. The American government has occasionally been interested in this traffic of peoples, keeping a record of entrances and departures from 1908 until 1932, when it was concerned with border crossings and naturalization.[5]

Immigration authorities disagree as to the actual number of Polish immigrants entering the United States. Some of the numerical confusion is due to differences in the dates and years being grouped together by the examiner. The various sets of figures are presented in Table 3–1. The *Annual Report* of 1950 summarizes prior decades, and the numbers are added for the 1950s and 1960s. The figures in Table 3–1 are, however, highly questionable, in spite of constant use (Emmons, 1971). Schermerhorn (1949:265) pointed out that there were 174,365 Polish immigrants in the year ending June 30, 1913 alone. The underreporting during the 1890s, the blanks during the time when the immigration was highest, and the contradictory figures given in different sources warranted an examination of each *Annual Report* available in several major university libraries.[6] For the purpose of this discussion summary figures will be used, which establish the parameters within which the actual numbers of Poles who came to America as immigrants and who remained here are apt to be located. The totals of Poles listed by "race or peoples" can be used as the

[5] Turn-of-the-century immigration officials tried for several years to make official a policy of recording departures. In 1902 the report included the following statement: "The Bureau can only reiterate with emphasis arising from an additional year of experience, its recommendations of the past three or four years with regard to keeping a record of departing aliens. . . ."

[6] For details of the immigration, see Lopata (1975).

TABLE 3–1

DECADE SUMMARY OF IMMIGRANTS IDENTIFIED AS POLISH BY THE
U.S. IMMIGRATION AND NATURALIZATION SERVICE
BETWEEN 1820 AND 1970

Decade	Number of Immigrants	Decade	Number of Immigrants
1820	5	1819–1900	96,700
1821–1830	16	1901–1910	——— a
1831–1840	369	1911–1920	4,813 b
1841–1850	105	1921–1930	227,734
1851–1860	1,164	1931–1940	17,026
1861–1870	2,027	1941–1950	7,571
1871–1880	12,970	1951–1960	9,985
1881–1890	51,806	1961–1970	73,391 c
	TOTAL	1820–1970	505,682

a The immigration officials were instructed to list Poles under the political
state—Austria, Prussia, or Russia—within which their community was
located.
b These figures must be due to changing policy in 1920.
c The figures are not accurate; they do not add up to the total and are different in different tables. The 1961–1970 total on pp. 60–61 of the *Annual
Report* is 53,519; on p. 64 the total is 73,286; by adding and subtracting
I come up with 73,391.
Source: U.S. Immigration and Naturalization Service, *Annual Report for
Fiscal Year ending June 30, 1951* and *1970*:60–64. (See also Emmons, 1971:
38).

minimal parameter since we know that these people can be counted as
first generation Poles in America (see Table 3–2).

The totals in Tables 3–2 and 3–3 offer us the maximum parameter
of 1,670,536 for the number of Poles who immigrated to, and stayed in,
the United States from 1885 to 1972. Of course, Polonia as a community
has been strongly influenced by the even temporary presence of 297,590
immigrants who then emigrated, and the 669,392 nonimmigrants and
temporary residents who lived in America for varied amounts of time

TABLE 3–2

TOTAL NUMBERS OF POLISH IMMIGRANTS TO AND EMIGRANTS FROM THE
UNITED STATES IDENTIFIED BY "RACE OR PEOPLE," AS RECORDED IN
THE IMMIGRATION AND NATURALIZATION SERVICE *ANNUAL REPORTS*

Years	Number of Immigrants	Number of Emigrants	Total Immigrants
1899–1907	556,025	———	556,025
1908–1919	677,620	174,602	503,018
1920–1932	90,815	120,824	—30,009
	1,324,460	295,426	1,029,034

during its history. They were probably some of the more educated and cosmopolitan participants in American life but were also highly dependent upon the Polish community for personal contact, thus serving as a bridge between it and the societies of origin and settlement. The outflow of Poles from America was, at times, sufficiently larger than the inflow to result in an actual loss of persons to the community, particularly immediately following World War I. All in all, there were 592,568 Poles departing from America in the years between 1908 and 1932, when the continuous record of departures ceased being reported. This includes both immigrants and nonimmigrants.

The political situation of Poland during and after World War II is reflected in the reports of the arriving and departing immigrants and nonimmigrants who gave Poland as the *country of last (or future) permanent residence.* Only a trickle of persons came directly from, or were going to, Poland during the "prethaw" years. Poles were not leaving the Polish political state and coming to America for a variety of self- or other-imposed reasons, and they were definitely not leaving America for Poland as late as 1959.

Present estimates of the total Polish stock in the United States (including the foreign born and the native born whose parents, one or both, were of Polish birth) range from two to three million (see Table 5–1). The problems in estimating the total "Polish descent" or "Polish heritage" group are even worse; if we do not know how many people were identified with the Polish national culture society because of birth in Poland and self-identification at immigration, we can only speculate how many third or fourth generation descendants there may be. We will examine the figures and the known characteristics of these Polish Americans in chapter 5.

TABLE 3–3

TOTAL NUMBERS OF IMMIGRANTS TO AND EMIGRANTS FROM THE UNITED STATES
GIVING POLAND AS THEIR COUNTRY OF BIRTH AS RECORDED IN THE
IMMIGRATION AND NATURALIZATION SERVICE *ANNUAL REPORTS*

Years	Number of Immigrants	Number of Emigrants	Total Immigrants
1885–1898	131,694	——	131,694
1933–1946	46,573	——	46,573
1946–1972	301,709 a	——	301,709
1947–1972	164,292 b	2,766	161,526
1885–1972 (total)	644,268	2,766	641,502

a Includes immigrants.
b Includes displaced persons and excombatants.

The Immigrants

The United States Immigration and Naturalization Service (as it is now called) defines an immigrant as "an alien, other than a returning alien, admitted for permanent residence" (United States Census, 1969:87). A profile of the immigrants from Poland at different periods of its and American history indicates changes in their basic characteristics, and thus in the characteristics of the population from which Polonia could draw its members.

There were over seventy-seven thousand immigrants who entered America in the fiscal year ending June 30, 1909 who were listed as Polish, and three-fourths of them were farm laborers, unskilled laborers, and servants. Only one seventh were women and children without any occupational designation. This means that very few immigrants were of skilled occupations. There were only sixty-six professionals, who were accompanied by skilled workers typical of village economies; blacksmiths, carpenters, locksmiths, miners, dressmakers, shoemakers, and tailors (U.S. Department of Justice, 1909:41–46). These people brought with them resources for starting service establishments in the newly developing Polonian communities. They were also accompanied by over eight thousand visitors, who were more sophisticated than the farm laborers. Few urbanites or farm owners were included in the immigrant group, because they had more invested in staying in Poland. Most of the immigrants were young males between the ages of fourteen and forty-four and the outflow of almost thirty thousand people officially declared immigrants or visitors was also heavily male dominated.

The U.S. Immigration and Naturalization Service in those years was worried about the ability of immigrants to sustain themselves in this country, so it asked the entrants many questions. One of these was the amount of money each person carried with him or her, and the Service reported that only three percent of the Polish immigrants were entering with $50.00 or more in their possession. Most of the money had gone for the purchase of transportation here, since only one fourth had the cost covered by someone else, usually relatives. Only 14 percent of the entrants were not going to join relatives, with 13 percent joining friends and a few others venturing forth as pioneers or at the initiative of people whom they had not known from the homeland. Although economically destitute, only about a third to a fourth of the immigrants did not know how to read or write (U.S. Department of Justice, 1909:22–23; 68).[7] Unfortu-

---

[7]Those who could read but not write included 595 males and 585 females; those who could neither read nor write included 17,438 males and a disproportionately high 9,384 females.

nately, the language skills they had were not suited to American society.

As the years went by, immigrants came with greater occupational and financial resources, reflecting what was happening in Poland. In 1929 they were still, however, heavily rural in background. There were far fewer people coming that year than in 1909 (3,500 compared to 77,000) and their arrival was somewhat offset by the number who were leaving in order to return to Poland. The highest proportion, 89 percent, of emigrants to immigrants had been in 1926. By 1929 this percentage was down to 66, although this is still a significant number (U.S. Department of Justice, 1929: Table 90:202). The occupational distribution shows an almost doubling of the proportion of nonfarm immigrants from 20 years before, and a sizable number of "no occupation" wives, children, and even some older parents (U.S. Department of Justice, 1929:Table 33:90). The entrants carried with them more money than that of their 1909 predecessors, half of them having $50.00 or more. More had their passage paid by relatives than by themselves. This distribution shows the greater affluence of the American based relatives of the 1929 entrants than of the 1909 immigrants, and the difference in their connection to the people already settled here. The earlier group came to stay with other male relatives or pioneer families; the 1929 immigrants came to join their families of procreation or orientation. Thus, the 1929 immigrants were brought over to fill in family units, although there were still a few pioneers and returnees who had tried life back in the homeland and decided that they liked it better in America. Very few of the immigrants could not read or write (four percent), reflecting the expansion of mass education by the independent Polish government.

The refugees who were admitted by special acts of the American government in the years between 1946 and 1969, totalling more than 160,000, were different from their 1909 predecessors. The 1949 influx of twenty-seven thousand included almost half with "no occupation," indicating a movement of whole family units, usually ones with young children. Only 7 percent of them were listed as operatives, household workers, nonhousehold service workers, farm laborers, and laborers (U.S. Department of Justice, 1949: Table 8, no page). An additional fourth had been farmers or farm managers, and professionals, sales workers, people in clerical occupations, and in crafts composed the rest of the immigrant group. Thus, in terms of occupations and other characteristics, the Polish immigrant group was heterogeneous and changing over time.

This, then, is the base upon which Polonia was built and maintained over the years. The early emigrants from Poland primarily represented the various strata of peasants, but enough professionals and skilled craftsmen came to help in the formation of a relatively self-sufficient community. They were then joined by more and more professionals, skilled workers, and the intelligentsia, first represented by priests and political émigrés. The "new emigration" was dramatically different from the old, being more urban, industrialized, and representative of all social strata and occupational skills. In recent years there has been an increase in temporary emigration, composed of young people who are studying or working illegally while on temporary visas. They are not active, however, in most of Polonian life.

BUILDING POLONIA

The Beginnings of Settlement

The foreign born Poles settled in a few New England, Middle Atlantic, and East North-central states, particularly in Connecticut, New York, New Jersey, Illinois, and Michigan (Hutchinson, 1956:41) in highly concentrated communities (Lieberson, 1963). They were also one of the most urban of the immigrant groups in their manner of settlement; over 86 percent of them were found in cities, the percentages not varying much over the decades (Hutchinson, 1956:26). The location they chose for settlement in this vast land was not haphazard, but followed the migration chain established by early pioneers who had been successful in finding residence and employment. The villager in Poland heard (via letters, the grapevine, potential fellow migrants, agents of steamship companies, employers looking for cheap labor) of opportunities in America where equal or less effort produced economic benefits far outweighing what he was able to wrest from the homeland (Curti and Birr, 1950; Thomas and Znaniecki, 1918–1920, 1958). Young men were usually first to venture on the long journey overseas. They had a better chance of finding employment than older men and were freer to experiment than were men bringing their families over in the first crossing. Young single women also came to stay in homes of relatives, but they were much fewer in number.

A young man usually left Poland in the company of other men from the same family or village and headed for the American town or city in which he knew someone already established. Upon arrival, he obtained work in a factory, steel mill, mine, or other industrial organization accepting unskilled labor and providing foremen or others who served as marginal links between the foreigner and the American system. He usually boarded with friends or relatives. The few women who were part of the early migration waves ran such boarding houses. This was considered women's work and highly appropriate for those who were married because it allowed them to stay home while contributing to the family income. "The boarders were frequently brothers or other near relatives of the husband or wife, or fellow townsmen from the old country, and so the household was something in the nature of an enlarged family" (Zand, 1956:79). Strangers could find boarding houses through local newspaper advertisements. As a man became economically stable, he went back to Poland to help his family migrate, or sent for a few members at a time. Some men deserted their wives and children in the homeland, making new alliances here, but there are no figures as to the frequency of this practice.

The immigrant family unit focused around the initial male migrant. The family tended to settle near the friends or relatives it had initially joined, gradually building a community of Poles from the same village, or at least the same region. Eventually, the community became so large as to attract new immigrants from other parts of Poland or Poles from other parts of America. These local ethnic settlements were located near large industrial work sources and in the poorer sections of the city; the newcomers could not afford better housing or higher transportation costs. The history of Polonia records much movement among the localities, accompanied by repeated family separations as the men sought greener pastures in other parts of America. Hamtramck, Michigan, for example, attracted Poles from other settlements during "the first and second decades of the present century as the automobile industry expanded its needs for unskilled workers" (Wood, 1955:16).

The lack of facilities and resources to which the Polish immigrants had been accustomed back home, and the needs arising out of the new circumstances of life in the rapidly industrializing and urbanizing foreign country encouraged the many members of the community, even those with limited funds but with special skills such as shoemakers or dressmakers, to open businesses and provide services, thus contributing to the growth of an increasingly complex, diversified, and self-sufficient economic and social structure. The immigrants were unable to transplant from Poland all they needed to build a new life. They had to build their own churches; import their own priest (if the Irish one assigned by the Roman Catholic hierarchy in America was not to their pleasing); start and man schools in which their children could learn their language and culture; organize mutual aid societies for emergency needs; insure that objects necessary to traditional life were available in stores where Polish was spoken; find doctors and lawyers who understood their needs; even find scribes who could write letters and read the replies if a member were illiterate. In addition, at all times and in all places, they needed to locate translators to mediate between them and the strange world to which they had migrated.

Building a
Social Structure

The Polish Americans were able to build a complex and organized ethnic community, with sufficient institutional completeness (Breton, 1964) to last more than a century, although its local subunits vary considerably in size and complexity. This community consists of several layers of social order:

1. The *local neighborhood* is often organized around a parish; it allows direct contact, personal knowledge of the lives of others, and the use of informal methods of social control and social integration. The neighborhood uses gossip to crystallize reputations (see Thomas and Znaniecki, 1918–1920) with sufficient flexibility to allow for de- and re-crystallization of status with the addition or loss of major clusters of status points. Social mobility is made possible through the dynamics of change in status packages. People see each other as neighbors, customers, parents, spouses, earners, participants in religious ceremonials, students, contributors to and leaders in local associations, etc. (see also Suttles, 1968; 1972)

2. The *settlement* is larger than a single neighborhood; it contains a greater institutional complexity or completeness and has a definite boundary in which a single ethnic group is dominant. For example, there were originally three main Polish American settlements in Chicago: the near northwest, the "back of the yards," and the south side near the steel mills. Each contained several neighborhoods and "community areas" (see Kitagawa and Taeuber, 1963), or the initial one compiled by Louis Wirth, Eleanor Bernert, Margaret Furez, and Edward L. Burchard in 1938; see also Emmons, 1971:56–58).

3. The *local ethnic community* consists of all members of the ethnic group who participate in the superstructure at any level. Members may be dispersed over several noncontiguous neighborhoods, settlements, or even ethnic boundaries. Thus, there are local Polish American communities in Detroit, Chicago, Buffalo (New York), Erie and Scranton (Pennsylvania), and Panna Maria (Texas).

4. The *regional* or *"district" ethnic community* consists of several local communities but shares some form of organization and communication. Many, but not all, ethnic communities are organized on a regional basis. The regional Polish American groups hold meetings and facilitate inter-group communication as well as regional reputations.

5. *Polonia* is the ethnic community itself; it encompasses all those who identify with it and are engaged in some form of interaction and activity contributing to its existence. The members can be scattered in a variety of work and residential centers; the community is maintained through superterritorial organizations, mass communication, and personal contact (see Thomas and Znaniecki, 1918–1920 for the concept of superterritoriality). As mentioned before, our concern here is only with American Polonia. The lack of unification and similar life style among Poles living in America, England, Australia, etc., makes it more realistic for us to refer only to American Polonia and to shorten its designation to Polonia.

An important factor contributing to the Polish Americans' ability to build a complex social structure, locally and superterritorially, was their divergence from the dominant society. A second factor was the need to innovate in order to meet the demands of life in a foreign country. American society allowed social experimentation, not really caring what the Polish Americans did among themselves as long as they continued to provide labor and did not cause too many problems. Accustomed to the oppressive controls of the Russian and the German occupations, the immigrants welcomed this internal freedom. They were uninterested in the American scene; thus, they directed all their attention to building their own world on the new ground.

Another factor contributing to the creation of Polonia was the relatively rapid affluence gained by peasants who had been merely surviving on a near subsistence level in Poland. As Abel (1929:216) explains:

"The ability of the immigrant to establish himself so quickly and to pay off staggering mortgages in a short time, was owing to the cheap labor offered by a numerous family, and to the willingness to do hard work, and to his low standard of living" (p. 216). He did not spend his money on luxuries in order to maintain a competitive standard of living with non-Polish neighbors; rather, he depended on the status symbols he had learned back home. As soon as he became sufficiently free of the mortgages, he bought more land and contributed to the building of "Polish houses."

The main base for the formation of Polonia, granting the facilitating factors, was the combination of heterogeneity of population with the strong heritage of status competition. Although most of the immigrants were originally of peasant background, they were internally heterogeneous, belonging to all the substrata of the peasantry discussed before, and varied in many other ways. Regional differences were strong, since the German occupied territories were more industrialized than were the Russian, and the Austrian area was poorer but less oppressed. Accents, vocabularies, and styles of life varied considerably. There is still much joke-telling and teasing in Polonia along regional lines. Villages differed not ony in size but in degree of urban sophistication. Villagers varied by leadership skills. In fact, there was sufficient leadership ability among the peasants to start many social groups, mutual aid societies, parish clubs, and so forth (Thomas and Znaniecki, 1918–1920). In addition Polonia contained, permanently or temporarily, many other members of the Polish national society and descendants of earlier immigrants and political émigrés. Socialists came to revolutionize the communities, intelligentsia refugees started a wide range of periodicals, nationalistic leaders organized to prepare for the liberation of Poland, priests started Polish parishes, and restaurateurs provided opportunities for an exchange of ideas and organizational plans.

Because of the interest in status competition and the individualism within each subunit of Polonia's communities, there developed a proliferation of groups of all sizes, functions, and complexities. These gradually became united with similar units into larger federations and, at all levels, provided experiences and training to new members and new leaders. Local leaders, who started local groups and then trained other members in organizational procedures and leadership roles, were themselves being trained by more sophisticated organizers at community-wide or even superterritorial levels. Local groups sent representatives to neighborhood, settlement, or national congresses, and social events which were being organized at every level of the developing social structure. They learned, and in turn, brought back information about new activities or procedures for undertaking cooperative action. To this day there is a great deal of attention paid during organizational meetings to formal rules of procedure.

Certainly the effects of the more nationalistically inclined residents and visitors to Polonia contributed to its creation. The ex-villager probably did not have the organizational *savoir-faire* needed to form a Polish National Alliance, a Polish Roman Catholic Union, or any of the other superterritorial, literary, or economically based groups, but the community included enough people who were able to develop these, build an ideology justifying their existence, and convince even the parish-bound peasant to join the local branch and contribute time and money even to abstractly idealistic causes. As mentioned in chapter 2, a major factor contributing to the success of these groups was Poland's genuine need, a need communicated in many different ways from the leaders to the mass of immigrants. Few ethnic communities in America have experienced this highly dramatic ideological justification for building a complex social structure, or the opportunities for such a large segment of their population to gain social interaction skills.

Status Competition in Polonia

In addition, of course, the former Polish peasant was willing to spend so much time, money, and self in active participation in the social structure of Polonia because of his or her interest in the status competition. Status competition in American Polonia was even more engrossing than it had been in Poland at all levels. The many and expanding opportunities for gaining status *vis-a-vis* other members of this community has served as a motivator not only in establishing Polonia, but in maintaining it for a century. The strong interest Polonians have had in status competition, and their ability to use available resources to build numerous status hierarchies have provided them with many of the characteristics of social movements: an esprit de corps, or "we-feeling," a source of morale, because daily and more dramatic activities are given meaning within the system, a justification for action, an institutionalization of internal conflict, and a certain joi de vivre accompanying engrossing activity.

What is sociologically interesting is that the status competition and the complex structure of the community have served an integrative function throughout Polonia's history, while the ideological base has been able to shift from religious identity, to national identity, to ethnic identity. Even the criteria for the status competition have varied with Polonia's changing ideologies, as the people involved over generations in different companionate circles have varied. Throughout, however, the competition itself has supplied a meaning to life, a means for feeling important as an individual being, and a method for keeping strangers outside of interest boundaries. The success of Polonia as an ethnic community had been to a major extent due to its flexible ideological base—it is not the content of the ideology itself, but the status competition that gives it vitality. The changes in Polonia over the years within which the community has been developing, maintaining, and justifying its existence have been extensive, so that its continued existence has surprised many observers not cognizant of the complexity of the structure and its status foundation. It has changed from a basically two class Polish folk and national culture based community, into one devoted to helping Poland with little concern for the American society, to a very acculturated but not assimilated ethnic community with changing ethnicity. It will continue to exist as a unique ethnic community to the extent that its members find their status competition within their static or mobile companionate circles interesting enough to prevent them from moving out into the broader society.

DEVELOPING INSTITUTIONAL COMPLETENESS

A major criterion of ethnic survival is the institutional completeness the group is able to develop within its community (Breton, 1964; Gordon, 1964). Let us examine the contention that Polonia's organizational activities are local variations of the major institutions in total societies.

There are six basic types of institutions in human society: religious, economic, educational, political, family, and recreational. In addition, there are (in varying degrees of complexity) language, the scientific-technological institution, welfare, and art (see Hertzler, 1961). Together, these provide the foundation and organizing structure for the societal culture.

An ethnic community must always operate within a broader national, religious, or political society. Very few communities have been independent enough to meet all of their own individual and group needs. This is particularly true of an extensive and urbanized ethnic community like Polonia. For example, although Polonia's web of social relations contributes to the distribution and consumption of economic goods, few Polish American communities produce consumer objects from their own raw materials, using only Polish American workers who are paid with local currency which is then spent for goods produced locally. On the other hand, Polonia does adapt to American practices and builds them into unique packages, typical of Polonia alone. Thus, there are many Roman Catholics in America, but Roman Catholicism in Polonia is unique to Polonia. Many people in America dance the Polka, but it has a distinctive meaning for members of the "Polka Federation," who use this dance for social and competitive purposes and weave it into a whole folk culture (Emmons, 1971). Earlier in the chapter we discussed Polonia's family structure. Let us now look at the other five institutions in Polish American communities.

The Religious Institution

The first institution which was consciously developed by the Poles in America and which formed a base for the social structure, brought them into immediate conflict with American society. Polish peasants, particularly during the decades of heavy migration, combined a Polish version of Catholicism with pagan and magical beliefs in animated natural objects and spirits (Thomas and Znaniecki, 1958, Vol. 1, 205–88). In Poland, they took for granted their church buildings and sacred objects for whose maintenance they did not need to sacrifice heavily. However, there was some ambivalence in the attitudes toward the priest who was a stranger, a representative of outside powers, and a member of the intelligentsia. On the one hand, the priest was central to community life; he mediated on behalf of his people with the heavenly system and held power useful to any villager in the status competition. On the other hand, his power created strong negative feelings whenever the highly independent and competitive villagers felt that the priest "overstepped" his bounds by trying to control secular matters (Reymont, 1925). Also, the very nature of Roman Catholicism contributed to much of the latent and manifest tension with the villagers because of the doctrinnaire insistence on conformity to norms which were interpreted by the priest. Two tendencies emerged in village life and were transmitted to Polonia: anti-intellectualism, and disregard for theological ideology and norms if they interfered with other beliefs or status competition.

The mixed feelings of the peasants became more complicated when they settled in America, Negative feelings toward priests of other nationalities (usually Irish) often ran so high as to prevent the priests from carrying out their duties. Part of the refusal to cooperate, of course, resulted from the difficulty in communication because of language barriers, but the feelings ran even beyond this aspect. Eventually, ethnic parishes were created, Polish priests and nuns were imported, and schools were developed to train religious personnel in Polish Catholicism.

In the early years of Polonia's life the parish served more than religious functions—it combined the parish and the *okolica* as a community and was the focus of life within the neighborhoods (Thomas and Znaniecki, 1918–1920). Often it was developed with much sacrifice since, in addition to contributing financial support, the people literally had to erect the buildings themselves. These efforts to build the church, parish house, and parochial school provided the former peasants with an important training ground for organizational and leadership abilities. The priest could not manage everything; he had to delegate authority. While the structure was taking shape, a web of social groups was being formed and prepared for leadership roles. Once trained to be leaders, the former peasants started competing with the priest and resenting the structure of the church which gave the lay members little actual power. Thus, as is typical of Polonia, the strong unifying bond of religion also became the source of conflict. Much of the conflict was due to the status competition and the stubborn individualism the immigrant brought with him to America.

The protest against the Roman Catholic power structure took three major forms. The first of these protests took place on the local level. Many of the parish mutual aid societies joined the Polish Roman Catholic Union (PRCU), organized in 1873. The PRCU focused on the religious institution to the extent of giving priests the right to "free admittance to all meetings of the church societies, . . . to approve all candidates for office and membership in these associations . . . and to approve each decision in matters not anticipated in the constitution of the Union" (Haiman, 1948:85). Many groups broke away from the PRCU because of these provisions. Others did not join, preferring the more nationalistic Polish National Alliance (PNA).

A major protest against the Roman Catholic control over parishioners was the formation of the Polish National Catholic Church (PNCC) in the years between 1897 and 1904. The organization of the PNCC, which was so popular it spread even to Poland in a rare example of re-

GARDNER WEBB COLLEGE LIBRARY

verse diffusion, illustrates the sources of friction between many of the Polish Americans and Roman Catholicism. The power of each parish is located in the combined hands of lay leaders and elected priests, who can marry. The top governing body, the Synod, consists of six priests and six laymen. Polish rather than Latin is the official language and the doctrine of papal infallibility was replaced by the doctrine stating each man has the right to interpret "the work" for himself. Hell was abolished from the belief system.

Another illustration of the inability of the religious institution to unify Polonia on a community-wide level lies in the long, strong, and eventful competition between leaders attempting to organize it under the banner of religion, and those focusing on nationalism and other themes. Although there have been many instances of this competition in the history of Polonia, the most dramatic example is the relationship between the Polish Roman Catholic Union and the Polish National Alliance. The PRCU was organized earlier on the religious theme and grew quite successfully on the foundation of the local parish groups. The PNA was founded in 1880 around a nationalistic theme. The competition was so extensive between these two groups as to amount to open conflict, with the PRCU losing its position as the main unifying group to the PNA. Over the years, these groups have reached a compromise, mainly because they realized by the 1930s that both themes were needed to maintain Polonia and draw the youth to it.

There have been many other attempts to unify Polonia along religious lines, including several lay and clerical congresses whose aim was to improve the position of Polish clergy in the American Roman Catholic hierarchy. The competition among groups, and the clergy's concern over pressure from above to decrease such activity, led to a lack of effective protests. Even today, the Roman Catholics among the Polish Americans complain over the lack of representation of their ethnic group in the hierarchy. As of the late 1960s, there were "only seven bishops and one archbishop of Polish descent" (Wytrwal, 1969:74). The headquarters of Roman Catholicism in Rome is seen as a source of power with which the Polonians hope to influence the American hierarchy. In the meantime, Polonia still maintains "an estimated 800 Polish American Catholic parishes" (Wytrwal, 1969:73).

The Educational Institution

Education has long been closely associated with religion in Polonia. Most Polish Americans found American public schools unacceptable in terms of their emphasis on American culture, language, history, geography, etc.

Also they were more concerned with discipline and the learning of moral virtues than they felt American schools were teaching. In the 1960s, Obidinski (1968) found the Polish Americans of Buffalo still firmly convinced that parish schools provided a superior education than public schools. Polish Americans, therefore, have entrusted the education of their children to the Catholic parish schools in spite of the financial costs to the community and to individual families, and in spite of their ambivalent feelings toward religious personnel. The early schools were quite restricted, being mostly concerned with transmitting Polish Catholicism and morality (Bolek, 1948; see also Miaso, 1971). Little emphasis was placed on the teaching of Polish or American secular, literary, national culture. The curriculum was often unstandardized, the schools inadequately equipped, the teachers relatively uneducated, and the students poorly taught. The Polish peasant had little interest in formal education, desiring instead the strict moral upbringing his children received in the authoritarian classroom. The nonpeasant based Polish immigrants made other provisions for their children, very often sending them to public schools.

Around 1918 America began to pressure Polonia to accept the standardized schedule of classes and to use English in its schools, charging that too many young men in the armed services did not understand or speak English. As it was, some schools were already beginning to convert to English. This trend increased as fewer children came to school with a background in Polish and as the need to function in the American work and school systems increased. The curriculum eventually phased out all Polish subjects and language training which was taken over to some extent by the Saturday or "continuation" schools, usually organized by the major voluntary organizations.

Because of the parental insistence on the part of so many Polish Americans that their children attend Polish American schools, the community has supported a relatively large number of such educational groups. Recent figures are unavailable because of the dispersal of the children to non-ethnic parishes, but as of the late 1950s there were an estimated 250,000 elementary school students being taught by Polish American Catholic nuns and over 100,000 students registered in special programs, the largest of which were catechism classes (Sister Tullia, 1959: 603). As late as 1942 there were 585 grammar, seventy-two secondary schools, and fifty-eight institutions of higher learning which were purely Polish American, as well as 300 grammar, seventeen high, and thirty-seven "other" schools which had major courses of relevance to Polonia (Bolek, 1943).

As of 1969, Polonia's main institutions of higher learning were Alliance College in Pennsylvania and the complex of Orchard Lake Seminary,

St. Mary's College, and a high school in Michigan (Wytrwal, 1969:75). The seminary teaches future priests and lay students the Polish language in spite of the fact that Polish churches now say mass in English. The priests are able to use Polish in their contacts with parishioners in generationally mixed parishes. Of the present students at St. Mary's School in Orchard Lake, however, 23 percent never spoke Polish at home and 39 percent spoke it rarely (Chrobot, 1969). The seminary and related schools of Orchard Lake also contain a relatively new Center for Polish Studies and Culture, offering courses in Polish, a library, and an art gallery.

A recent move in Polonia has been to pressure American schools for the inclusion of Polish language and literature courses. As of 1957, forty-eight American universities and colleges and sixty-eight public secondary schools offered such courses (Miaso, 1971:38), but the pressure has intensified in recent years with mixed reports of success. Many schools have started such courses only to quickly remove them from the curriculum for lack of students.

Other groups contribute to Polonia's educational institution in the creation or dissemination of Polish and Polish American culture. These efforts are directed toward Polish American adults, Polish American youth and/or American society. Almost all the multifunctional groups include a youth division aimed at educating descendants of the immigrants in the Polish language and culture. Some organizations, such as the Harcerze (Polish scouts), are aimed at the youth audience exclusively. The Polish Falcons combine physical and national culture development of their members. The American Council of Polish Cultural Clubs sponsors many "cultural events" (see list of associations in Appendix A and chapter 6). The Kosciuszko Foundation devotes most of its energies to assisting scholarly work through the exchange of students and scholars between America and Poland. In addition, it grants stipends, supports students, and others working on special scholarly projects, and publishes the products of such work.

Most of the other existing organizations dealing with the development and dissemination of Polish culture were founded during and after World War II by a combination of the intelligentsia of the old emigration and their descendants, and their counterparts among the new emigration. The Polish American Historical Commission, founded in 1942, meets in conjunction with the American Historical Society and publishes *Polish American Studies*, a scholarly journal and newsletter in the English language. The Polish Society of History and Museum of America, founded in 1943, has as its main function the maintenance of the Polish Museum of America which is headquartered in the Polish Roman Catholic Union building in Chicago's old Polonian neighborhood. The museum houses archival and artistic products of Polish and Polish American culture, and is connected with a library and a periodical collection. The Polish Institute of Arts and Sciences in America was formed by refugee scholars in 1940, on the model of the very prestigious Polish Academy of Sciences in Poland. It is headquartered in New York with branches in the Midwest and Canada. It publishes *The Polish Review* and a number of books dealing with Polish subjects. It also holds periodic scientific congresses and cultural events. The institute is currently planning an extensive study of the Polish Americans. Finally, the Joseph Pilsudski Institute of America, founded in 1943, devotes itself to research in the modern history of Poland. Its functions are similar to those of the PIASA.

The history of Polonia records many cultural and educational associations which have not survived into the 1970s. The Polish People's University, which organized lectures drawing an audience of as many as 1,000 Polish Americans at one time, has only one remaining branch on the east coast. Polonia even developed an Esperanto club for people interested in building a cosmopolitan culture. The Polish People's University, the Esperanto Club, and the very active Polish Socialist Party usually drew the same people to their events, forming a substratum of intellectually oriented Polish Americans that was likely to be socially isolated from members of the village parish clubs.

This history of Polonia's development of its educational institution beyond the parochial school indicates that, although most Polish Americans have not used schooling as an important criterion in status competition and have even been hostile to the intelligentsia, there has been a change in its attitude in recent years. There are several factors contributing to Polonia's increased emphasis on the development and dissemination of Polish national culture and on its encouragement of youth to participate fully in educational organizations. First, the new emigration is less anti-intellectual and more oriented toward achievement through education than the old emigration had been. Second, Polonia is becoming more interested in status competition with other ethnic communities in America. Third, Polish Americans are becoming more willing to use American criteria of success in competition with others. Finally, Polish Americans are becoming increasingly aware of the disadvantage of being ignorant of the culture of the national society of their origin. These points will be developed further in future chapters.

The Political Institution

Political institutions are sets of procedures by which a society or community regulates its internal relations and its relations with other groups. Observers of Polonia in America have noted two main tendencies in its political life: internal strife and conflict, and a lack of unified involvement in the political life of the larger society (Thomas, 1921; Park, 1928; Wood, 1955). Thomas and Znaniecki (1918–1920) observed and predicted increasing social disorganization, evidenced in conflict on the individual, family, and community levels as the traditional forms of community control typical of the village dissolved and were not replaced by sufficient control from agencies outside of the community. Poland, the country in which the immigrants had been socialized, lived under very strong social controls imposed on all classes by the occupying powers, so that deviation brought reprisals, and escape was possible only through emigration. Most villagers were not involved in protesting this externally imposed social control, but lived under a system of strong internal controls. Socialized into a shame culture by families demanding continued contributions to their reputations, most villagers lived within narrow behavioral limits (Lynd, 1965). However, socialization into a shame culture results in minimal deviation because of fear of having things known and used against one's reputation, rather than because of internalization of norms and self-control.

Thomas and Znaniecki (1918–1920) expected people dependent on a small, highly controlling village to become "hedonistic" and morally disorganized when these controls were weakened by the migration process and by many characteristics of American society, including its size and democratic norms. Observing conflict within the communities and families, they interpreted this as evidence of, and a contribution to, social disorganization. The point being made here is that the political institution which had emerged in Polonia was built upon competition and conflict to such an extent that its incidence had a community building rather than destroying consequence.

The internal conflict was itself an outgrowth of status competition, which is a competition for power, for economic goods, and for reputation. The conflict occurs when the competition becomes so strong as to result in open action between the competing parties. The history of Polonia is replete with numerous, publicly expressed schisms within groups in the struggle for leadership roles or a voice in the formation or reformulation of organizational goals and procedures. The mass communication media constantly carry stories of such conflicts, and letters by people denouncing their political or organizational opponents have appeared for as long as there has been a Polonian press. The groups formed this way continue involvement in the community, competing now with their former "enemies." This is one of the main reasons for the proliferation of groups in Polonia. The same is true of conflict-ridden families and other social units.

The institutionalization of conflict as part of the status competition in Polonia and the neglect of reputations outside of its boundaries is evident in the external social control agencies used by many groups and individuals to enforce conformity of one's own group. Thomas and Znaniecki (1918–1920) expressed shock over parents who took their own children to court for failure to contribute to the family's economic status base. Wood (1955) made frequent reference to the use of courts and mass media to settle "squabbles" among politicians in Hamtramck, a predominantly Polish American subcommunity of Detroit. The leaders' struggle for political power, as a means of acquiring status, was combined with an utter disregard for the poor reputation Hamtramck gained in the larger society for its political in-fighting. Each candidate for office tried to discredit and disenfranchise all opponents through all possible means. To a lesser degree, other Polish American organizations have tried to force their competing opponents into submission or cooperation through the use of the courts and mass communication, even at the cost of lowering the community status in the society at large.

The status competition within Polonia has had another effect on its political life and that is the avoidance of the recognition and assistance of the deviant. Finestone (1964) found that family members who shamed the unit by criminal behavior were simply ignored while in prison and had to reestablish their relations with each of the other family members upon release, on the promise of contributing positively to their status in the future. Public avoidance of the deviants is seen in the lack of admission that they exist and in a lack of social agencies designed to help them reintegrate into society (Thomas and Znaniecki, 1918–1920; Park, 1928).

The internal focus on status competition has contributed to a lack of unified involvement in the American political scene in two ways, through a lack of interest in committing resources to winning political office and in an unwillingness to support one candidate. Hamtramck, for example, has had an extremely large turnout of voters for many of its elections, but the competition leads to a splintering of votes among the numerous candidates (Wood, 1955:72). The same is true of Chicago, as we shall see in the next chapter.

The political life of the community has been deeply dependent upon the actions of the organizational leaders who have formulated policy and provided the backing for the few candidates for public office who are members of Polonia or who promise to support its causes. These leaders have changed as the first generation has retired or died off and been replaced by a second generation. These newer leaders are apt to have an educational background in law or economics and often lack knowledge of the Polish language and Polish culture. Fishman (1966) found strong generational differences among leaders of four ethnic communities; Polish, Ukrainian, Jewish and German. He finds the new generation to represent "organizational leadership."

"This shift from personal involvement in ethnic cultures to involvement in ethnically-peripheral organizations is of crucial significance here. It prompts us to conclude that native-born leaders, far from being ethnic *cultural* leaders, should more properly be considered ethnic *organizational* leaders. Of course, by actively participating in ethnic organizational life native-born leaders may be trying to reassert their attachment to ethnicity. But organizational participation does not necessarily lead to personal and creative involvement in the ancestral culture. In point of fact, native-born leaders are largely de-ethnicized (both linguistically and otherwise) while, at the same time, they remain extensively involved in organized ethnic life" (Fishman, 1966:178).

There is evidence, however, that Polonia's political leaders may have changed their orientation toward the importance of ethnic, and particularly national, culture. Ever since the spread of "Polish jokes" in the early 1970s the main leaders have developed a policy of attacking them and trying to change the image of Polish Americans by stressing and idealizing Polish national culture. How effective they become and how permanent this shift is, remains to be seen.

The Economic Institution

Economic functions are performed by many organizations. Any group can serve as an economic support system for its members by providing information about sources of economic goods, be they jobs or excellent buys. Such groups can help members become established in professions or occupations by providing sponsors in the form of already established colleagues. As Hall (1975) points out, men's careers—and probably women's, although they are not discussed as often—are strongly influenced by the people they know and the opportunities these people make available to them. Medical, dental, legal, and other professional organizations have a referral system by which a new professional gains a set of clients. Many professionals with Polish backgrounds chose to practice within Polonia because of the status benefits coming from affiliation with the ethnic professional group. Other organizations provide economic opportunities directly or in the form of exchange of services.

Mutual aid has been very important in maintaining Polonia and was central to the development of fraternal insurance organizations. Although most of the superterritorial associations (including the Polish Roman Catholic Union and the Polish National Alliance) started with ideological goals, they added insurance within a short time. This function has contributed to the maintenance of at least eighteen such groups as powerful, multimillion dollar business enterprises. The money collected in insurance is used for loans, mortgages, and stocks and bonds; each investment brings in additional capital. These insurance groups are sociologically interesting because they combine a multimillion dollar business and a large voluntary association with numerous functions.

The stability of the voluntary association is maintained in two ways. First, the top officers form a bureaucratized *cadre* or nucleus of trained personnel, and retain their positions for long periods of time. They are paid officials and managers located in the central headquarters of the organization. Their continuity of office is due in part to the unwillingness of members to trust neophytes with large sums of money. The leaders prefer to remain in office as long as possible since the salaries are good, and the status benefits of the positions are high. Few social leaders are willing to enter positions of such responsibility for short terms of office, since they are full-time jobs and require temporarily dropping former occupations (with possible reentry problems after being voted out). Generally speaking, these leaders are very visible on the political scene, which brings reflexive status to the members, who thus continue to vote them into the office.

Second, the business itself is so complex that it would be very difficult to dissolve. For example, the Polish National Alliance has 332,962 policies, each one guaranteeing membership, and assets and loans in the millions. Unravelling these would be such a tremendous task that once such an insurance-fraternal group passes a certain financial size, it tends to perpetuate itself.

The Recreational Institution

"Recreation" refers to any patterned, stabilized set of procedures having no other primary function but leisure activity or companionate interaction. People have been known to convert a variety of activities from work to recreation and vice versa, but there are some traditional leisure activities. In Polonia, recreational subinstitutions have been class stratified, each social stratum selecting an almost mutually exclusive aspect of the culture as a focal point for getting together and socializing. These activities will be discussed at length in chapter 4.

DEVELOPING ASSOCIATIONAL COMPLEXITY

Although each of Polonia's settlements has its own local groups, the community abounds with a variety of associations that weave the numerous smaller units into complex federated structures. There are three types of such superterritorial structures: those combining single interest groups, the multipurpose associations and the interorganizational structures purporting to represent all of the community.

Single Interest Groups

Single interest groups can contain one category of people or be devoted to a single type of activity. Some of the lasting voluntary associations of similar people have been the veterans groups, organized into local units by and for ex-combattants of either the Polish or the American armed services, with auxiliaries for wives and daughters. The Polish Legion of American Veterans is open to "American Citizens of Polish descent who served in the United States Armed Forces during World War I and II or the Korean or Vietnam Conflicts" (Gale, 1972:101). The second such group is the Polish Army Veterans Association of America and it is open only to men and women who served with the Polish Armed Forces. These veterans groups offer companionship to people who went through similar dramatic experiences, protect rights accrued from these experiences, and take care of members who are hurt or disabled. Care of disabled or elderly veterans of the Polish armed services is particularly important and problematic since they are not recipients of help from either the Polish or the American government (see chapter 5).

The associations combining local groups named after specific villages or districts in Poland have also been long-lasting. The federations are mainly regional: the mountaineers have their own assocation, distinct from that of "Small Poland" or "Large Poland." Members of a group named after a particular village do not necessarily come from that village (Lopata, 1954). The category of single purpose federations includes all those devoted to limited and specific activities, such as singing, playing, and listening to the Polka, organizing cultural and artistic events, etc.

Multipurpose Associations

The multipurpose federations of local groups usually have a unifying set of purposes but a variety of functions meeting the needs of different categories of members, organized either territorially or by function. All are insurance-based businesses, in addition to being ethnically oriented voluntary associations. Most of the major organizations did not start out as insurance fraternals, but originated as idealistic religious or patriotic groups. The addition of insurance gave them a stable base, and they expanded their size by bringing into membership already existing local mutual aid "groups" or "societies;" later they assisted the creation of new locals. At the turn of the century, mutual aid groups had already mushroomed in the Polish neighborhoods, particularly in the parishes (Thomas and Znaniecki, 1918-1920). Each such group insured its own members, guaranteeing a "nice funeral" or protecting them from the costs of lengthy illness. Each member would come weekly or monthly to a central location and pay the local treasurer a standard premium. The occasion provided opportunities for contact and socializing. When the mutual aid society joined the federated fraternal group, the contacts became more formalized and the tasks of the local officers broader. The dates designated for the payment of premiums turned into business meetings. The money collected from the insurance premiums went to the central office, along with special "taxes" levied in order to maintain associational activities. For example, in 1906 the Polish Women's Alliance added a one cent increase per month for each member for "cultural aims," half of this money going to the national headquarters and half remaining locally (Karlowiczowa, 1938:50). The members of each group sell new insurance policies. Cash prizes have been periodically awarded to people bringing new "members" to their local group, membership being an automatic benefit of taking out an insurance policy. Actually, such prizes are economically beneficial to the organization since members serve as insurance agents without salary but with commissions.[8]

The expansion of the fraternal groups resulted in two types of organizational subunits. First, regional divisions integrated groups in the same district or region, depending on the density of members. These territorial units, still in existence, have served as intermediary links between the local group and the national headquarters, relaying communication and authority, helping to launch new groups, handling relations among the locals, and pooling resources for special events which most locals could not carry out independently. Second, functional or special membership divisions work through the existing local groups or set up specialty "societies." For example, women were given equal rights in the Polish National Alliance in 1900, and a Women's Division emerged with a set of women-only societies.

The superterritorial organizations have three channels of communication and integration for member groups scattered across the country. The house organ disseminates news of coming events, offers status opportunities for local and national leaders, trains and directs

---

[8] The practice still continues to this day and most of the insurance companies sell their policies through their members, often in contest situations. For example, the Union of Polish Women in America had a "Very Important Member of the Year" contest which involved the selling of insurance, with additional incentive in cash returns in proportion to the amount sold by each group (*Gwiazda Polarna*, Jan 31, 1974).

members in political action, crystallizes the associational ideology, and in general reminds members of all the benefits of being affiliated with such a strong and prestigious group. Personal contact with regional and local branches through tours by leaders or the telephone solves acute problems requiring joint decisions. One of the functions of associational leaders is to visit local and regional branches not only at times of crisis, but for special events of these groups. Neglect of that obligation creates indignation, because of the assumption that the offender did not consider the group "sufficiently important" to make an effort at attendance. Fortunately for the system, the hierarchical structure of status is generally known, so that the expectations of leadership presence are usually realistic. Problems arise only if there is a gap between the status the group thinks it has reached and the personal attention it achieves from the appropriate hierarchical level of leaders.

A third method of integrating member groups has been through congresses. These perform a number of functions similar to those discussed by Durkheim (1915) in reference to ceremonial events bringing members of a religious group together. They reinforce the "collective representations" the group has of its self, its ideology, and shared values. They afford opportunities for personal contact among delegates coming from a variety of locations and, through mutual socialization, they encourage group identity. The socialization also involves formal and informal training of new group leaders as they witness the very parliamentarian procedures and the more sophisticated methods of handling strife and even conflict than those available for observation in smaller groups. In addition, they reinforce or, if need be, change and crystallize definitions of Polonia and accentuate the judgment of the organization as important by sheer size and complexity of the congress. Finally, the congresses serve to broaden the local member's awareness of the wider world which is concerned with national policies and politics. The delegates later return to their home groups and disseminate all these sentiments to fellow members, each of whom experiences the congress vicariously, or plans for the future to insure becoming a delegate. The organization usually pays the costs of transporting, housing, and feeding the delegates, which contributes to their identification with the superterritorial organization and through it, with Polonia. The importance of the congresses, publicized months before and after in the ethnic press, should not be undervalued as a means of maintaining Polonia by crystallizing and shifting its ideological base.

On the other hand, the congresses can have dysfunctional consequences for the organization, in that they offer opportunities for any latent or sectional conflict to become manifest and to draw converts to the dissenters. The public arena of the congress serves as a platform for opposing views of organizational functions or procedures and for the struggle for power. Splinter groups are provided a central location to engage in mobilization efforts and, if unable to obtain satisfaction from the central authorities, to leave the meeting place with their followers to start their own congress and form a new group. This has happened several times in Polonia's history. Fear of such events leads to tightly planned congresses, with strong control of the proceedings by the leaders, and a careful screening of delegates.

Because of the positive and negative consequence which can accrue from the congresses and the costs involved in organizing them, most associations have them infrequently, usually every four years. Conflicts over mandates of delegates and all conflicts in organizations are supposedly resolved internally, but the history of Polonia records frequent uses of external courts to settle them. Most of the larger organizations have judgment tribunals ostensibly formed to settle internal conflicts, but these usually consist of the representatives of the power elite within the group, and the conflicts are created by dissident groups attempting to change the power structure.[9] As a result, the tribunals are not resorted to in really traumatic cases.

Interorganizational Associations

Attempts to unify Polonia behind a single federated organization have been unsuccessful or short-lived until recent years.[10] There are two major

---

[9] Many of the organizations try to prevent an open display of conflicts by forbidding such action in their constitution. The constitution of the Polish National Alliance states: "It is treason to the Polish National Alliance for a member to incite or try to persuade other members, groups or departments to break away from the Polish National Alliance or violate its laws and rules; it is treason to slander the Alliance or to harm it by representing in speech or writing the aims, tendencies or interests of the Alliance in a false light" (Renkiewicz, 1973:71–72)." The penalty is expulsion, which, in the case of successful 'inciting . . . to break away' would be likely to happen anyway. Rather than stopping such action, this declaration gave the Alliance the right to expel the unsuccessful revolutionaries. In any case, this is a strong statement of loyalty demands. The 10th point is equally strong: "No member, officer, group, committee, commission, department or part of the Alliance has the right of appeal to the courts of the country in affairs concerning the Alliance or any part of the Alliance until all the stages of jurisdiction and appeal within the Alliance, the diet included, have been exhausted (in Polish)."

[10] Interestingly enough, while the Polish Americans consider themselves fragmented and uncooperative, assuming that other social groups are better able to organize or solve their problems, the Canadian Poles feel they are unique in cooperation difficulties (assuming that Polonia in the United States is integrated). Makowski (1967) states that the immigrants to Canada were so diversified that "Complete unity was never really achieved because there was dissention between nationalists supporting the pre-war government, the liberals, the socialists and the clerics. In this regard the Poles in Canada differ greatly from their copatriots in the United States. In the United States

reasons for this failure. The Polish American community has been so heterogeneous that it could not agree on common goals that were important enough to warrant putting aside the status competition. Therefore, it did not establish an ongoing structure, in spite of creating many short-lived ones. Part of this lack of agreement on goals is an inevitable consequence of Polonia's marginal position. Lacking power in both the Polish and American societies, its members have often been hesitant to join groups taking a strong stand on subjects which may place them in jeopardy with the power structure. For example, organizations to exert pressure on the Roman Catholic hierarchy were unable to obtain the support of the clergy, let alone of groups strongly controlled by hesitant clergy. The powerlessness itself is a source of frustration and competition among groups, each convinced that it has the best solution for alleviating the problem.

Of course, the status competition itself has led to an unwillingness to subject one's own group to leadership by another. Each of the major associations within Polonia feels that it should have its leaders head up the interorganizational association and its ideology guide the direction of the new unit.

There have been at least eighteen attempts to unify Polonia, starting with the Polish Roman Catholic Union in 1873 and the Polish National Alliance in 1880 (see Lopata, 1954 for details). Neither succeeded, but no other interorganizational assocation has been able to survive without the cooperation of these giants in the community.

The longest lasting unifying asociation has been the Polish American Congress, formed in 1944 but somewhat dormant during the 1960s. It has recently become revitalized and its success is mainly due to cooperation among the Polish National Alliance, the Polish Roman Catholic Union, and the Polish Women's Alliance. In fact, the president of the Congress is the president of the PNA, the most powerful group in Polonia. The Congress defines itself as a political organization aimed at influencing American society and American politics in favor of Polish Americans (detailed analysis of its activity will be given in the next chapter). The Congress is supported not only by powerful groups, but by individual Polish Americans who are very conscious of the importance of having their status raised in relation to other ethnic groups and in America in general. Members of Polonia have become increasingly concerned with presenting a united front to the outside. This does not mean that conflict is absent within the Polish American Congress or that the community is unified in its attitudes or actions, only that there is general

---

a mass of Poles were, and still are, united within the Roman Catholic Church, or to a much lesser degree around the Polish National Catholic Church" (p. 176).

agreement that the Congress should be a strong organization in order to have some politically effective means of pressuring the American society.

THE POLISH
AMERICAN PRESS

The foreign language press has performed many functions in Polonia. It originally helped the nationalistic leaders to develop patriotism among the former peasants and at least an awareness of the Polish national culture society, although it was not able to impart knowledge of the content of this culture. Periodicals devoted to Polish national culture existed, but their format drew only such readers as were already oriented toward intelligentsian subjects. The foreign language press helped to develop a broader religious identification than is typical of village parishioners. In general, it facilitated the process of converting the villager into at least an "urban villager" (Gans, 1962), though usually not into an urbanite, and helped his child to move even more in the direction of "urbanism as a way of life" (Wirth, 1938). The press assisted in the development and crystallization of the ideology explaining Polonia and its relation to Poland and to the American society. It introduced changes and reconstructed reality for community members, defining the world in terms they could understand, not just once, but many times in Polonia's history. It helped the parents socialize their children into the rudiments of Polish language and its folk subcultures. Fiction published by the press described life in Poland and widened the readers' limited perception of the country. The Polish American press also helped to develop and record the new marginal culture and in its pages the gradual changes can be seen.

Another important function of Polonia's press has been the recording of community life, the record itself indirectly accentuating trends and building role models. People would read that a certain family or group introduced a new form of social entertaining or succeeded in a new money-raising activity and would reproduce it, thereby adding new cultural items to Polonia's life. In these functions the press was assisted by, and in turn fostered, the active interest in status competition. Leaders at all levels could have their names listed as officers or organizers of an "event." Groups could compete by making known their successes in gaining members, carrying out their goals, or being honored by the presence of famous leaders. It also provided an open forum for the competition when it reached conflict proportions by recording organizational strife. The press was used politically to encourage community members to support candidates or stances, or to refrain from such support. Candidates often used its pages to accuse opponents of all sorts of crimes and moral delinquencies—few internal struggles passed unnoticed.

The Polish language press has reflected the heterogeneity of the community, not only in the source of the publications, but in the content and even the language. For example, many of the daily and weekly papers and house organs catering to the lower classes had slipped into such a combination of regional, lower-class, and Americanized language by World War II as to shock the new emigration. There was a marked improvement in the "purity" of the Polish in papers when some of the war refugees with intelligentsia backgrounds joined their staffs. Other periodicals direct themselves to other audiences, the intelligentsia itself, a professional group of dentists or doctors, the "Polka world," or women. They exist side by side with newspapers devoted to mining or farming.

A high proportion of the Polish publications which did not survive for long were started by members of the intelligentsia who had no training in the business management of journalism, and the publications were sufficiently esoteric as to draw a limited number of readers. In addition, many were unable to obtain sufficient advertising to cover the gap between publishing costs and subscriptions. Many Polish American businessmen had small margins of profit and were accustomed to the word of mouth advertising typical of small communities. The social distance between Polonia and the rest of American society resulted in a neglect by English speaking businessmen of the economic potential of advertising in the Polish American press.

Table 3–4 shows the frequency of publication for the 1,356 *Polish American Serial Publications:*

TABLE 3–4

THE POLISH AMERICAN PRESS BY FREQUENCY OF PUBLICATION, 1842–1966

Newspapers		Parish Bulletins		Other Publications [a]	
Daily	51	No Date	14	No Date	130
Weekly	325	Daily	None	Weekly	145
Monthly	12	Biweekly	None	Biweekly	20
	388	Weekly	18	Semimonthly	21
		Monthly	47	Monthly	328
		Bimonthly	1	Bimonthly	15
		Irregular	1	Quarterly	45
			81	Irregular	80
				Semiannual	4
				Annual	94
				Yearly Intervals	5
					887

[a] Includes internal organs, journals of all sorts, special interest periodicals, etc.
Source: Compiled from Wespiec (1968).

Table 3–5 shows the frequency with which the three major types of publications—newspapers, parish bulletins, and other types of periodicals—were started at different periods in Polonia's history. The period of 1940 to 1954 covers World War II and the intensive anticommunistic mood of Polonia as well as the strong attempts of the new emigration to propagandize its cause.

In spite of the high level of activity in Polonia's press, there has been a gradual decline of the number of separate publications, some of them being consolidated into more stable periodicals, but most of them simply dying without replacement. In 1925, there were almost 100 Polish language publications with a circulation of 1,320,000 copies (Wachtl, 1944:219). Fishman (1969: 51–71) found a 56 percent decrease in the number of Polish language dailies between 1930 and 1960, accompanied by a decrease of 47 percent in their circulation. The number of weeklies decreased by 72 percent and their circulation by 74 percent. On the other hand, the number of monthlies increased 150 percent and their circulation 259 percent. An increase was also experienced in English language publications aimed at Polonia's members, and Renkiewicz (1969:58) estimates that the number of publications the community supported in 1960 was proportionately higher than that for other ethnic groups. Although the Polish Americans formed only 12 percent of the people who spoke a non-English tongue, they maintained "22 percent of the foreign press circulation." By contrast, the 488 hours of average weekly Polish radio broadcasting were lower than that for other groups, forming only 6.4 percent of all foreign language broadcasting.

Those periodicals that have survived into the 1970 are most apt to be supported by organizations. Few Polish American publications have been able to maintain themselves through subscriptions and advertising alone.

TABLE 3–5

THE POLISH AMERICAN PRESS BY YEAR OF FOUNDING, 1842–1966

	Year Not Given	Prior to World War I	1914–1918 (During World War I)	1919–1939 (Between Wars)	1940–1954 (World War II Aftermath)	1955 to Present	Total
Newspapers	5	229	32	104	13	5	388
Parish Bulletins	4	6	9	43	14	5	81
Other Publications	40	167	113	254	198	115	887
Totals	49	402	154	401	225	125	1,356

Source: Compiled from Wespiec (1968).

SUMMARY

Polonia has developed as an institutionally and organizationally complex ethnic community, with a dynamic life of cooperation, competition, and conflict with the help of a large number of Polish immigrants and their descendants. The old emigration came to America mainly in the years between 1880 and 1924. Most of them came from villages but they represented a variety of types of peasants, differentiated by sub-class, degree of urban influence, and region. Most of the early emigrants used whatever money they were able to obtain to buy their passage, arriving in America with less than fifty dollars in their pocket. Most of them were young men who imported their families, or went back to get them, after becoming established in a job and a community here. Most settled in urban centers, near other Polish immigrants, thus helping establish the local settlements. As these grew in size, Poles of other social classes and skills were drawn to them, and the institutional complexity began developing. Polish priests and nuns were imported, and later trained here, to take care of newly formed parishes. These parishes became the center of the *okolica*, not only of religious, but of total community life. Mutual aid societies and groups helping in the functioning of the parish and its school increased, giving opportunities for parishioners to develop organizational and leadership skills. Nationalistic Polish leaders, many of them members of the intelligentsia, came to these centers, started other types of groups, and founded a variety of different periodicals and radio programs. Parents sent their children to Polish language parish schools, primarily hoping they would learn the rudiments of Polish Catholisism and moral values.

The ethnic communities developed some economic services for their members such as stores in which Polish was spoken and Polish goods were sold, doctor's and dentist's offices, legal and writing services, and larger businesses such as coal or sausage companies which employed some workers. Most of the Polish immigrants, however, worked for American industry, as miners or unskilled and semiskilled steel and automobile workers. The Polish Americans did not involve themselves in American politics very extensively and the status competition within the community prevented unification *vis-a-vis* the rest of the society. The status competition institutionalized conflict and the use of all available resources, even external social control agencies in order to gain reputations, power, or other sources of status. The status competition, and even the conflict which splintered groups and contributed to the formation of new ones, helped prevent the extensive and predicted social disorganization which could easily have followed migration and settlement in such a foreign country. The development of competing groups, clustered around competing ideologies and status-concerned leaders, with constant splintering to create new groups, each convinced that it was better able to meet the needs of the community than its competitors, has been the essence of the dynamism keeping the community together. The creation of a complex economic base under some of these groups helped their survival rate, but many other groups were able to survive without that base.

Most small groups have joined federations devoted to one or more functions and drawing either a special kind of member or several categories organized territorially or functionally. Attempts have even been made throughout Polonia's history to unite all the major groups but these failed until recent years. The forming and reforming of groups brought in new members and leaders, providing opportunities for participation in the community life and in its status competition for a very large segment of the population, including working class and even lower class people who are generally alienated from urban associational life. Even second generation, and in some cases, third generation Polish Americans have joined these groups, or formed new ones, as has the new emigration. This last wave of immigrants kept apart in early years, feeling very alienated from the ethnic culture that the old emigration had created in Polonia which they found "archaic" and too low class for the most part. Heterogeneous to an extent exceeding even the prior emigration and reared in a different kind of Poland than remembered or learned by the Polish Americans already living in Polonia, their presence and behavior had a profound effect on the community, increasing its interest in the Polish national culture society, changing the language in the Polish press, and shifting the content of the status competition.

Throughout Polonia's history, the ideological identity and rationale for the community has shifted considerably from folk culture to Polish patriotism, from the "identity crisis" of marginality to increasing Americanization. The dynamism of the status competition and organizational flexibility and complexity carried it through the changes and has maintained it in spite of the fact that, at present, there are relatively few characteristics of this ethnic community which distinguish it from the larger society. Decreasing Polishness has not necessarily decreased the organizational and institutional complexity of the ethnic community. Yet, there are evidences of a decrease in Polish American involvement in Polonia, or at least a shift from daily concern to more specialized interest in the demise of the daily newspapers which are being replaced by English language monthlies.

"To gain influence and stature in the American society Polonia must involve itself in the mainstream of American life"
(Piwowarski, 1970:8).

This conclusion, reached by a Polish American conference (Washington, D.C., 1970), reflected several aspects of Polonia's current definition of its situation,particularly its status as an ethnic community within a larger society. First, it implies that Polonia has not been in the "mainstream" of American life, but that it should now move in that direction. (This assumes that the mainstream consists of ethnic communities rather than a core of nonethnic American life.) Second, it implies that Polonia wants to gain influence, since the statement is preceded by the strong declaration: "Another deplorable circumstance is the limited influence of Polonia in American political life" (Piwowarski, 1970:8). Finally, it points to dissatisfaction with Polonia's stature in American society.

Polonia's Relations With The Rest of American Society

In the PAC newsletter of July 20, 1970, its Commission on Civic and Political Activities reported "shocking discrimination" against Polish Americans in the state government of Illinois, and Congressman Pucinski in the federal government. Pucinski recommended that "all State Divisions (of the PAC) start a 'talent bank' which would give all of us a steady reservoir of capable Polish Americans who are willing to take on responsible positions, both in the Government and in the private sector (p. 12)." Other stories concern themselves with "anti-defamation" activities" and the concern that "There is so much to be done to uplift the Polish American image;" including "stimulating the interest of our youth in the Polishness" (p. 3). The board of PAC was told of the "action and steps aimed at enhancing Polonia's standing and prestige in American life" by the organization's president.

THE BASES FOR INTERACTION

While Polonia was developing its unique structure and culture and formulating its relations with Poland, it also had to interact with the American national society and the political state within which it is located. Relations of an ethnic community with the country of settlement can be on the community or individual level (Gordon, 1964).

Several characteristics underlie these relations. In the first place, Polonia is not an independent community, able to survive without interaction with the larger society. It is a functional component of the society, regardless of how much it has identified itself as a separate sub-society. The members of the community are influenced in their private and community life by the political, economic, religious, educational, and recreational life that is emerging, existing, and changing in the larger society and its other social groups. In spite of the ideology developed in Polonia in the 1930s that pictures American society as a mosaic of different ethnic groups with no central core, there *is* a distinctive American way of life. It would be hard to imagine anyone in urban America claiming total independence from American institutions and associations. The culture pervades the home through radio and television and the actions and reactions of those members of the family who return home after participating in school or work roles on the outside. Although Polonia has developed a complex set of institutionalized alternatives to segments of American institutions (Breton, 1964), the lives of its central core of organizational personnel and leaders are heavily American in structure and action. The recent revitalization of interest in Polish national culture rather than folk or ethnic culture does not negate the fact that Polonia is an ethnic community whose life style heavily resembles the rest of America. Movement from folk or national Polish culture to American culture has been gradual, but definite (see also Kramer, 1970).

A second characteristic of Polonia's relations with America has been an underlying acceptance of the greater society and of the democratic political process (see also Symmons-Symonolewicz, 1966). Whether applying pressure on the society, or objecting to some of its actions, Polonia has functioned as a reform group rather than a revolutionary group, aiming to change, not to overthrow. Unlike Poles living in Germany or Russia (who, for many years organized extensive efforts to sabotage the society), Polish Americans identify with the system and operate within its political institutions, even when they feel angry (as over the Yalta agreement), or hostile (as over prejudice directed against them). Part of the general friendliness toward America has been due to the fact that the larger society left the immigrants alone to build their own community. The Poles came here voluntarily and the American society accepted them, made room for them in its cities and factories and allowed them to build their own churches and schools.

In fact, the third characteristic of Polonia's interaction with America has been until recently a mutual neglect (not entirely benign) except at times of emergency. Polonia neglected America because of the awareness that it was difficult for the foreign-born and even second generation Polish Americans to achieve status in American society. Only during wars and over peace settlements did Polonia attempt to change or direct the action of American society. In addition, there were some sporadic attempts to elevate Polish Americans to positions of higher prestige in the religious and political systems. This neglect of America has diminished in recent years due to the improved probability of positive responses and to the changing composition of the Polish American population (see chapter 5).

Mutual Prejudices of Poles and Americans

The in- and out-flow of prejudice has colored much of Polonia's life. Since they first settled in America, Polish Americans have been aware of the prejudice of non-Polish Americans toward them and toward other recent immigrant groups. Prejudice against immigrants has a long history in America; Benjamin Franklin stated that although America needed the Scotch, Irish, and Germans, he was worried about having so many of them and about their behavior (Cross, 1973:4). Forgetting that they themselves had been the objects of prejudice, or perhaps still reacting to it, the descendants of the groups now considered the "old immigration" in turn expressed strong negative attitudes toward the "new immigration" from southern and eastern Europe. In the first quarter of the 20th century the Immigration and Naturalization Service and many nongovernmental agencies sponsored or conducted studies which negatively portrayed immigrants of those years as illiterate, often mentally deficient (see Mullan, 1917, *The Mentality of the Arriving Immigrant*), and criminally inclined or victimized by their own people (see Claghorn, 1923, *The Immigrant's Day in Court*; Thrasher, 1927, *The Gang*). In addition they were said to be experiencing serious health problems (Davis, 1921, *Immigrant Health and the Community*), individual and family demoralization (Thomas and Znaniecki, 1918–1920, *The Polish Peasant in Europe and America*; Thomas, Park, and Miller, *Immigrant Traits Transplanted*), and to be inwardly clannish and unwilling to Americanize (Park, 1922, *The Immigrant Press and its Control*). Sociologists and other supposedly value-free scholars often expressed negative judgments regarding the new immigrants, a large number of whom were Polish. W. I. Thomas, an eminent American professor at the University of Chicago, used a policeman's stereotype as one of the reasons for wanting to study Polish Americans:

> They were the most incomprehensible and perhaps the most disorganized of all the immigrant groups. This may be illustrated by what the American police call "Polish warfare." A policeman might enter a saloon where there was a noisy crowd of Poles and say, "You men be quiet," and they might subside immediately or one of them might draw a gun and kill him. This was due to the fact that the Pole in America has two attitudes toward authority. One of these reflects the old peasant subordination to authority. They were called "cattle" by the landlords and submitted like cattle. The other attitude reflects the conception that there are no limits to the boasted American "freedom" (quoted in Blumer, 1939:104–5).

Bias is indicated in Thomas' report of his first contact with his future co-author, Znaniecki, who "was in charge of a Bureau for the Protection of Emigrants, which means advising all who planned to emigrate as to the desirable destinations and guarding them again[st] exploitation, especially in South America. Incidentally, it meant also, as I understand it, keeping the best elements in Poland and facilitating the departure of the remainder" (pp. 5–6).

Even an American historian, Woodrow Wilson, advocated the reduction of Polish immigration to the United States:

> . . . but now there came multitudes of men of lowest class from the south of Italy and men of the meaner sort out of Hungary and Poland, men out of the ranks where there was neither skill nor energy nor any initiative of quick intelligence; and they came in numbers which increased from year to year, as if the countries of the south of Europe were disburdening themselves of the more sordid and hapless elements of their population, the men whose standard of life and of work were such as American workmen had never dreamed of hitherto (quoted in Gerson, 1953:55).

On the other hand, some social scientists questioned the validity of such portrayals of the new immigrants. Taft (1936, see also a more detailed discussion of his findings in chapter 5) analyzed criminal statistics of the 1930s and reiterated a prior finding that the foreign born were not highly criminal, having rates lower than the native born. He also concluded that the high second generation rates were due to the age distribution of the population. The new immigrant groups' second generation males were highly concentrated in the "criminally significant" ages, as compared to the old immigration second generation youth. Hourwich (1912) attempted to dispel the myths concerning the labor force and social behavior of the new immigration, including the Poles. However, their efforts were not very successful in decreasing prejudice against the Polish immigrants and their children.

Initial Reactions
to American Prejudice

The Polish Americans could not be oblivious to the statements made about them nor to the significance of the quota acts which were, after all, designed to keep people like them from entering America in any but minimal numbers. They reacted at first by ignoring the society of settlement and turning their attention to Poland and to Polonia's internal life. Withdrawal from identification with Poland was very difficult for Polonia while it faced negative prejudice from Americans, and it took many years. Polonia's realization of its low status in relation to other groups was reflected in the anger and frustration of its pronouncements of the 1930s and 1940s:

> The great declarations of freedom in the United States are only empty watchwords. Statements are made by the Nordics: "You Pole are as good an American as I." However, when the same Pole wants to take a place on an equal level as this Nordic, then he meets another side of his character: "What, you foreigners want to be equal with?" The Pole is supposed to be satisfied with slogans. That is why the [Polish National] Alliance must widen its services and waken the emigrant group to a recognition of itself and the role it has to play in the land of Washington. The Alliance must make the slogans become real (Zwiazek Narodowy Polski, 1940:27, in Polish).

Changing the status of Polish Americans in the American society was, however, very complicated. One internal problem was that the Polish Americans did not have a positive image of themselves; in short, they suffered from a major inferiority complex (Kolm, 1969, 1971, 1971b; Nowakowski, 1964). Rather than dealing with prejudice through positive action, the Polonians simply became angry, withdrew from competition in American society, or dropped all ties and identities with Polonia and created a non-Polish family history (see also Novak, 1972).

According to a Polish writer of the new emigration, Alexander Janta (1957), the Polish American's feelings of inferiority were due to their ignorance of Polish culture and the anti-intellectualism which prevented them from breaking through this barrier of ignorance (Janta, 1957). "At the root of this deficiency lies a profound misunderstanding of the meaning of culture among the majority of Polish leaders, and, consequently, among the masses as well (p. 83). . . . In spite of the efforts of a few national culture intelligentsia, . . . an overwhelming majority of Poles in America can express their 'Polonism' in relation to the American background by little more than costume, dance, or food" (p. 86). Thus, the Polish Americans lived as a separate entity within society, preserving the folk culture and the language, but ignoring the literary and artistic culture of Poland. The latter could have been of interest to Americans and might have helped change the image of Polish Americans and also of Poland as a limited and peasant-dominated land. "It is disappointing to realize that between the two wars too little was done to reverse this trend. No solid educational program has been conceived and developed [in Polonia] and no investment into its establishment was attempted from the Polish side" (Janta, 1957:94).

The inability of the Polish Americans to fight prejudice resulted in one Polish author (Kuniczak, 1968) writing a book about them entitled *The Silent Emigration.* The few attempts to change the passivity did not have a profound influence on Polonia. Bishop Rhode pleaded, "If we forget our Polish heritage we become nothing but ships in the wind without anchors" (Haiman, 1948:433). The Polish National Alliance kept telling the Polish Americans, "We can not change ourselves into hybrids, because then our worth would be completely lost. We must convince ourselves of the worth of our spiritual possessions and of our Polish history . . ." (in Polish, *Zwiazek Narodowy Polski,* 1948:35). However, only recently have observers of the Polonia scene reported an interest by youth in learning more about the Polish national culture.

One accomplishment of the Polonian leaders assisting the preservation of the community was the development of an ideology defining America as a pluralistic society as early as the 1930's, long before such a view became popular with the waning of the melting pot theory.

The ideology looked at the United States as a group of subcultures—minority groups with no highly visible, permanent, and distinct majority. (Bujelski, 1952:3) Accordingly, not only did American society lack a central core of nonethnics, but the other ethnic and racial groups had been aware of this, were well organized, and had effectively concentrated their attention toward improvement of their relative statuses. Polonia in the meantime, was involved only in Poland and in its own internal affairs. Within this frame of reference Polonia's low status in the society was admitted but was attributed to its long-lasting insistence on being the "fourth province of Poland" and its failure to establish a satisfactory community status in this society, rather than to any "inherent" inferiority. The other ethnic groups were internally better unified and organized in their efforts at status achievement, and the lack of "Polish power" (as it is currently being called) is thus reversible with proper effort and cooperation.[1]

It is here in the ideology, however, that some hesitation is voiced, as to Polonia's ability to unify. Many Polish Americans who still identify with their Polish background believe in a Polish national character that makes sustained cooperation difficult, if not impossible. The main features of this national character are individualism, independence, and competitiveness. The ideology thus provides a loophole for the lack of status achievement in the outside society. Not only were other groups more established on the status ladder than were the late arriving Polish Americans, but they benefited from the absence of the "Polish character" which was likely to handicap Polonia in its bid for superior or at least equal status in the future.[2] On the other side of the coin, the positive consequence of the national character was an internal appreciation of the

---

[1] The assumption that other ethnic groups are better organized and united than are the Polish Americans, and that this contributes to their success in American society, is contained in pronouncements of the leaders of the "Wisconsin Plan" asking readers of the Polish American ethnic press to support "a candidate of your own choice for a congressional or senatorial seat." (*Gwiazda Polarna*, February 16, 1974:5). Although indefinite as to the means by which the "Wisconsin Plan" will accomplish the goal of united action, the appeal for membership contains the following statements:

> A more specific example [of united efforts which bring results] is the success story of the Jewish community in America. While small in members, they have become extremely effective through united action. . . . Americans of Polish heritage have built America, obeyed its laws, and contributed toward making it the great nation it is today, but they have been ignored. . . . Our brothers have labored long and hard to correct these injustices, but they have not been successful. Why? Part of the reason is that the average Congressman and Senator knows little about Poland and our problems, and probably cares even less.

[2] The persistence of the idea that there is a national character and that it prevents internal cooperation is evident over decades. Tomczak (1933) states that they are considered clannish by others but that "a queer paradox is observed in this respect. For clannish though they may be, they are still divided among themselves. While distinctions and policies are not very sharply drawn, there is nevertheless an intense rivalry and competition between organization and between commercial houses" (p. 70). Tomczak continues: "It is said also that the Poles are unable to self-govern, that they are by nature independent and self-seeking, and that their achievements in sciences and the arts are merely accidental and not representative of the people as a whole" (p. 79). The current President of the Polish American Congress and the Polish National Alliance referred to this "national character" in a speech entitled "The Poles—a National Group Full of Dynamism and Individualism" (Mazewski, 1973:5) at a banquet following the unveiling of the Copernican Statue in Chicago: "It has been said and written many times in the past that Americans of Polish origin tend to weaken and fragmentize their strength and potential through internal discords." His argument was that although this "diversity and, at times, cross purposes, were the rule rather than the exception" in Poland's history, the presence of so many representatives of so many organizations and individually prominent Polish Americans in the audience is evidence of their ability to synthesize and reconcile.

dynamism of individualism and competitiveness. Feeling these sentiments and beliefs about themselves, recognizing their status in American society as low, and assuming a powerlessness to change it because of their very "character," the Polish Americans who continued to identify with the community (from World War II until recently) were mainly concerned with individual and family participation in community life and in its lively and engrossing status competition.

Efforts at Participation in the American Status System

Although Polish Americans have not concentrated all their efforts on changing their status in American society, they continue to remind people of their cultural contributions to American society. They do this in three ways. First, they select individual Polish Americans for dramatic publicity as positive representatives of the community; second, they make declarations of loyalty; and third they try to "enrich" American culture with elements of Polish culture.

The first of these activities was based on the assumption that certain types of people and certain activities are more highly valued in the society than are others. Early in Polonia's history, the two persons most often selected as reminders of Polish contributions to America were the Polish generals Pulaski and Kosciuszko who became heroes in the American Revolution. References to these men in mass communication media and the erection of statues to them attempted to anchor American memory of Polish contributions to the past, capitalizing on the society's idealization of its own history and length of residence or involvement by members on this side of the ocean. It also served as a reminder of the historical presence of men of upper classes in a land from which most of the Poles who emigrated were of the lower classes. More recently, outstanding sports figures, film stars, successful businessmen, artists, and scientists have been chosen as representatives.[3] The publicity emphasizes that these individuals have achieved not only American but cosmopolitan reputations. Their

---

[3] The Poles and Polish Americans most frequently mentioned include pianist Artur Rubenstein; conductors Leopold Stokowski and Artur Rodzinski; harpsicordist Wanda Landowska; singer Bobby Vinton; Pola Negri and Gilda Gray of films; Helena Modjewska of the theater; Henry Sienkiewicz, author of *Quo Vadis* and *Portrait of America*; Wieslaw Kuniczak, author of *The Thousand Hour Day*; sociologist Florian Znaniecki; political scientist Zbigniew Brzezinski; political leader Edmund Muskie; former Postmaster General John Gronouski; baseball stars Stan Musial and Carl Yastrzemski; and football players Ed Rutkowski, Larry Kaminski, and Bob Kowalkowski (Wytrwal, 1969). A recent addition to the list is Jerzy Kosinski, author of *The Painted Bird* and *Steps*.

idealization is expected to infiltrate the image of the total community.

Declarations of loyalty have also been used in attempts to change the image of Polish Americans. As one of the speakers at a 1938 joint Convention of the Polish Medical and Dental Association of the United States of America and the Polish Lawyers Association of the U.S.A. stated:

> Our first and most important duty is to be good Americans, take an active part in all phases of life here, and take advantage in full of all opportunities and privileges, as are rightfully ours, not as a numerous minority but as mutual originators and participants in the common good of the American Republic (Kostrzewski, 1938:18).

At this same convention Starzynski stated that Polish Americans have another set of obligations:

> Our second and no less important duty is to enrich our common American life and newly forming culture. This American culture is the total of contributions of all those national groups which live here. We can not be beggars, with hat in hand. We cannot take, giving nothing in return (Kostrzewski, 1938:18).

Several groups such as the American Council of Polish Cultural Clubs (see chapter 3 and 6) or the Kosciuszko Foundation undertook the selection, development, and dissemination of cultural items to the broader society. However, not until very recently has there been a concerted and dramatic effort to change the status of Polonia in American society by changing the image of Polish Americans. As far as can be determined from Polish leaders and the ethnic press, this effort is a direct consequence of the "Polack" or "Polish" jokes (although other factors played an important role). The humor of these strongly negative stories centers on the lower class background and peasant culture of the immigrant. Use of this humor increased dramatically in the late 1960s and early 1970s when most Polish Americans had moved away from behavorial aspects of peasantry (which are exaggerated by the jokes) into the upper segments of the lower class and into the middle class. This increase has been attributed to the mobility itself which has made the ethinic group more visible in the society. It has also been attributed to the anti-Polish sentiment of the Jewish community, many of whose members are writers and performers (*Dziennik Zwiazkowy*, 1973, in Polish). "More and more Americans of Polish descent are complaining of the malicious anti-Polish articles written by members of certain Jewish groups, and to the constantly growing discrimination against Poles and Americans of Polish descent by these groups. The more judicious individuals of the Jewish community are ready to help in the goal of changing this situation, but they need facts on this subject" (p. 12). The Kosciuszko Foundation in New York asked the readers to send data documenting discrimination or prejudice with names, dates, places, and descriptions of the event. Although the Foundation could not directly follow up each indicident, it promised to find ways of helping other groups to do so.

Whatever the real and attributed reasons for their emergence, Polish jokes have had a profound influence on Polonia—more so, in fact than all of Polonia's previous efforts at expanding the Polish American and American knowledge of its Polish heritage. The campaign against these jokes has been taken very seriously in Polonia for several reasons. In the first place, they were a jolt to a community that had been comfortably involved in its own status competition, only vaguely aware of and responsive to prejudice from the outside. Second, success in acquiring American status symbols served to increase interest in status competition outside the community. Third, the jokes affect not only the active members of the community, but *anyone* who identifies himself or is identified by others as Polish American. They have reportedly been told to people with Polish names as if they would be specially meaningful, even when the recipient considered him- or herself successfully acculturated and, in Gordon's terms, structurally assimilated. The jokes thus come as reminders of the imperfection of such assimilation. They also serve as a rallying point for those who want to retain Polish or Polish American identity. The leaders are now able to say, "I told you so . . . You must support us and the community to change this prejudice." The leaders are aware that the jokes may have a beneficial effect in forcing the youth and adults to identify and cooperate with Polonia. They have, thus provided a source of re-vitalization of community efforts, a specific goal and sources for sentiments of peoplehood.

An official reaction to the current status of Polonia in American society is fully expressed in the report of the Committee for the Defense of the Polish Name (Anti-Defamation Committee) and states:

> Slandered, ridiculed and misrepresented in the media as "dumb Polacks," Polish-Americans have, for the most part, remained silent. This silence, with all its implications of ineffectuality, fear and intimidation, is the greatest problem facing the Polish American community today.
>
> Too many of us are content to cart around for a lifetime the psychological and emotional damage that has been done to us by a continuing barrage of negative images, slurs and so-called "Polish jokes." . . .
>
> What the Polish-American community needs more than anything else is an effective process of consciousness raising. . . . (Kowalski, n.d.:3)

Polonian leaders have tried to change the image of their ethnic community in five ways. First they consulted members of the intelligentsia (previously somewhat isolated from the community) to create ideologies and select cultural items which could be used outside the community to project a new image. The first meeting of the political leaders and the intelligentsia resulted in a set of recommendations as to such ideologies and items, and the methods to use in disseminating knowledge of Polish and Polonian culture internally and externally. Some of the recommendations were a push for high school and college courses in the language, history, and cultures of Poland and Polonia, teacher training programs at Orchard Lake Schools and Alliance College; publication of books and journals on the above subjects, a survey of attitudes of youth with a Polish background, excursions to Poland by the youth, the creation of speakers' bureaus, the hiring of a professional public relations expert, the collection and dissemination of information on all publications dealing with Poland or Polonia, and support of the Polish Museum in Chicago. The proposed studies of Polish American communities and organizations by the Polish Institute of Arts and Sciences in America is a direct movement in the direction of the recommendations, but many of the other ideas of the conference have not been acted upon due to a shortage of funds.

While these proposals and plans were being crystallized in the minds of Polonian leaders, other members of the community were undertaking public relations actions. For example, the Polish president of Mrs. Paul's Kitchens (a financially successful producer of frozen foods) decided to change the image of his ethnic group through direct advertising. The content of the advertisements was developed by the president of the Orchard Lake Schools and Seminary. Together, these men devoted a year to an intensive publicity campaign, reported on the front page of the *Wall Street Journal* (October 12, 1973) as follows:

POLISH AMERICANS HIT
ETHNIC SLURS, PRAISE
THEIR CULTURE IN ADS

Was Copernicus Trying to Tell
Us Something? Yes, and It's
Far From a Joking Matter

By Greg Conderacci
Staff Reporter of the *Wall Street Journal*
ORCHARD LAKE, Mich.—Have you heard the story about the Polish Millionaire who spent $500,000 to help stamp out Polish Jokes?
It's no joke.
It's "Project: Pole," an effort to place a half-million dollars worth of pro-Polish advertising in newspapers across the country.
"Polish jokes should set up in a man a determination to prove

they're not true," says Edward J. Piszek, president of Mrs. Paul's Kitchens, Inc. of Philadelphia and the man bankrolling the campaign. "In a positive way, it's an answer to the jokes—instructively. You eliminate the opportunity to originate the joke by proving it's not true."

So today a pilot campaign, in the form of a half-page advertisement will appear in Detroit newspapers with the headline: "The Polish astronomer Copernicus said in 1530 that the earth revolved around the sun. What was he trying to tell us?" The answer, Mr. Piszek says, is that Polish Americans are every bit as good as any other Americans.

A third form of action designed to change the image of Polish Americans is the joint celebrations of important Polish events. In 1973, Poland and Polonia celebrated the Copernican Year, declared as such throughout the world by business, religious, intellectual, and political leaders of Poland and its "colonies" in other countries. The celebrations took place in many cities (including Chicago and Philadelphia in America) and involved the unveiling of statues of the Polish astrologer. Many leaders of the larger societies as well as the ethnic leaders gathered for the ceremonies. The very erection of such statues, an expensive venture, involved concerted effort and a great deal of publicity and cooperation with various individuals and organizations. In addition, Poles are participating in events significant to Americans. In trips to Jamestown and other American cities in connection with the bicentennial celebration, Polish American leaders stress that "the Poles have been in the United States since 1608" (*Dziennik Zwiazkowy,* 1973:7).

Besides stressing Polish contributions to American society and shared culture, Polonia's efforts at changing its image in the society includes many gestures of inter-ethnic cooperation. The Polish Americans have repeatedly been accused of prejudice against other minority groups, particularly those with which they are apt to have come in direct contact at community boundaries. The history of relations between Polonia and the Jewish community is one of mutual dislike and attempts at cooperation are relatively infrequent. In recent years Polonia's members have been increasingly angry over what they define as a deliberate attempt by Jews in mass communication media to prejudice the rest of society against them, and the relations between these two communities tend not to be very cordial, especially in recent years.

Initial settlement of Poles in America placed them in virtual isolation from blacks (Lieberson, 1963) but recent years have evidenced a movement of blacks as well as Puerto Ricans into traditionally Polish neighborhoods, accompanied by an increase in anti-black and anti-Puerto Rican prejudice on the part of Polish Americans. The expansion threatens the status-invested property so painfully gathered by the immigrant, his proof of success of upward mobility. The value of the property diminishes as the black community expands, due to the panic selling and moving, and the negative feelings in older Polonian communities that have been dissolving is very strong. The status loss created by the geographical expansion of groups the Polish Americans consider below them in the American status hierarchy and the black civil rights movement of the 1960s and the societal response to it angered the Polish Americans. They had worked hard to bring themselves up to their present position and now society was threatening these gains by helping the blacks up to a similar position while Polish Americans were losing money and property because of the expansion of the black community (see also Novak, 1973). Aware, however, of the accusation of anti-black prejudice in, for example, Greeley's (1974) work, community leaders have attempted both to decrease that feeling in Polonia and to develop and document instances of black-Polish cooperation. If fighting blacks and ignoring Italians and other groups in a similar position did not benefit Polish Americans in the past, then cooperation in solving community problems deserved a try. An example of cooperation to solve common problems without a history of cultural contact is the Black–Polish Conference of Greater Detroit—a combining of forces of two low-status groups to increase the status of both.

Polish organizations have met on numerous occasions with representatives of other ethnic groups for special events or in order to meet specific goals. For example, the Poles, Czechs, and Hungarians distributed 10,000 fliers with an open letter to the Secretary General of the Soviet Communist Party, Leon Brezniew, demanding freedom for the "captive nations." The joint effort included the three countries which had tried to revolt against the Soviet influence or power in Europe (*Dziennik Zwiazkowy*, June 29, 1974:2). Other intergroup activities which have been institutionalized include participation in the Intercollegiate Council by members of Polish students, decoration of a Polish Christmas tree in museums, participation in ethnic festivals (Detroit), international trade fairs (Chicago), and singing and dancing competitions.

The current popularity of the ethnic movement in America and the society's interest in it is documented by the Ford and Rockefeller Foundations grants and governmental support of such centers as Andrew Greeley's Center for the Study of American Pluralism and the Center for Immigration Studies at the University of Minnesota. The Poles themselves received a Rockefeller grant to study Polonia through the Polish Institute of Arts and Sciences in New York. This interest has guaranteed greater cooperation between Polonia and other ethnic groups or the society at large. The society, in fact, is now coming to Polonia and its organizations and representatives, asking to xerox its files of newspapers for permanent preservation and to obtain information as to its ethnic identity and the content of the ethnic culture.

The final form of action aimed at changing the image of the Polish Americans has been the active protesting—by mass communication or through public representatives—of any known prejudicial statement. The antidefamation committee's guide specifies what data are needed to start a protest, the best methods of doing so, and the best methods for communicating with the committee so that it can reinforce the protest. For example, strong protests have been sent to NBC for sponsoring "Laugh-In" because its comedians repeatedly use "Polack jokes." In fact, the case against the company has been brought before the Federal Communications Commission.

Thus, Polonia is now very actively involved in efforts to prevent negative images of Polish Americans from spreading in American society and to create its own positive image of Poles and Polish Americans, and Polonian and Polish culture.

PARTICIPATION IN THE POLITICAL INSTITUTION

There are two major forms of political participation available to interest groups in a democratic society: direct and indirect pressure upon outside public officials, and the election of their own members to political offices. Direct pressure may be applied if officials are dependent upon the interest group for their election or if officials have declared themselves in favor of the interest group's point of view. Indirect pressure involves convincing other groups, even in the cosmopolitan world, of the justice of an interest group's demand. The representatives of the interest group in public office have to use the same means of influencing their colleagues, unless there are so many of them that they can pass or kill important legislation with the cooperation of other legislators. Few, if any, groups are that well represented.

Polonia has more often applied political pressure (the effectiveness of which is hard to measure) than it has elected its own representatives (an action with a more easily apparent consequence). Also, most of the pressure applied to high public officials has been on behalf of the Polish state and national culture society rather than on behalf of Polonia itself.[4]

4 Krakowska (1955) emphasizes that the appeal these groups sent to President Wilson before the end of World War I on behalf of Poland contained a specific disclaimer of self-interest: "The Poles in America want nothing—they need nothing—but we beg you to keep Poland in mind when the opportunity comes" (p. 16).

The Use
of Political Pressure

The two types of political pressure that Polonia uses on public officials can be termed acute (or "event" focused), and continuous (using all available methods and occasions to try to change a chronic undesirable situation or to introduce a change in policy). Acute events frequently occur within a chronic situation and Polonia uses them to draw attention to the fact that the acute event would not have occurred had the underlying chronic situation been removed. An example of a chronic situation is the position of Poland in relation to its neighbors. Throughout its early history, Polonia has tried to pressure America into forcing the three occupying powers to rescind the partitions and move back to their pre-1795 borders. During World War I there was extensive pressure on Congress, cabinet members, and President Wilson to this end. The inter-war years involved some pressure concerning the "Polish question" which was the access to the Baltic ocean, in terms of the narrowness of the "corridor." During World War II, Polonia again applied pressure on behalf of Poland. Pressure was intensified when the Yalta and Potsdam agreements were made public in Polonia; members were angry over the demands of the Soviet Union and the fact that America agreed to them. These treaties, and in later years the Yalta treaty, have been subjects of continuous political activity. The takeover of the Polish government by the Communist party, under obvious influence of the Soviet Union, had intensified the chronic situation, and anniversaries of historical events in Poland, visits of Soviet dignitaries to America, special international conferences and similar events bring forth acute activity directed at denouncing not only the event but the chronic situation. In recent years, Polonia has accepted the inevitability of Communistic control in Poland, and has concentrated on applying pressure on the American government to force the Soviet Union to withdraw troops from Poland, cease censorship of the press and the mail, and release political prisoners. The current relations between Polonia and Poland (as discussed in chapter 2) are reflected in the kinds of demands being made upon the American political system.

The Polish American Congress (the longest lasting of the inter-organizational groups) had facilitated and routinized the application of political pressure. Although headquartered in Chicago, it has branches in many states; the Washington, D.C. office keeps track of current and projected programs, and other governmental actions which could affect Poland, Polonia, or Polish Americans. The office also helps in political lobbying. The presence of an interorganizational association has other advantages: first, it can claim representativeness in that it presents a unified front to the outside. Its leaders can begin all communications with a statement of voting power. For example, "We six million Americans of Polish Descent . . ." Second, its responses to acute events can be more rapid than can the pooling of responses by separate groups. Third, it can spend its time between acute emergencies in formulating basic ideologies and sets of policies. Since most acute events fall within chronic situations, such a crystallization of stances and procedures gives the leaders confidence to act rapidly and to communicate a call for action to Polonia without having to argue out the whole issue. Fourth, it has continuing operational budget of sufficient size to cover most of its "normal" activity. Finally, it has a very broad, but definitely political, focus. The Polish American Congress was created in order to mobilize political pressure and it does not have distracting functions which might sometimes be given higher priority.

The methods Polonia uses to apply political pressure on the American government at the federal, state, and local levels have increasingly turned to personal influence upon selected leaders. Previously, Polonians sent communications to governmental representatives directly involved with specific bills in Congress of interest to Polonia; they publicized any bills which were favored or opposed by the community; and they used any means available for dramatizing their cause. Personal contact is being used by the second and third generations because of their familiarity with the American political system and many of its representatives, and their willingness to invest funds in such efforts. The increasingly sophisticated methods of political influence are evidenced in the greater number of positions open to Polish Americans, and are predicted to have even more effect in the future.

Political Action
through Voting

The most effective method of exerting political influence in a democracy is by voting. In order to be effective, however, the vote must be sizable and predictable. This means that an interest group must be eligible to vote, must refrain from action countervening this privilege, must actually vote, and must vote as a "block." For example, the more Polish Americans there are in the United States and the more integrated and politically manipulative they are in their voting behavior, the more likely it is that their vote will influence public officials. A major problem of the Polish Americans has been that they make up only a small proportion of the total American population. However, their concentration in certain geographical areas could be of significance in local politics though this potential influence has not been used effectively in Polonia's past. One of the factors contributing to this ineffectiveness was the immigrants' hesitancy to become naturalized; they planned to return to Poland and therefore wanted to retain their Polish citizenship.[5] Others did not pass the naturalization tests, being unable to speak English, having "incompetent witnesses," being ignorant of the Constitution, and lacking evidence of date of arrival since they were unaware of the importance of obtaining such evidence (Gavin, 1922). For example, "In 1920 only about 35 percent of the 127,254 Polish immigrants in Chicago twenty years of age or over were naturalized (Thurner, 1971:122).

A later problem in influencing the American political system has been Polonia's internal status competition. The competition leads to a proliferation of candidates and split votes. Thurner (1971), for example, found the Chicago Polish American candidates independent, fighting with each other, and losing the positions for which they ran because of a split vote. "Like most ethnic groups in Chicago, people of Polish birth and descent developed various competing sub-groups, often openly antagonistic to one another. Although distinguishable by certain common cultural qualities, the Poles in Chicago were hardly a cohesive, well organized group bringing political pressure to bear for the advancement of their mutual interests" (p. 20). The status competition, an integral part of the life of the community, accounts both for the liveliness of the participation in politics and for the unwillingness to give up the competition for community gains vis-a-vis other interest groups in American society. The coming years will show whether the newly consolidating power base of the Polish American Congress and increasing concern with community status in the society will lead to cooperative backing of a few candidates chosen for political reasons rather than personal competitive reasons.

Political issues can swing the Polish American vote if they are sufficiently vital to Polonia's interests. The Harris Poll analyzed the 1952 election returns and concluded that the Democrats had lost much of their

---

[5] Manning (1930) reported that Polish immigrant women in Philadelphia and Lehigh, Pennsylvania in the late 1920s were not apt to be citizens. Only 18.2 percent were U.S. citizens and they were mainly in their 30s or 40s; 51.9 percent were unable to speak English. There has consistently remained a 20 to 30 percent of foreign-born Poles who have not become naturalized because they either hope to return someday to Poland, or because they are here for only a limited time according to their own plans. The American government forbids people who enter on a visitor or student visa to work in this country but those who come as immigrants can work even without becoming citizens. Eighty percent of the half million foreign-born Poles living in the United States in 1970 were naturalized, with those remaining registered as aliens (Bureau of Census, Detailed Characteristics, 1970: PC(1)-Di Table 195).

support (estimated at roughly 70 percent) among Polish Americans because the latter believed that Poland had been betrayed at Yalta and in succeeding years.

PARTICIPATION IN OTHER AMERICAN INSTITUTIONS

As we saw in chapter 3, Polonia has been able to build and maintain a relatively complex system of ethnic institutions which parallels the American system and capitalizes on many of its features. Maintaining the Polonian economic institution are those who provide services, such as doctors or lawyers, and objects, such as Polish American newspapers or foods. Most Polish Americans work for people of other ethnic groups or for Americans and buy the society's products and services. But participation in the American economic system has been said to be limited by discrimination. The Institute of Urban Life documents the absence of a proportionate "representation of Poles, Italians, Latins, and Blacks in the executive suites of Chicago's largest corporations (Ruggiero, 1970:1)." The conclusion concerning Polish Americans in particular was that "although Poles make up 6.9 percent of the metropolitan population, only 0.3 percent of the directors are Polish (p. 3). . . . One hundred two out of the 106 corporations had no directors who were Polish; 97 had no officers who were Polish" (pp. 3–4).

Polish Americans have been slow to join unions although their early involvement in strikes in Pennsylvania is part of that state's history (see Greene, 1968). Napolska (1946) stated that "out of a Polish population of 300,000 in the state of Michigan in 1911, at best only 5,000 were union men" (p. 39). She goes on to explain:

> There were several factors responsible for these conditions: first, the inadequate knowledge of the American labor problems; second, the lack of adjustment of the Pole to the American system of organization; third, the unsympathetic attitude toward non-Polish organizations; fourth, the distrust toward such organizations resulting from the inability of understanding the English language freely, and the consequent impossibility for looking into initiation into these associations depends often on the official policies of the parental organization.[6]

---

[6] The interesting thing is that the American society was very worried that the "new" immigrants were "radical" and would join or form unions and cause great problems for management. Hourwich (1912) defended them against this accusation and Rosenblum (1973) develops this thesis further. The immigrants were not radical; they just wanted a job and once here did not complain about wages. Although often not accustomed (from prior life) to wage labor, in fact they were against unionization if it were

Studies of local Polish American ethnic communities have found both types of membership in otherwise American groups (Gould, 1966; Jurczak, 1964; Obidinski, 1968; Sandberg, 1974). Both types of lodges are present among American veteran groups, but one or the other can also be found among the Masons, Elks, Kiwanis, Lions, etc. Involvement in these organizations is class related.

Polish American participation in the religious and educational institutions of America is increasing in spite of the continued trend toward parish schools for children. A recent survey in the Chicago area indicated that even Catholic schools with a relatively high percentage of Polish American children were so Americanized that they did not teach Polish. Most Polish Americans have remained with the Roman Catholic Church, rather than going over to the Polish National Church or to American Protestant groups. However, those now living in secondary or tertiary areas of settlement are not apt to form Polish parishes, they blend instead with Catholics of other national origins. Participation in the recreational institutions of America is not documented, although there is some evidence of continued leisure-time socializing by segments of the community along class lines (Gordon, 1964).

SUMMARY

Polonia as an ethnic community has interacted with the larger American society through official and individual action. The community has been maintained in spite of the fact that most individual Polish Americans cross the ethnic boundaries many times to enter the flow of economic, educational, recreational, and other aspects of American life. The community itself spent the early decades of its existence attempting to influence the American political powers on behalf of Poland. Engrossed in its own status competition, the community was aware of prejudice

---

to control the labor market. In addition, the immigrant did not identify with the society and its problems. "His contact with Native Americans was likely to be within an employment relationship and that relationship was predominantly rational, functionally specific, universalistic, avoidant and individualistic" (Rosenblum, 1973:125). Also, the new immigrants often did not expect to stay in this country. Between 1908–1910 the "immigration commission found a greater rate of departures for new (73 per hundred admitted) than for the 'old' (13 per hundred admitted)" (p. 125). They were thus unlikely to spend time and interest forming unions, preferring to work hard and live frugally. "We suggest that the failure of a major working-class challenge to capitalistic economic institutions to mature in the United States is partially attributable to the fact that a large portion of those in the lower reaches of the occupational hierarchy at the time mobilization was most likely to occur simply did not identify themselves with the society in which they carried out their work lives" (p. 177). Thus, the Poles were not the only ones to refrain from joining the American unions.

against it and other new immigrant groups in the wider society. This awareness usually resulted in a neglect of attention to what was going on outside the community boundaries, unless an acute event reawakened concern over a chronic situation such as the condition of the Polish political state or the underrepresentation of Polish American clergy in the upper rungs of the American Roman Catholic hierarchy. Relations with other ethnic and racial groups were generally nonexistent or hostile if contact threatened the social position of the Polish Americans.

In recent years, however, Polonian leaders have become increasingly interested in changing the image of Polish Americans in the larger society. The negative nature of this image was brought into focus by Polish jokes, and the community leaders in a variety of companionate circles have been organizing a concerted effort to change this image. In the meantime, Polish Americans have not been very active in American political life, under-using their potential influence on the local scene where they were numerically concentrated, because of an initial lack of citizenship or because of the status competition among candidates for public office. They have, however, recently organized on the national scale in order to use a variety of methods of political pressure.

The Polish Americans have also been underrepresented in the upper echelons of the American economic and voluntary association hierarchies, for a variety of background and attitudinal reasons. The antidefamation campaign and the attempts to change the Polish American image through new ideologies and cultural items, and dissemination of Polish culture internally and in the larger society, may modify the position of this ethnic community in America. It is also probable that the changing demographic characteristics of Polish Americans, particularly their increasing use of American educational resources will assist this process. Thus, we turn to a description of the past and present characteristics of Polish Americans.

In the 100 years since the Poles started coming to America in large numbers, Polonia has undergone many changes in the education, occupations, social life styles, and "ethnicity" of its members. In discussing these changes we must first ask, "Who is a member of the Polish American ethnic group?" Unfortunately, the inaccuracies and inconsistencies in the immigration figures (discussed in chapter 3) also confound census information. All past analyses have been based on country of birth and have lumped together Polish Catholics, Polish Jews, Lithuanians, and other groups. The census does not contain questions dealing with religion; mother tongue is not a reliable source of information.[1] This is particularly important when the country of birth figures include, for example, Polish Jews who do not identify with Polonia and who have gone in a different direction as far as educational and occupational achievement. Since 1969, fortunately, ethnic origin, "determined on the basis of a question asking for self-identification of the person's origin or descent and is, therefore, a report of what persons perceive their origin to be" is included in the census (*Statistical Abstracts*, 1973:3).

Patterns of Change in Polonia

THE POPULATION

Table 5–1 shows that the peak year for Polish "foreign stock"[2] in America was 1930 with a recorded total of over three million people. By 1950 the total decreased, indicating deaths of older members and movement into the third generation. The "new emigration" was not large enough to offset the continuing decline. Since Table 5–1 is limited to the first two generations (as determined by country of birth rather than ethnic identification) and to mother tongue, we must look elsewhere to determine the parameters of the Polish American ethnic group. The special supplement to the census undertaken in 1969 asked for country of birth of grandparents and reported 1,776,921

[1] More Polish Americans list Polish as their mother tongue than list parents as having been born in Poland. This indicates that some members of third and later generations are being raised in homes still using the Polish language (see Table 5–1).

[2] "Foreign stock" includes people born in Poland, and children born in America whose parents (one or both) were born in Poland. Many Polish families in America are still made up of immigrants (some of whom identify as "Poles") in addition to the second generations (usually identified as "Polish American" but occasionally referred to as "Americans of Polish descent") and the newest generation (whom Polonia likes to refer to as "Americans of Polish heritage").

TABLE 5–1

TOTAL NUMBERS OF FOREIGN STOCK POLES AND PEOPLE LISTING POLISH
AS THEIR MOTHER TONGUE IN THE UNITED STATES 1910–1970,
WITH URBAN, NON-URBAN RESIDENTIAL DETAILS FOR 1970

| | Country of Birth | | | Polish Mother Tongue | |
Year	Foreign Stock	Foreign Born, White	Native of Foreign or Mixed Parents	Foreign Born	Native Born of Foreign or Mixed Parents
1910 * Total	1,663,808	937,884	725,924		
1930* Total	3,342,198	1,268,583	2,073,615		
1950 * Total	2,786,199	861,184	1,925,015		
1970 Total	2,374,244	548,107	1,826,137	419,912	2,018,026
Urban	2,138,531	512,522	1,626,009	385,567	1,743,121
Rural:					
non-farm	197,899	29,912	167,987	29,021	225,775
Rural: farm	37,814	5,673	32,141	5,324	49,130
Metropolitan					
Total	2,098,912	502,245	1,596,667	376,572	1,713,997
Central city	1,127,853	331,543	796,310	223,596	790,473
Other urban	857,505	154,410	703,095	127,248	793,416
Rural:					
nonfarm	98,386	13,751	84,635	13,453	113,943
Rural: farm	15,168	2,541	12,627	2,275	16,165
Nonmetropolitan					
Total	275,332	45,862	229,470	43,340	340,029
Urban	153,173	26,569	126,604	24,723	159,232
Rural:					
nonfarm	99,513	16,161	83,352	15,568	111,832
Rural: farm	22,646	3,132	19,514	3,049	32,965

Source: U.S. Department of Commerce, Bureau of the Census: Sixteenth
Census Reports, *Nativity and Parentage of the White Population*; U.S.
Census of Population, 150, Vol. IV, Part #A, and 1960, Vol. 1, Table 36;
U.S. Department of Commerce, Bureau of the Census; United States *Sum-
mary, General Social and Economic Characteristics*, 1970, Table 97–108
and Table 136.
* *Historical Statistics of United States, Colonial Times to 1957.* Washing-
ton, D.C.: U.S. Government Printing Office, 1960. C185–217; pp. 218–83.

third generation Polish Americans (see U.S. Census, *National Origin and
Language* PC-2-1A). The three generational total, obtained by adding
this figure to the 1970 foreign stock is then 4,151,165. In addition, the
number of people who gave "Polish" in response to the "ethnic origin
question since 1969 census, raised the total number of Polish Americans
in 1972 to 5,105,000 or double the foreign stock total for 1970. (*Statistical
Abstracts,* 1973:T-41). This is probably the most realistic figure available.

Other data on Polish Americans are unreliable since they come from surveys of the American population conducted by a variety of scientific bodies because the number of people so identified in the samples is small. Conglomorate samples uniting several surveys conducted in a block of years camouflage changes over time.[3]

Keeping the problems of identification in mind, we can examine the makeup of the Polish American population today. The original immigrants who are still living (most have died) have a median age of 66.7, up considerably from 41.3 in 1930, and 57.3 in 1950 (*Statistical Abstracts*, 1973:T-41; Hutchinson, 1956:17). The median age of the second generation was 32.7 in 1950 so that it is now in the late 50s. The median age of the *total* Polish ethnic group, including succeeding generations was 32.9, indicating that younger people are identifying with this group when given a chance to do so by the census question. The ratio of second to first generation Polish Americans has been increasing at a rapid rate from 114 in 1920 to 224 in 1950, offset only by the "new emigration" arrivals (Hutchinson, 1956:14). The ratio of men to women has also changed considerably: there were 131 men for every 100 women in 1920, 116 in 1930, 111 in 1940, 102 in 1950 (Hutchinson, 1956:19) and 90 in 1972 (*Statistical Abstracts*, 1973:T-41). The ratio dropped between 1920 and 1930 due to the importation of families of the original male immigrants and between 1950 and 1972 due to differential death rates. Polish American men 65 years of age and over, formed 9.9 percent of the male component of this ethnic group in 1969; women of that age formed 13 percent.

GEOGRAPHICAL CONCENTRATION AND DISPERSAL

The Polish immigrants and their children settled in the urban northeast and north central United States. Few immigrants went south or west.[4] As late as the 1950s, the heaviest concentration for foreign-born and second generation Poles was in the New York-New Jersey metropolitan area. Chicago housed more Poles than any other city outside of Poland and the immigrants and their children also settled in Detroit, Boston, Buffalo, and in several cities in Pennsylvania and Ohio. Within these cities, they concentrated in their own communities and segregated

---

[3] Of special relevance here is the conglomerate sample developed by Greeley (1969; 1972; 1973; 1975) out of studies conducted by the National Opinion Research Center and the Michigan Survey Research Center.

[4] There was an attempt to relocate "displaced persons in the Deep South" after World War II (Heberle, 1951) and there has been a recent dispersal into the more leisure-oriented temperate regions of California, Arizona, and Florida.

themselves from both whites and blacks (Liberson, 1963).[5] In the 1960s, the foreign-born Poles were still highly concentrated in a few American localities in which they formed a high proportion of the total population ranking fifth out of 23 groups on their concentration scale (Fishman and Hofman, 1966:48). Their local communities tended to be in central cities and, in spite of the recency of their arrival and the presence of a large number of persons who did not even speak English, they rapidly acquired home ownership (Lieberson, 1963). The tendency to invest all money and efforts into home and land ownership is documented in a variety of informational sources.

Recent census evidence indicates that the Polish Americans are moving out of the central cities into other communities within the metropolitan areas (see Table 5–1). Although the census figures recorded here are of the first two generations only, half of the children of immigrants were already living outside of the central cities in 1970, while two-thirds of their parents remained in the cities. Very few Polish Americans live in rural farm locations of either metropolitan or nonmetropolitan areas. The same conclusion emerges when we examine figures of young (aged 15 to 44) Polish American women. Only 2 percent of the young women who identified their national origin or ancestry as Polish lived in farm areas, and 58 percent of those residing in metropolitan areas were outside of the central city. In addition, only 9 percent of those living in metropolitan areas of 520,000 people or more were in low income areas. (Bureau of Census, *Current Population Survey* F20–226:13)

EDUCATIONAL PERSISTENCE
AND CHANGE

There are numerous references in the literature to negative attitudes toward formal schooling among Polish peasants in pre-World War I Poland (Reymont, 1925; Szczepanski, 1962; Thomas and Znaniecki, 1918–1920). The social class system of those years provided a foundation of nonintellectualism bordering on anti-intellectualism which was accentuated by the great social distance between the peasant and the nobility. Although the upper classes idealized education as a necessary background of "the cultured man" (see chapter 2), the peasant classes did not adopt this idealization of education. Their anti-intellectualism is evident in the labeling of a person who enjoyed reading as a deviant, rather than as a

---

[5] Their index of segregation from the natives of native parentage ranged from 57.1 (out of 100 which would be complete segregation) in Boston to 70.5 in Buffalo as late as 1930 (Lieberson, 1963).

wise man (Thomas and Znaniecki, 1958:Vol. 2, 1135–36). Catholicism did not encourage scientific curiosity or the love of learning; it was an authoritarian and dogmatic religion, and the lay person was expected to accept it verbatim without question. There was nothing in the village culture which would make learning, abstract thinking, or experimenting with knowledge a pleasurable activity. Nothing defined education as an important means of contributing to the vital spheres of life.

The attitudes of the Polish peasants toward education—which defined it as a waste of time at best, and as a dangerous thing undermining the traditional way of life at worst (Benet, 1951:222)—were transplanted to the American soil. Ideally, the children of Polonia began working at an early age to help the family in its endless struggle for money. The United States Immigration Commission, which undertook an intensive study of immigrants in 17 American cities in 1911, found the children of Poles following this typical educational career: parochial school from the ages of 8 to 12, first communion, public school for two years, and then work (Miaso, 1971:35). The idea of higher education was foreign to Polonia's first or second generation youth: only 38 men and 6 women of Polish birth or descent were studying in the 77 schools of higher learning in the United States in 1911. (See also Abel, 1929:216–22). Higher education usually did not refer to college, but to schooling above the minimal level required in America at that time.

Although a dramatic change in educational achievement among newer generations of Polish Americans has taken place in recent years, the median year of schooling for the total group is pulled down by first and second generation members. First generation members born in Poland received very little formal education. The children born here suffered from having to go to work early in life. As late as 1960, Polish Americans aged 50 to 74 were ranked seventh out of eight major language groups other than English in median years of schooling, the only lower group being the Italians (Fishman and Hofman, 1966:49). Only 9 percent had gone beyond grade school, 59 percent had attended primary grades, and 31 percent had never obtained any formal schooling.

These uneducated older persons handicap the newer generations when their median schooling achievement is compared to other ethnic groups. This is particularly true when the Polish Americans are compared to the total white population, most of whose members are already in the third, fourth, and later generations.[6] Greeley (1974b) noted that "among

---

[6] This is the main reason for the deviation of the Polish American mean educational achievement scores in the Duncan and Duncan (1968) and Nam (1959) analyses of deviations from the non-Negro national mean.

the English-speaking white gentile groups, the Poles are almost a year beneath the national average" (p. 65). This deviation goes up to 1.1 years when the figures are standardized by geographical location since the Polish Americans are concentrated in large cities of the North "where there is more opportunity for education and educational achievement is higher" (p. 66). However, age is an extremely important factor in understanding this deviation. "The Italians over age 60 are almost a full year beneath their cohort mean in education, the Slavs a year and a half beneath the mean. The Italians and the Slavs in their twenties, on the other hand, are both about one-tenth of a year above the mean and the Poles about half year above the mean" (p. 68).

The 1969 census, which first asked for "ethnic origin," further documents the expanding use of higher education on the part of young Polish Americans. Men and women between the ages of 25 and 34 who identify with this ethnic group have reached a median level of educational achievement of 12.7, second only to the Russians' amazing 16 + median (U.S. Bureau of the Census, P–20:221, 1971). The Poles now surpass the English, the Germans, and the Irish—all of whom had a higher median than the Poles among the older age groups. The proportion of young people who have finished college is more than double that of older Polish Americans, and the proportion of young people who at least attended college is triple. Thirty-one percent of the younger Polish Americans have gone beyond high school.[7]

Educational changes in Polonia involve not only the number of years completed by the Polish Americans but also the source of this education. Most of the older people attended parochial schools and received training that did not guarantee knowledge of either Catholicism or Polish culture. Greeley and Rossi (1968:37) found that attendance at parochial schools did not affect the Polish American Catholics' knowledge of Catholic doctrine, respect of church authority, or of the church as a definer of moral issues; nor did the products of these schools fare well on a "general knowledge" index. One of the main leaders of Polonia has accused the clergy of inadequately educating the youth into Polish culture, because of their own lack of knowledge about it[8] (Kusielewicz, 1973:104).

[7] The Greeley analyses of the Catholics in America would indicate that this change is more than a reflection of the presence of Polish Jews in the census sample. Admittedly, I would feel more comfortable about the assumption that non-Jewish Polish Americans were contributing a major part of this increase if the table contained a Jewish ethnic origin group, since the Russian median is probably influenced by the presence of people socialized in the Jewish culture.

[8] Kusielewicz (1972:104) specifically stated, "Is it any wonder, then, that our young clergy of Polish American background look upon their Polishness as a liability

If these allegations of inadequacy of parochial training in Polish American schools are true, then the movement of the young outside this system can be expected to produce a change in knowledge and attitudes. Findings indicate that such education does in fact have an important influence on Polish Americans. Greeley and Rossi (1968) studied differences among Polish Americans who did and did not complete high school, and found that those who finished high school were more apt to have attended public (rather than parochial) schools for at least the last few years of education. Those who finished high school among all Catholic groups (Irish, Germans, Italians, and French) were different from their less educated fellow ethnics in many life situations and attitudes. But the differences between these two groups of Polish Americans were dramatic. The high school graduates were four times as apt to be in the top three occupational categories of the Duncan prestige scale, almost five times as apt to be in professional or managerial positions, and twice as apt to be among families earning $14,000 or more in 1962. The proportion of people reporting that they were happy increased from 22 percent for the less educated to 32 percent for the more educated; the probability of scoring low on an anomie scale increased from 38 to 50 percent. Although what Greeley calls "religious extremism" and "antisemitism" indeces are considerably lower among the educated, the "racism" index was not affected by education. The latter set of attitudes reflects the current situation in Polonia in terms of status competition and anger of the type described by Novak (1971).

OCCUPATIONAL PERSISTENCE
AND CHANGE

Without knowledge of English and the "American way of life" and without industrial skills, the majority of Poles who emigrated to America were not equipped to enter the occupational structure at any but the unskilled level. They entered the Chicago packinghouses, the steel mills of Indiana, Detroit's automobile assembly lines, and Pennsylvania's coal mines much as other immigrants had done before and would do after them. The second generation tended to put themselves at a disadvantage by limiting themselves to the occupations of their fathers. They did this partly because they were unwilling to use education as a means of learn-

---

and that they reflect this view in the administration of their parishes and the schools attached to them. The teaching orders themselves, according to Kusielewicz, "suffer the same feeling of inferiority that is characteristic of the greater part of the Polish American community" (p. 101). His point is that there is a vicious circle of ignorance of Polish culture being transmitted by the teachers of parochial schools to students, some of whom then become seminarians and future teachers of the young."

ing new skills, and partly because the strong patriarchal family system provided entrance into the father's work place early in life. The unusual structure and culture of the American society almost guaranteed horizontal outward and even upward mobility for sons of immigrants. Lieberson (1963:189) concluded that the Poles were dissimilar to other ethnic groups, being below the expected rate of generational mobility. Duncan and Duncan (1968), in analyzing the 1962 Census data by ethnic origin, concluded that second generation Polish Americans started with a serious handicap in early life in that their fathers' occupations deviated more from the prestige mean of the total population than did any other group's included in the analysis. Additionally, they found that Poles "suffer a modest handicap" in achieving upward mobility from the first job to the current one (p. 362). Occupational inheritance occurred more frequently among Poles than among other groups, not necessarily in terms of actual job but in level of prestige; that is, the occupational distribution among the second generation tended to be more concentrated than among the second generation for other groups. This reinforces Hutchinson's (1956) conclusions that second generation Polish Americans were held back by following their limited parental occupations while the country as a whole had moved away from such occupational inheritance.

The current occupational status of Polish American men reflects the continued presence of the first two generations in the concentration within four occupational categories: craftsmen, foremen and kindred workers (23 percent), operatives and kindred workers (19 percent), professional and kindred workers (18 percent) and managers, officials, and personnel (13 percent). These conceptions indicate a white and a blue collar polarity (*Current Population Reports,* U.S. Bureau of the Census, 1971, P–20:249, T-7). This polarity deviates from Greeley's findings which were based on a composite of ten years prior to 1973 and indicates a recent trend away from blue collar toward white collar jobs by Polish Americans. In general, most studies show that older Polish Americans of the old emigration are at the top rungs of the blue collar world, and recent generations are at lower rungs of the white collar world. An increasing number are entering the professions, shortcutting the traditional rung by rung movement of prior generations.

The percentage of Polish American women aged sixteen and over in the labor force is still relatively low (37.9 percent) to the national (44 percent) (U.S. Bureau of the Census P–20; 22, 1971). The lack of emphasis on higher education for women in Polonia is reflected by the fact that 36 percent are in clerical jobs, 19 percent work as operatives, 13 percent are in professional jobs, while 16 percent are still in service occupations.

SOCIAL LIFE STYLES

Internal differentiation among Polish Americans makes it hard to describe their "typical life style." Members of the old emigration have village and regional identities in common. New emigration Poles share common experiences of displacement. Each group identifies differently with Poland, America, and Polonia. Other important variables distinguishing one Polish American from another include generation in America, age, sex, marital and parental status, education, occupation, and presence or absence of an extended kinship group. These traits affect a Polish American's (1) social class life style; (2) involvement in Polish, Polonia, and American variations of this life style; and (3) content of life. We will discuss the first generations of the old and new emigrations separately, and then deal with class and community variations of later generations.

Life Style of the Old Emigration's First Generation

Those members of the first generation of the old emigration who have survived until the 1970s tend to have been brought here as children in the pre-World War I years or to have come to join relatives of already established family members after that war but before the imposition of the immigration quotas and other events stemming the immigrant tide into a trickle. Of course, in many cases it is only the accident of birth on the other side of the ocean which places them as first generation members of a sibling or age cohort, while their brothers and sisters born on this side of the Atlantic are considered members of the second generation. For this reason we are extending our comments to that generation which was born outside the United States or whose siblings were born outside the United States although they themselves were born of recent immigrants in this country.

The life styles of the immigrants and their young children were heavily influenced by their class background, place of residence in America, sex, and age at migration. Their backgrounds were varied in that not everyone had been a peasant, and not all peasants were alike. Some came from small isolated villages, unable to read or write; many did not know how to prevent the spread of diseases in new crowded conditions (Davis, 1927). Others found cities such as Chicago almost barbaric with its wooden sidewalks and high crime rates, being accustomed to the more established communities back home. Most were taken aback by the great heterogeneity of peoples from all over the world and by the hostility they met because of of their own behavior which they considered normal. Although one-third the Poles emigrating prior to World War I were illiterate, each local community had many temporary or even permanent residents who were relatively educated; these people started organizations, published newspapers, and helped develop the complex social structure. Community leaders at all levels wrote and read letters, taught the children, found jobs for others, and acted as role models for those trying to learn the best way of living in a strange new land. Reports of Poles in Detroit (Napolska, 1914), Hamtramck (Wood, 1955), Chicago (Thomas and Znaniecki, 1918–1920), the Connecticut Valley (Abel, 1929), and other local communities document the problems of rapid urbanization—hard work, frequent victimization, and overcrowding as people shared quarters or rented rooms to help family income. But they also document lively interaction, status competition with increasing resources, organizational activity in each neighborhood, and mobility from community to community in search of better jobs and nicer places to live. These reports also document internal heterogeneity with many mutually exclusive companionate circles. Except for the few immigrants and temporary visitors who function partly or exclusively in the wider American society, the boundaries of Polonia were socially, if not always territorially, clearly drawn.

Family Structure. The life styles of a large proportion of Polish immigrants were influenced by age and sex roles. The traditional Polish family was not only patriarchal but limiting of the social life space of girls and women.[9] In a Polish village, the new bride usually moved into or near the home of her husband's family (Benet, 1951; Thomas and Znaniecki, 1918–1920; Zand, 1956). Girls never inherited property unless there were no sons to take it over, and then the arrangement involved an "adoption" of a son-in-law into the bride's family. The woman's power within the family was very low at first and did not increase until she was older and had children of her own (particularly sons), and until the introduction of younger women into the unit relieved her of physical tasks and elevated her to a managerial position. Her status also increased with the increase of status of her husband. Her behavior and direct contribution to the economic welfare of the family unit were important for its reputation, so that although the patriarchal authority was absolute, her status was not as low as it might have been under such a system. Her husband and his family, and later her children, needed her constant contribution to their status *vis-a-vis* other families. "The bond [family] is

---

[9] The concept "social life space" refers to the social territory within which a person moves during his or her involvement in all the social roles which form his or her role cluster. The boundaries of the social life space are at the cut-off of the web of social relations in which he or she is involved.

not necessarily one of affection . . . There appears to be as much concern for economic status and stability and for 'face,' as for emotional bonds. The family is an economic unit and it is also a social corporation, reinforced by the strongest traditional sanctions" (Benet, 1951:144; see also Thomas and Znaniecki's description of village life [1918–1920]; Reymont's [1925] *The Peasants* and Finestone's [1964] analyses growing out of this literature).

Zand (1956:77) claims that the immigration process resulted in female hegemony within the Polish American family for several reasons. Wives were often left back in Poland while husbands migrated to America, or were left in one city of the new world while the men sought better working conditions in another. They, therefore, became accustomed to leading and managing their families. The kinds of jobs the men were able to get often kept them away from home long hours six days a week; the children did not have much time with their fathers and turned, instead, to their mothers. The fact that each woman could establish her own household rather than having to move in with her in-laws helped increase her influence over the family. Being freed from the male kinship group, women acquired much greater importance than young peasant women had traditionally enjoyed. Zand (1956) also indicated the possibility that, since there were so few women among the immigrants, some of the single men married the daughters of the more established families. In such cases, the woman's family had the major influence over the new unit, particularly if the couple lived in her family's home until the husband became economically self-sufficient. In addition, American laws protected women and dealt with family members individually rather than as part of a unit (Thomas and Znaniecki, 1918–1920). These authors concluded that the Polish-American combined marriage, in fact, had little chance of survival because the woman could refuse to be coerced by the man and could resort to external control agencies in order to force him to do her bidding, punish him for transgressions, and demand full economic cooperation. Marriage tended to become, under those circumstances, a matter of civil and legal rights rather than subject to community and extended family controls. Entrance into marriage remained, however, a matter for status matching and building.[10]

---

[10] Zand (1959) explained in "Polish American Weddings and Christenings" that the importance of status matching extended to the selection of couples to form the wedding party as bridesmaids and ushers. In choosing their attendants the bride and groom had to "match personality, appearance, social standing and wealth (p. 25). One reason for the concern was that "each couple was photographed separately at its own expense, with the man giving the girl six of the customary dozen photographs. Naturally, no one wanted to be thus immortalized in photographic print with a distasteful partner" (p. 25).

Regardless of the influence women have gained on American soil, each family exerted strong patriarchal control over the children, particularly the daughters.[11] A girl's reputation affected her marriage chances and the family status. Constraints were placed upon young women's involvement in school and work.[12] Schooling was not valued positively for girls, and work away from the immediate neighborhood was equally undesirable. "Domestic service, while recognized as hard and humble in social scale, was valued for the training and experience it gave a girl. . . . Young men married a girl who had been in domestic service more readily than one who had worked in a factory, partly because they expected that she would be a better girl morally, partly because she would be a better housekeeper" (Zand, 1956:85). Factory work was less favored, but might be permitted depending on the kind of work it involved. "The location was also a factor in the community's appraisal of the factory; if it was located within or near the Polish settlement so that most of the people who worked in it were Polish and the girl was, in a sense, under the eye of her friends and neighbors, the community approved it. The greater the distance and the opportunity for strange contacts, the less the community approved of factory employment for girls" (p. 86). Married women ideally remained at home to care for their husbands and children. This is why keeping boarders was a favored means of helping the family earnings, as was running small businesses such as grocery stores. The labor statistics of Polish American women until recent years reflect that unwillingness of the family to have them work once they are married.

Social interaction between man and wife, generally, was limited to matters of common interest, such as sex, household management, and child rearing. Men were expected to be concerned mainly with male matters, to seek the company of other men, and, among the former peasants in America, to use alcohol as a means of recreation and emotional release. Drinking on special occasions, such as pay day, Saturday night, or a wedding was traditionally heavy and accompanied by outbreaks of violence. Taverns formed an important meeting place for Polish men in the village and then in the American city (Thomas, 1949).

[11] Petras (1964) also concluded that the Polonian family was patriarchal. "Early studies characterized the Polish American family as authoritarian and extended, i.e., relatively unchanged from its form in Poland" (p. 17). "In the period of 1927–1929 there was still a belief in the absolute paternal authority" (p. 22).

[12] Schooling beyond the requirement set by law was particularly rejected for women and "obviously the old belief that a girl does not 'need' much education is still active among Polish Canadian families" as late as the 1970s (Dunin-Markiewicz 1972:98). Dunin-Markiewicz found that "the females outperformed the males" in high school in Windsor, Canada, by getting good grades, "yet when it comes to planning a university education, the situation is completely reversed and the boys outnumber the girls fifteen to nine." (p. 98).

Most foreign-born Poles married foreign-born Poles (except when newcomers married daughters of more established families), and the tendency to stay within the ethnic group carried over to their children. Fertility rates for Polish women have dropped considerably over the decades. The fertility rate for foreign-born Polish women aged 35 to 44 dropped from 5,868 children having been born per 1,000 women in 1910 (compared to 4,102 for all foreign-born white women) to 2,076 for foreign stock Polish Americans in 1960 which was below the total foreign stock rate of 2,195 (U.S. Bureau of Census, P–20, N.226, November 1971: Table 8).

As the immigrants reared their children they came into conflict with them, primarily over obedience and economic cooperation. The traditional Polish culture was based on a negative view of human nature: "The Poles are a censurious lot and have little faith in the continence or general moral fiber of their fellows" (Zand, 1956:79). Finestone (1964:126) concluded that "the Polish mode of interpreting experience is deeply imbued with the conception of sin; moral categories are widely applied in the judgment of human conduct." The result of such a mistrust of human nature was a system designed to rigidly control the behavior of children. Bennett pointed out a contradiction inherent in the Polish family institution: "Unquestioning obedience was expected of a child; at the same time the child was expected to become self-reliant, strong-willed and independent of spirit. . . . The dual emphasis on unquestioning obedience and independence subjected the child throughout the formative period of his life to two opposing pressures, creating strong tensions that often resulted in serious clashes between parents and children" (quoted in Finestone, 1964:150).

Children judged old enough were expected to find means of earning money, which was then to be turned over to the parents to use wisely in helping the family live and maintain or even increase its status. Thomas and Znaniecki (1918–1920) were personally shocked by the behavior of parents and children toward each other. Describing the disorganization of the family, particularly the parent-child relations over economic matters, they state, "The parents, for example, resort to the juvenile court, not as a means of reform, but as an instrument of vengeance" (p. 104 in 1958 edition). Finestone (1964) feels that this is proof of a basic lack of affection among family members. However, the status competition may also motivate such behavior. Thomas and Znaniecki (1918–1920) for example, report a case in the juvenile court in which a father who had been asked to cooperate in solving the problem of his daughter who had been living in the streets answered, "Do what you please with her. She ain't no use to me" (p. 104 in 1958 edition). He was referring to her failure to contribute to the family economic status. Finestone (1964) also found that parents, spouses, and other relatives failed to visit or write to men who had been caught in criminal acts and sent to prison. Unlike the Italians, who welcomed their exprisoners with a party and automatic help in reestablishment, the Polish family required a man to reestablish relations with each family member independently by promising not to bring dishonor to him or her again. Thus, not only do family members have to earn their right to belong to the unit through initial cooperation, but they must continue earning it throughout their lives by contributing positively to family status.[13] Those who dishonor or shame the family are either written off, legally disowned, or simply ignored until the time when they can reestablish themselves as effective contributors to the status competition. Those family members who because of birth or accident are incapable of ever helping in the status competition are simply ignored as much as possible. Conflict with uncooperative children was emotionally charged since failures to take part in the competition created anger and even hatred (Thomas and Znaniecki, 1958 edition: 104).

The immigrant generally had many children. In addition to contributing to the family social status, the children were also expected to maintain their parents in their last years. Wood (1955) found Hamtramck parents to be disappointed in the changes within their families brought about by Americanization. "After they finished school, they got married, and they are no help for the parents at all. They leave home and forget about their poor old parents." (p. 215). The second generation Polish Americans thus came into conflict with their parents as they adopted ways of relating to them which were not typical of the traditional obedient child role. Their demeanor toward their parents and other elderly persons lost the quality of "respect;" they became concerned with developing their own social status independent of their parents. In fact, establishment in the community or the society at large meant, in the case

---

[13] Finestone (1964) repeatedly points to the difference between the Polish and the Italian cultural values, including the relation between role behavior and sentiment, emphasis on privacy, expression of interpersonal hostility, the relationship of work and play, and family membership. "The criteria of membership were much more explicit in the Polish than in the Italian peasant family. Among the Poles, except for infants and the very young, continued membership in the family presupposed that each individual would make a regular contribution to the material sustenance of this group. The application of this criterion tended to render ambiguous the position within the family of the deviant, the inefficient, and the aged. Within the Italian peasant family, in contrast, the terms of the transaction between individual and group were somewhat mitigated for the young, the aged and the deviant. A member could choose to sunder his tie with his family but it is unlikely that other family members would voluntarily impose such a condition upon him because of some disability on his part" (pp. 488–90). In addition, "among the Polish peasants human nature was regarded as dominated by evil impulses and the human organism as fragile" (p. 490).

of second and sometimes third generations, becoming unlike the parents, rejecting their style of life, and moving away from the community. The parents had been allowed to establish themselves independently because their families had been left behind in Poland; however, they now attempted to impose the traditional forms of control. Conflict between the aging parents and the adult children, often over the way the grandchildren were reared, continued in three-generation households. Some parents retained contact with one child more than others by living in the same housing unit, in the same building, or within "soup carrying distance" (Townsend, 1957; Lopata, 1972b, 1973a, 1973b). Contact with other offspring and their families became limited to holidays which had always been very important and gradually became the only items of Polish folk culture that younger generations experienced (Gould, 1966).

One of the ways in which life in America affected the Polish immigrant and his family was through the de-crystallization of sibling status. Each brother, and, mainly through marriage, each sister, established his or her own life, following economic opportunities or problems. Although helping each other in the initial stages of settlement and sometimes in emergencies throughout life (Shanas and Streib, 1968), many families became sufficiently divergent and involved in their own nuclear families as to decrease interaction.

Geographic Location. The old emigration's first generation Polish Americans are apt to be still residing in the older sections of American cities, while their children and/or grandchildren have moved to the outskirts or the newer suburbs. In these older areas they are apt to be located in racially changing neighborhoods. The villagers' traditional fear of strangers combined with a lack of familiarity with people of different races (due to their absence in Poland) and the prior segregation of the Polish and the black communities has resulted in hatred and fear of the blacks. The Puerto Ricans and Mexicans are also met with hostility in that they represent different life styles and are symbolic of the break-up of the old Polonian community. Studies of residential areas of elderly Polish Americans in cities present a picture of sadness, anger, feelings of abandonment by neighbors, and family and social isolation. The "Needs Assessment of Chicago Elderly" survey found that Poles have negative attitudes toward their neighborhoods at a frequency higher than that of any group but the blacks, and consider safety to be a major problem (Lopata, 1975).

In general, the social life space of most of the old emigration's first generation expanded with immigration to America. Polonia as an *okolica* provided greater variation of social roles than had the Polish village *okolica*. The lower class Polish Americans tended to be limited in the geographical space their social life space covered, and the women still focused their major roles around the family institution. Men worked for large American organizations but generally refrained from active participation in their groups (even in unions), preferring their own ethnic associations. Organizational membership for both sexes was high even among the working classes, with parish groups, mutual aid "societies," and village clubs being most prevalent. The higher the social class of the Polish immigrant, the fuller the social life space, with involvement in social roles in several institutions and the more apt was even the first generation man or woman to be involved in at least some American institutions outside of Polonia.

Life Style of the
New Emigration's
First Generation

The first generation of Poles who came to America as part of the new emigration was an even more heterogeneous group than had been the old emigration. They were admitted by the special Displaced Persons Act of 1948 and subsequent laws. Many had spent up to five and six years in labor or other concentration camps and prisons in Germany. Others spent years fighting with the allied armed services in Europe or wandered the world after being deported by the Russians. Their background and the procedures they followed in resettlement were very different from those of the earlier peasant, middle class, or intelligentsia immigrants. They had been reared in independent Poland which had made concerted efforts at mass education; they came from urban communities more frequently than from rural; and they had been involved in a variety of occupations. The intelligentsia was over-represented among them, due to the German and Russian attempts at liquidating this segment of the population and its tendency to nationalistically participate in the underground government and the Warsaw uprising, which resulted in its frequent dislocation. The experiences of uprooting, survival, participation in the fighting or underground inside and outside of Poland changed their outlook and concerns with world affairs, the unwillingness of most to return to communistic Poland created a strong motivation for success in the adopted country. Their adjustment to American society was facilitated by a complex social system created to screen applicants in Europe, obtain guarantees of housing and employment or at least temporary financial support from sponsors, arrange for the trip, and obtain the cooperation of local communities in meeting settlement problems (Kolm, 1961: chapter 7). The refugees were predominantly young, with a sex ratio of 119.3 males for 100 females and a much lower marriage rate than the American population (Kolm, 1970:225). Most settled in the largest cities of the Middle Atlantic, East North Central, and New England states.

All indications point to a more rapid and successful acculturation and adjustment of the new emigration than of the old (Kolm, 1970; Mostwin, 1971). The newcomers did not initially join in Polonia's status competition; they preferred to develop their own subcommunities or to turn instead to the American sources for self-establishment such as education, occupation in white collar positions, and residence in nonethnic neighborhoods. The most extensive analysis of this emigration was conducted by Mostwin (1971) whose respondents form a self-selective sample in that they were found through Polish American groups and only a relatively small proportion of distributed questionnaires were answered (p. 143). Keeping in mind the probability that the more educated and successful Poles were the most apt to answer the questionnaire, we can learn some aspect of their life style from the 2,049 respondents. This was mostly a political immigration; few came for economic reasons. The majority is now between 40 and 50 years of age having come to America between 1948 and 1952. Mostwin found that:

> The respondents who tend to be more satisfied with their living arrangement in this country are married, have longer years of residence in the U.S., immigrated to this country already trained in a profession, live in the suburb or in the country, do not live in a Polish section, have never lived in a Polish section, own their homes, and have comparatively low ethnic commitment (p. 196).

It is interesting to note that living in a Polish section of a city did not lead the respondents to residential satisfaction Those people who knew English upon arrival, who have a higher educational achievement, and who have developed a successful "American" life style are apt to be satisfied not only with their residence but also with their employment. Employment satisfaction is related negatively to living in a Polish neighborhood, immigration for economic rather than political or familial reasons, low income, and strong ethnic commitment. The higher status Poles of the new emigration are the most satisfied with all aspects of their lives. However, Mostwin found that although there were more upper strata than lower strata emigrants among her respondents in terms of status prior to the war in Poland, the two top classes paid a price in status drop for migration. In fact, it was mainly the middle class that suffered—over

50 percent of them moved downward to the lower middle class. Many had been owners of small businesses or required prolonged retraining made difficult by their age. The Poles who came directly from Poland after the 1956 political "thaw" were highly over-represented among the professionals.

Although Mostwin's (1971:256) respondents reported that they had less conflict with their children than did the first generation of the old emigration, certain behavior patterns typical of American youth were picked up by their children which bothered the new emigration's parents. What bothered them most was "lack of respect for older people" (63 percent), "laxity in social manners" (56 percent), and "early dating (under 16 years of age)" (48 percent).

Like other social groups, the higher the social class of the new emigration, the fuller the social life space, and (even more than in the case of the old emigration) the more likely it is that that space involves roles within the American institutional system. Contact with Poland is maintained by many of the former displaced persons and excombatants, in spite of a continuing strong stand against its communist government. Polonian affiliation is strong among a segment of the new emigration. The intelligentsia among this emigration lead a life typical of the Amercan intelligentsia if they are affiliated with American organizations. There are many former members of the Polish intelligentsia who are unable to reproduce this life in the American society and these people tend to gravitate to each other in friendship patterns.

Life Styles of the Second Generation

The second generation of Polish Americans is now (with the exception of the children of the new emigration) in the middle years of life. The offspring of the old emigration reputedly suffered much social disorganization because of their position as the marginal generation caught between the Polish culture of their parents and the American culture of the society around them (Park, 1928; Stonequist, 1937). In fact, most scholars predicted social disorganization in the community and the family, resulting in increased demoralization, "hedonism," and antisocial behavior among members. (Claghorn, 1923; Thomas, Park and Miller, 1921; Thrasher, 1927). Thomas and Znaniecki (1918–1920) expected this disorganization to follow the inability of Polonia to reproduce the Polish village culture and social organization, with its strong use of shame and other personal forms of social control.

The predictions of high rates of social and individual disorganization proved to be exaggerated. In fact, a few social scientists tried to convince the others that some of the indices of disorganization, such as crime rates, were being misunderstood and misused. Taft, (1936:726–730) argued that "the foreign born as a whole are committed to penal institutions for felonies in proportion far below their normal ratio," although the children of foreign-born parents had high rates. The main reason for this, according to Taft, was their disproportionate age distribution. Many second generation Poles fell within the "criminally significant"ages of 15 and 24. The age distribution of the Polish foreign born placed only six percent of them in these criminally significant ages in 1930 while the native born of foreign or mixed parentage of Polish background contained 63 percent between 15 and 24 years of age and an additional 33 percent between the ages of 25 and 44 (Taft, 1936:726). The corrected rate, adjusted for population distribution, found Polish felons committed to state institutions in 1933 at a rate higher than that for the older immigrant groups but lower than that for Lithuanians, Greeks, Italians, and Spaniards (p. 734). Thus, Taft's point was that the Polish Americans were not any more contributive to American crime rates than were other groups with a similar population age profile and similar newness of immigration.[14]

Unlike the Italian Americans, the Polish Americans engaged in little organized crime (Finestone, 1964). Robbery and burglary were the most frequent causes of arrests and were usually "one-man jobs." The youth, on the other hand, were active in gangs; Thrasher (1927:9–10) reported that the main Polish business street in Chicago had "a gang in almost every block. The majority of gangs in Chicago are of Polish stock, but this may be due to the fact that there are more persons of Polish extraction in Chicago than of any other nationality except German."[15]

The Polish Americans also did not seem to have a disproportionately high divorce rate—the only real measure we have of family disorganiza-

[14] The American government was periodically concerned with the probability of its immigrant population contributing to the crime rates, particularly in its cities, and asked for investigations in 1911 and in 1931. According to Bowler (1931), the foreign-born Polish criminal rates were decreasing in the years between 1925 and 1929 from a higher level between 1915 and 1919 (pp. 83–193). In the late 1920s their rates were below the rates of the Mexicans, Negroes, native whites, Lithuanians, and, in some places, Greeks. In 1926 the Poles were underrepresented in relation to their proportion in the population, both in terms of total figures and in all categories but rape (p. 154).

[15] Certain Polish neighborhoods had very high second generation youth juvenile delinquency rates (Fleis-Fava, 1950:11). The area around the settlement house began to be heavily Polish by 1899 and remained so until the 1920s. In the 16th ward, "80.7 percent of the foreign-born whites [were] Poles, while the Poles made up only 17.7 percent of the foreign-born white population in the city as a whole" (p. 18). Crime rates were very high in those years.

tion. In spite of the dire predictions of family disorganization, there is no outward evidence of it in the history of Polonia, except for the use of courts to force conformity on family members, or to punish them for failure to contribute to the family status. Thomas (1950) and Rooney (1957) have questioned the assumptions of family disorganization, but they unfortunately had recourse to only a limited amount of divorce data. The Greeley (1974b) composite sample also shows relatively average divorce rates for the Polish Americans. Finally, the 1972 census shows that only 1.7 percent of the Polish males 14 years of age or over are divorced, a rate lower than the total 2.5 percent (U.S. Bureau of Census, 1970 PC(2)–4C:Table 2). The female rate is 2.2 percent for the Polish Americans and 3.8 percent for the total population.

The low divorce rates for the Polish Americans does not imply the absence of family strain and conflict, but those phenomena are very hard to prove one way or the other.[16] It is one of the theses of this book that the internal structure of Polonia's subcommunities prevented and cushioned some of the conflict, or at least institutionalized it into the status competition. The first generation helped the second to develop its own status package by providing a good family reputation and by starting them on a level at least equal to the one on which they were reared. Furthermore, the same forms of social control that had kept families together in Poland operated in Polonia; parishes and mutual aid groups provided the foundation for status competition; many status hierarchies were available in the social life of the community; it was easy to gain financial success in traditional terms. All these developments allowed parents to socialize their children, in spite of conflict and rebellion, into a similar concern with the community they shared. Rather than living in an anonymous urban center visualized by Thomas and Znaniecki (1918–1920) as inevitably disorganizing, the second generation was born into and contributed to reputation-giving communities offering numerous rewards by decrystallizing and keeping flexible status packages. The young generation eventually broke from their parents but this does not mean that they became alienated throughout life. In spite of all the literature on assimilation which claims a rapid "melting" of second generation ethnics, recent studies of Polish Americans indicate that the second generation is a "transitional" rather than a highly acculturated generation (Gould, 1966; Obidinski, 1968; Sandberg, 1974). The continued existence of Polonia for over a century indicates involvement of the second generations in family units.

---

[16] Zand (1959:30) also states that "divorces and separations were indeed rare among American Poles, while desertions were more frequent" but she gives no statistics to support this contention.

Second generation Polish Americans exhibit several different life styles depending on whether or not they had been brought up in and identified with Polonia, had been able to synchronize family resources in striving for upward mobility, and also on their inherited position in the community. Those who remained in Polonia gradually became Americanized in their behavior and appearance, if not in all attitudes. Although they did not become involved in higher education, they began to look at it more positively for their children (Wood, 1955). Their demands on the younger generation were much less severe than had been their parents' demands on them (Obidinski, 1968). Much of their life centered around the community with varying levels of participation. Other Polish Americans moved away from the area of first settlement, but often to places where other Polish Americans lived (Agocs, 1971). Commuting at first back to the old neighborhood to buy Polish foods, attend meetings, visit relatives, and even attend sacraments in the Polish parish, they gradually created their own neighborhood structure in the area of secondary settlement. Still other Polish Americans moved entirely away from Polonia, often changing their names and disassociating themselves from their ethnic identity.

Of course, not all second generation Polish Americans were reared in Polonia. Many, particularly children of the new emigration, grew up in nonethnic communities or those with only a scattering of Poles. An interesting life diversification by such children is reported by Mostwin (1971).[17] The children of the displaced persons, excombatants, and other refugees of World War II often live in two separate worlds: Polish and American, but not Polonian. Most are antagonized by the lack of knowledge of the Polish national culture by the descendants of the old emigration whom they consider obligated to share the heritage. Contact with Polish American offspring of the old emigration tends to occur only among professionals or members of organizations. Those who live completely outside of Polonia have not been sufficiently studied to know their distinctive characteristics.

Succeeding Generations of Polish Americans

Later generations of Polish Americans do not appear as a distinct unit in any collections or analyses of data on American society. We are thus limited to partial information from specific communities in which gen-

---

17 See also Johnson's (1969) description of the youth of Polish parents in Australia and Dunin-Markowicz's (1972) study of Canadian children of Polish parents.

erational differences have been the subject of special studies. Fortunately, there is an increasing number of these studies (Emmons, 1971; Gould, 1966; Jurczak, 1964; Mostwin, 1971; Obidinski, 1968; Sandberg, 1974; Wagner, 1964).

Obidinski (1968) found several important attitudinal and behavioral differences between second and third generation residents of Buffalo, New York including increasing approval of ethnic intermarriage (38 percent to 64 percent respectively); decreasing support for a political candidate on the basis of Polish American identity (85 percent to 65 percent respectively); and decreasing preference for use of the Polish language during the entire Roman Catholic service (67 percent to 31 percent respectively). The third generation is much less active in voluntary organizations, both Polish American and purely American than are prior generations. Fifty percent of the first generation, 42 percent of the second, and only 30 percent of the third belong to a non-Polish organization. Of course, the differences between the second and third generations may be due to age differences. It is interesting that the less educated older generation is very active. Church attendance also varies by generation: the second was much more likely than the third to report going several times a week (36 percent of the second to 4 percent of the third generation). We can hypothesize that decreasing identification with Polonia in each succeeding generation may lead to a decrease of associational membership and community participation in general. That is, Polonia developed because of the active participation of the first generation of all social classes. It has continued with the help of the established higher classes of both emigrations. The third generation, although already in the middle class, seems to be less involved in the community life and status competition, and may simultaneously be decreasing organizational and community involvement in any community. The higher the class the lower the associational involvement is a reversal of American trends.

Both Obidinski's (1968) study and Gould's (1966) analysis of data collected by Jurczak (1964) indicate that third generation Polish Americans have relatives and friends who are geographically more scattered in the community than are the associates of the second generation. The Polish Americans of the third generation of Buffalo, who tend to be young, are surprisingly more apt to live in the Polish area than are their parents. Obidinski explains this by their inability to "rent or buy homes in the more expensive residential areas outside of East Side" (p. 90). In addition, many third generation members are single and want smaller residential units. "Finally, younger respondents—both married and unmarried—may occupy the original family home with parents. Such joint residence in East Side homes sometimes involves dependent elderly parents who retain title to houses" (p. 90). However, both the second and the third generations have relatives scattered in the city and suburbs (42 percent and 34 percent, respectively) or living in the suburbs only (14 percent and 21 percent respectively). The same scatter holds for "best friends" except with greater concentration on the East Side for both generations (54 percent and 61 percent, respectively). On the other hand, the third generation is less satisfied with living in the East Side than is the second; although currently restricted to this area, it is suburban bound by preference.

While they are moving away from "ethnic islands," (Gould, 1966), members are apt to be simultaneously moving up on the socioeconomic ladder as they approach middle age. Such mobility is assisted by formal education and by marriage outside of the ethnic group. "There is upward mobility from the lower to the middle classes in the third generation and the third generation married to a non-Polish spouse has utilized education to a much more effective degree as an avenue of upward mobility than the third generation married to a Polish spouse (p. 26). Generally, however, "The third generation still tend to marry a member of their own nationality, and almost in every case a member of their own religion" (p. 26). The connection between higher education and marriage outside of the Polish group has many ramifications—most endogomous contacts were made in colleges and universities, and Polish American attendance at these institutions indicates at least partial independence of the community.

According to Sandberg (1974), the west coast has tended to draw a more assimilated or higher class Polish American into secondary settlement. In studying the Polish American community in Los Angeles, Sandberg found that with each generation of Polish Americans, membership in Polish parishes and in any church for that matter, has declined. In general, there were few differences in ethnicity and behavior between the third and the fourth generations, and there was a similarity between the post-World War II immigrants and the second generation of the old emigration. The greatest amounts of decreasing ethnicity (as measured by Sandberg) were between the first and the second generations, modified considerably by ethclass.

Immigration and generational changes have not been strong enough to destroy the image of a strong patriarch in the Polish American family, even if his actual control over it has decreased. McCready (1974) found that "the Polish father has been able to maintain the image of the patriarch even during times of great stress and social mobility" (p. 168). In fact, his being a "focus of attention" in the family resulted in a tendency for the mother to be "less salient for Poles than for the other groups we have seen" (p. 168). By saliency he means relative importance of the mother to the father, as measured by frequency of reference. "The young Polish women rate themselves high on domestic skills, attractiveness, and sex appeal, indicating that they do espouse the traditional values for women in society. . . . Their low saliency scores for mother indicate that they have received their values from their father rather than emulating their mothers as role models. In other words, they think of themselves as attractive competent women because their fathers told them they were" (pp. 168–69). His conclusions are based, however, on the 10 year composite sample of the NORC studies and the data is not analyzed by generation, so it is impossible to determine if this image is undergoing any changes.

ETHNIC IDENTITY

In order to introduce this book I had to stick to the labels of Poles, Polish stock and Polish Americans as they have been used by immigration officials or the Census Bureau, with just passing comments on variations among the self- and other-imposed criteria for labeling or identifying people rather than for establishing identity (see chapter 1). In other words, we had to agree on some basic criteria for reference to people as Poles or Polish Americans. This was done simply by using whatever labels have been used in Polonia. Now is the time to examine that elusive concept of Polish American ethnic identity. However, this is not an easy subject to investigate due to a lack of agreement over the dimensions, content, and pervasiveness which are "typical" or "necessary" (see Kolm's [1961, 1969, 1971a, 1971b] extensive discussions of ethnicity in general). How "ethnic" does a person have to be to be called an ethnic? Which traits of national culture or ethnic style of life does a person have to exhibit? How influential must such an identity be in the behavior of the person, in self-feelings, in the behavior of other members of the same ethnic group and of outsiders, toward him or her, before it is clearly identifiable? We will first look at some of the criteria used by other observers of the Polish American scene and then attempt to specify its components.

Ethnicity has recently begun to interest Americans. In the past, they were mainly concerned with "Americanization" as a process by which distinctive folk, national, or ethnic behavioral and attitudinal patterns were dropped and American patterns substituted. Various observers noted different "symptoms" of delay or failures in the "melting pot" process (Drachsler, 1920; Schermerhorn, 1949; Smith, 1939). Kennedy (1952) and

Herberg (1955) used intermarriage as a basic criterion of assimilation. Polish visitors to America have defined Polish Americans as Americans with no Polishness to them on the basis of their lack of knowledge of the Polish language. Several sociologists focused on legal changes of Polish sounding surnames as indices of a willingness to "pass" into the general society. Name changes end the last visible proof of identification with the ethnic group, breaking past family and ethnicity label ties, though not necessarily interactional ties (Zagraniczny, 1963; Kotlarz, 1963; Borkowski, 1963).

Recent studies of ethnic persistence have developed more complicated lists of criteria, but perusal of the literature shows that there is no consistent pattern to the measurement of this identity. Each observer's criteria tap only limited phenomena, and in the case of studies of Polish Americans, these criteria are heavily based on lower-class Polish peasant or folk culture, and ignore changes over time and the creation of a Polonian culture. As a result, studies of generational changes in ethnicity almost inevitably conclude that ethnic identity is fading since the children and grandchildren of Polish immigrants tend to score lower than the first generation on scales based on the folk culture of the first generation. This view of ethnicity—in terms of intergenerational loss of a limited number of cultural items—ignores the Polish national culture and the culture of Polonia. However, some of the studies contain interesting contributions to a potentially more complex set of indeces and they are of themselves reflections of the vantage point from which observers view Polonia. For example, a limited, folk-culture-bound "ethnicity index" was developed by Jurczak (1964). The index asks about the frequency of serving folk foods, and uses an ethno-religious practive sub-scale. Cultural habits which are used are limited to the sharing of the Christmas wafer, blessing of the Easter basket and blessing of the home after the feast of Epiphany. It also inquires as to the use of Polish language but, unfortunately, not the vocabulary and the occasion for its use.

Obidinski (1968) used a more complex scale. His respondents were given a choice of identities including: (1) Polish, (2) Polish American, (3) American Pole, (4) American, and (5) some other nationality. He asked, "What phrase on the card best describes how you think other persons consider you?" without specifying the "other persons" (pp. 65–68). The interview asked about participation in Polonia's life, persistence of residence in the ethnic community, attendance at Polish language religious services, and membership in Polish and non-Polish associations. Ideational items included the possession of a religious (Polish Catholic) picture in the house, belief in selected ideas deemed typically Polish, and familiarity with the term "Polonia" and with the Polish American Congress as an organization.

Mostwin (1971) reflected her own involvement in the life of the new emigration by entirely ignoring Polonian ethnic identity. She developed a five-fold classification emerging from answers to three questions: How did the respondents identify themselves? How did they think Americans identify them? How did they think Poles in Poland identify them? (pp. 51–58). The only alternatives are "Pole" and "American." The first category of respondents were shifting from Polish identity toward a two-directional identity, in that they "consider themselves primarily Polish, believe that the Americans consider them Polish, but think that the Poles in Poland consider them American" (p. 55). Then there is the person who "thinks of himself as primarily Polish, but believes that the Americans and the Poles in Poland consider him Amercan (p. 57). Finally, there is the person with inconsistencies within [his] own ethnic identity."[18]

In addition, Mostwin was interested in the "transmission of Polish cultural values and selected patterns of behavior to children in the new environment" (p. 251). She asked whether the parents talked to the children about their Polish heritage, sang Polish lullabies to them, and sent them to Polish language schools. In relation to social class and ethnicity, Mostwin found that, "the higher the respondent's previous social status in Poland, the more likely he is to retain Polish within his ethnic identity; that is to identify himself as a Pole rather than as an American (p. 289). On the other hand, "The higher the social class, [present] the stronger the probability of 'passing' directly from the Polish to the American identity" (p. 290). Some readers may say that this study is not relevant here because it does not deal with Polonian or strictly Polish American identity, but we must recognize that there are people of Polish birth living in America for whom Polonian identity is not a reality.

Just as Mostwin's (1971) study reflects the population she describes, Sandberg's (1974) ethnicity scale reflects the Polish Americans in the Los Angeles area who have a higher educational and mobility background than most of the older communities. Sandberg (1974) developed three complex scales, the first of which measured the importance assigned by respondents to the preservation of cultural ethnicity, including "Polish schools, centers, organizations and the press . . . as well as the perpetuation of the language, music, dance, history and traditions of the group"

---

18 This last group falls into three sub-categories:

1) the person who perceives himself as an American but believes that he is perceived as Polish by both the Americans and the Poles in Poland;

2) the person who considers himself an American and believes himself to be an American in the eyes of Poles in Poland, but thinks that Americans consider him Polish;

3) the person who consider himself American, believes he is perceived as American by Americans but as Polish by Poles in Poland (Mostwin, 1971:56–57).

(pp. 53–4). The religious ethnicity scale measured attitudes toward the Polish church, and the national ethnicity scale focused on the concept of "peoplehood," or ethnic solidarity.

> That scale probed at feelings of kinship, mutual responsibility, and a sense of belonging, with others of similar background. They also touched on the sensitive nerve endings of Polish identification, such as the concern with Polish jokes and the propriety of Anglicizing names (pp. 64–5).

His scales are thus much more able to flesh out ethnic identity.

The problems with many of the scales used to measure ethnicity in Polonia are that they flatten the wealth of heterogeneity, over-simplify the content, and obscure the changes over time which consist of more than just the dropping of folk culture items. Only Sandberg's (1974) scale does not fall into this trap. There are many indications of revitalization within this ethnic community brought about by a broader source of identity harking back to Polish national culture as well as new items of Polonian literary and artistic culture. Future studies should tap the richness of the Polish American background more adequately so that we can better understand how its various components are brought together into different identity packages. A study of the actual packages of identity can point to subtypologies if not limited to only a few items of the common denominator. We must keep in mind the three basic identities—Polish, Polish American, and American—and then see how these can be woven together into packages or typologies (see footnote 2, p. 88, for a review of the definitions of these terms).

One characteristic of nearly all Polish Americans is a strong belief in a Polish national character which can be transmitted over generations. Although Americans consider it undemocratic, most Europeans believe not only in a biological or cultural transmission of national character but also in regional variations (see also chapter 2). Actually, the Polish Americans have two images of Polish national character—one of the gentry or nobility, and the other of the peasantry although there is some overlap. Super (1939) describes the characteristics of the Poles as including: an emphasis on equality within the two main classes (gentry and peasantry) with a strong sense of individualism; tolerance of other groups; religiosity of predominantly Catholic identity; idealism, romanticism; love of the soil; a "knightly" tradition, with a sense of dignity and honor; intellectual culture; a strong family orientation; hospitality; interest in good food and drink of an international flavor; stress on courtesy, etiquette, and manner highly developed and strictly followed. The negative traits he defined as: restriction, until recent years, of the women to the home and to minimal education; lack of concepts of sportsmanship, fair play, team work, and efficiency; and a lack of directness of approach and openness in interaction. This view is more characteristic of the gentry, intelligentsia, and urban middle class self-image than the peasantry but even Reymont's (1925) descriptions of the peasants contain references to many of these items.

The overlapping characteristics involve the internal egalitarianism within each class although "the social cleavage between peasants and szlachta (gentry) was absolute and unbridgeable" (Benet, 1951:33). Within each class, however, there is an almost fanatical insistence on the quality of individuals. A Pole would rather bow to a foreigner than give authority to one of his own group" (p. 33). Like the gentry, the peasantry had elaborate rituals of social interaction. "The Polish peasant is probably the most polite and well mannered man in Europe. Rural etiquette prescribes certain expressions and even certain dialogues for everyday life and it is not permissible to improvise substitutes" (Benet, 1951:216).

At the same time, the peasant image of national character had some very strong negative features. It contained a negative and distrusting image of human nature, as prone to sin and evil action requiring a strong set of social controls, and the belief that shame was an effective means of socializing people. "Adult society is presented to the child as an arena in which social relations are determined by a constant and cruel interplay of domination and subordination" (Finestone, 1964; see also Zand, 1956). The peasant character was also portrayed as anti-intellectual and lacking the romantic, "knightly" traditions which deflected the directness of the individualistic status competition among the gentry.

The Polish American judgment of the national character combines elements of both the gentry and peasantry portrayals. The Polish Americans have internalized an image of themselves as the most individualistic and the least cooperative of all ethnic groups in this country; they thereby assume other groups to be different. As stated earlier this set of traits is used to explain failures in cooperative action. Any split in the community is fatalistically defined as a consequence of the national character.

In addition to the image of the national character, from which different traits can be drawn by Polish Americans, there are many other cultural items and group identity sources which can be incorporated in the identity packages. Part of the problem in studying ethnicity is the complexity of sources from which people can draw ethnic identities. There are basically three cultures and three groups of people who provide content for these identities. The cultures are the Polish and American national cultures and the Polonian ethnic culture which has grown from the merging of the national cultures and from its own dynamism (see chapter 1). Knowledge of these cultures can produce feelings of identity, as the feeling of Polish identification when hearing Chopin, or American identification when hearing the "Star Spangled Banner." Thus, part of Polish American ethnic identity can stem from the Polish national culture. As stated before, most Polish Americans have not expressed strong knowledge and identification with this literary and artistic culture developed and disseminated by nationalistic leaders and schools teaching Polish culture. Not enough is really known about the Polonian culture that has grown in this ethnic community to know how and when it provides sources of cultural, rather than group, identity. Cultural identity can be limited to a folk rather than a national Polish culture, as in the case of many Carpathian mountaineers.

Another major source of ethnic identity is the people. Again, there are three sets of people with whom Polish Americans can identify: the Poles, the Americans, and the Polish Americans. Such feelings of "peoplehood," of being a member of a group, can be very strong sources of a person's identity. This source can be complicated by divisions within the group, or by class, region of origin, etc. For example, a "new emigration" Pole who came from the traditional gentry class in Poland has a very different identity package when he or she is being considered as Polish American than does the descendant of the mountaineer immigrant of the "old emigration." His or her child also has a different identity package than does the first generation immigrant of either the old or new emigration. The Connecticut farmer sees himself as a Polish American very differently than does the official of a Chicago based superterritorial ethnic organization.

It is quite probable that each Polish American combines these sources uniquely, drawing different items of Polish, American, and Polonian culture and identifying with different groups of Poles, Americans, and Polish Americans in his or her ethnic identity package. This is particularly likely to have happened as generational, geographic, educational, occupational, and life style mobility have decrystallized the identity packages typical of the many subgroups of the Polish immigrants who have entered America within the past 100 years (see also Gordon, 1964; Mostwin, 1971; Znaniecki, 1952).

SUMMARY

The old emigration Polish Americans have progressed from the first generation of largely uneducated former peasants living in poor, urban, ethnic neighborhoods, to the financially well-off second generation that did not use higher education as a means of upward mobility and thus stayed in blue-collar jobs and life styles, to the increasingly educated third and fourth generations who can be expected to move up the socio-economic ladder. The ethnic community was able to survive the disorganizing and "demoralizing" effects of the migration, low status in American society, and loss of Polish folk culture as a unifying force, partly due to the strength of the status competition in a background of individualistic action requiring cooperation from social unit members, and partly due to the complexity of the new ethnic community. The new generations are physically, and for the most part culturally, indistinguishable from the dominant groups, and the choice of items for continued ethnic identification will depend to a great extent on the new social movements in Polonia. Encouragement of ethnic identification by Polonia's leaders is apt to affect even those Americans of Polish descent who do not know or identify with Polishness, possibly converting them into "Americans of Polish heritage."

Most of the studies of ethnic identity among Polish Americans have been very limited in scope. They conclude that mobility through generations and upward through the socioeconomic class system diminishes ethnic identity because they measure it by old emigration folk or peasant culture criteria. Inevitably then, movement out of the culture of the peasant into more middle class and upper class identifications and life styles must be defined as a loss of ethnicity. In other words, when Polish American ethnicity is measured by peasant folk culture criteria, those persons who are no longer, or never have been, peasants are apt to be defined as having lost their ethnicity.

If the activity of the intelligentsia and the organizational leaders in Polonia is successful, the whole base of this ethnic identity may change. We can assume that upward mobility will increase the social life space of Polish Americans, extending it through all three communities and cultures—the Polish, the Polish American, and the American—with a modification of the content of identity from folk to national, from generationally transmitted memories to learned national culture, and from a territorially circumscribed to an ideational ethnic community. If these trends are sufficiently strong, we would then need to change the content of the ethnicity scales being administered to the different generations of both emigrations of Poles, Polish Americans, and Americans of Polish descent into one that tested the meaning of the identity of Americans of Polish heritage.

A careful examination of life in Polonia reveals the significance of several sociological principles: the presence of ethclasses (Gordon, 1964) and other complexities of social structures (Hughes, 1934; Wirth, 1928; Kramer, 1970); the ability of an ethnic community to maintain itself in spite of territorial subdivisions and even dispersal (Etzioni, 1959), and the overlap between the life of an ethnic community and that of the larger society (Lopata, 1954). The concept of "ethclass" was coined by Gordon (1964) after an examination of the American scene which concluded "With regard to cultural behavior, differences of social class are more important and decisive than differences of ethnic group," and "with regard to social participation in primary groups and primary relationships, people tend to confine these to their own social class segment within their own ethnic group—that is, to the eth-class" (p. 52). Gordon (1964:51) thus refers to "the subsociety created by the intersection of the vertical stratification of ethnicity with the horizontal stratifications of social class as the ethclass."

Life in Polonia

Etzioni (1959) has pointed out to sociologists that ethnic communities do not have to be geographically or territorially bounded, with members of the same ethnic group inhabiting an area devoid of other people, or with all members living in such settlements. The community can function through interaction and identification by people who are territorially scattered, individually, in family units, or in many local communities and settlements. This is the main point of our definition of American Polonia as a superterritorial ethnic community.

There are several aspects of the Polonian situation which bear more detailed discussion. In describing life in Polonia we must limit ourselves to the activities of the community and its subgroups, not of people who could be identified as Polish Americans by descent but not by association. We limit our attention to people who belong to one or more of Polonia's organizations, participate in its web of polite companionship relations (Znaniecki, 1965: chapter 8) and interaction scenes, and maintain a community "reputation" in that their status in at least one of its companionate circles is known and compared to the status of their peers, people immediately below and people immediately above. Each local parish, neighborhood, settlement, and local community has its own circles of companionate relations, drawing in life style and interaction people of similar social status and involvement in Polonian life. Each level of community has its own set of hierarchies, depending on its size, length of establishment, internal differentiation, and location vis-a-vis other ethnic groups. The members of Polonia vary as to the size and complexity of the *okolica* within which their personal or family reputation is contained, ranging from the parish to Polonia as a whole, or even the cosmopolitan world.[1] People whose reputations are limited to a parish *okolica* are known only to a few people because they are not active in the web of organizational life beyond it, are not mentioned in the press of any but the parish newsletter, and have no other means of establishing themselves in a larger territorial and social arena. People with a Polonian reputation are active at national levels in the superterritorial organizations, have their activities reported in periodicals reaching members all over the country, and take advantage of many occasions for personal contact with local communities and other leaders.

POLONIA'S COMPANIONATE CIRCLES

The *okolica*—not territorially but socially circumscribed—within which a person's or a family's reputation is contained consists of three companionate relations circles; the one in which he is involved, the one immediately below, and the one immediately above. A companionate circle is a loosely bound group of people from the same ethclass who interact with each other, belong to the same organizations, lead a similar style of life, and are identified by others as belonging to the same circle. The circle contains peers, or near peers with whom people feel comfortable in both primary and secondary interaction. The boundaries of companionate circles are penetrable, and status decrystallization allows for mobility and overlapping, so that Polish Americans can belong to two or more circles and organizations devoted to their needs and composed of their members. There are identifiable circles in Polonia, which are differentiated by life style, personnel, and content of companionate activity. In general, the lower the social class, the more geographically limited are the companionate circles. The *okolica* is larger than the companionate circle because the circles at the upper and lower boundaries of that circle are usually aware of his or her reputation and membership within it.

The web of social relationships within Polonia involves Polish

---

1 Of course the intelligentsia, and the other elites as well, can be involved in interaction on a cosmopolitan Polonian level with similar elites from Canada, England, and other nations in which the Poles have settled, and with the intelligentsia or the comparable elites in Poland.

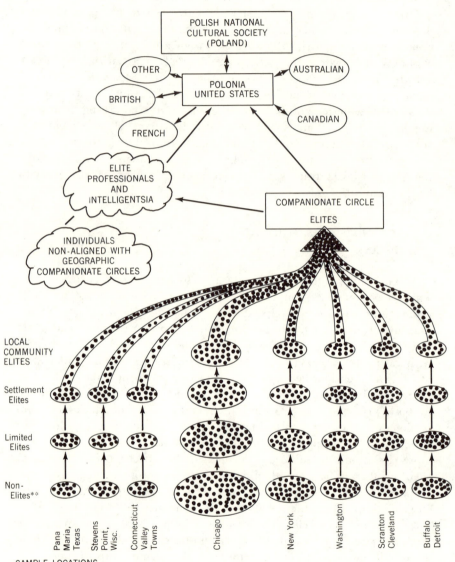

POLISH NATIONAL
CULTURAL SOCIETY
(POLAND)

OTHER

BRITISH

FRENCH

POLONIA
UNITED STATES

AUSTRALIAN

CANADIAN

ELITE
PROFESSIONALS
AND
INTELLIGENTSIA

INDIVIDUALS
NON-ALIGNED WITH
GEOGRAPHIC
COMPANIONATE CIRCLES

COMPANIONATE CIRCLE
ELITES

LOCAL
COMMUNITY
ELITES

Settlement
Elites

Limited
Elites

Non-
Elites**

Pana
Maria,
Texas

Stevens
Point,
Wisc.

Connecticut
Valley
Towns

Chicago

New York

Washington

Scranton
Cleveland

Buffalo
Detroit

SAMPLE LOCATIONS

**Actually Potential Elites, in that the Status Competition, Dependent Upon Status Decrystallization, Allows for Mobility
in the System at Each Level.

Americans to different degrees and at different levels. There is a core of organizational officials, people engaged full time in its economic life through businesses or the professions, the mass communication media workers, the priests, and the active members of the parishes. Without them and their replacements the community could not continue to exist. There are other people who participate only at certain hours, while working or in leisure, or only occasionally. They come to the headquarters of the activity, the "Polish Home," or organizational club rooms, and informal meeting locales from other neighborhoods, for special occasions, to contribute their skills or objects, or to buy or witness the skills of others; or they meet in outside locations with people of similar interests. They keep the flow of events possible, sometimes moving it outside the community's remaining geographical core, if such a core exists. The open boundaries of the community mean that even people who have moved away from the traditional Polish or Polish American neighborhoods are welcomed back at specific times or for acknowledged reasons. Some of those who participate in the community life never resided in localities with heavy concentrations of their fellow Poles or Polish American ethnics. The second generation Polish American doctor who lives in an integrated neighborhood and never contributes to Polonia's activities is simply not part of its life and we are not considering him here, but the doctor similarly located who is active in the Polish National Medical and Dental Association is part of the community's life even if it is not a major part of his life.

Several factors influence a family's reputation and membership in a companionate relations circle. Most members of Polonia are not status crystallized—their positions in different status hierarchies are sufficiently inconsistent to prevent an indisputable and permanent status package. This inconsistency or "status decrystallization" is the necessary condition for building Polonia's engrossing status competition. The old emigration tended to be more crystallized than their descendants, but according to internal standards there were definite status variations among the early immigrants which affected their willingness to share companionate relations. The place of birth in Poland was important. The emigrants from German occupied Poland and from larger villages or towns associated only with each other and looked down on the "more primitive" easterners and mountaineers. Due to the tendency of many Poles from the same area in Poland to migrate and settle together, personal and family reputations followed people across the ocean so that even small settlements in America contained their elites.

The first centers of community activity in America were the parishes (Thomas and Znaniecki, 1918–1920). These served as the *okolicas*, or the areas within which reputations were contained, for most of the emigrants. Gradually, with the development of nonreligious and territorially more expansive organizations, the community expanded the opportunities for social contact, drawing together those people who had common interests beyond that of neighborhood proximity or immediate needs. The internal differentiation of the community resulted in the formation of several loosely bounded or firmly limiting companionate relations circles, sometimes with overlapping memberships. Simultaneously, the uniting of neighborhoods into Polonia as a whole further broadened the scope of ethclass identification and association.[2]

In the meantime, of course, the internal differentiation produced by upward mobility of the former peasants and their descendants (Hughes and Hughes, 1952) filled empty rungs of the social status ladder. The push into middle class status was supplemented by those members of the community who arrived with higher status than the majority of the old emigrants, or who attained it through higher education or prestigious occupation. Most of the Polonians who entered with a higher status were political emigrees of both emigrations who stayed long enough to organize the People's University, the Socialist Party, or the Esperanto Club, and to start the national press (rather than ethnic press, which was limited to local Polonian interests). Some people, particularly of the new emigration, finally settled in America after years of expecting to return to Poland. Others of nonpeasant background participated in Polonia only marginally while generally living and keeping apart from the community which they branded as operating on a cultural level well below theirs. It is this feeling which has until recently kept the two emigrations apart in different companionate circles. The *temporary emigration*, still unstudied and made up of people who do not plan to stay after reaching

---

[2] Two styles of participation in Polonia's life, in mutually exclusive companionate circles, are demonstrated in two obituaries appearing side by side in the *Dziennik Zwiazkowy* (June 19, 1973:6). The first is that of a male, a doctor in South Bend, Indiana who was a member of the staff of a hospital, a national medical association, the Indiana State Medical Association, the American Academy of Family Physicians, the Pulaski Post No. 357 of the American Legion, the Schuyler Colfax Post 3194 of the Veterans of Foreign Wars, the Chopin Fine Arts Club, and Group 83 of the Polish National Alliance. His memberships are associated with past veteran's and professional roles, cutting across ethnic lines but with some Polish affiliations ranging from the "cultural" to the fraternal. It is impossible to determine the ethnic composition of some of his groups.

The woman whose obituary happened to be next to the doctor's was typical of older, lower class parish Polish Americans. She had belonged to the Brotherhood of Women of the Holy Rosary, the Jaslo Club, the Apostleship of Prayer, the Heart of Mr. Jesus, the Solidity of St. Teresa of Infant Jesus, the Society of St. Josef the Protector of the Novitiates of the Congregation C.R., and the Society of the Mother of God of Lourdes and St. Ann.

a certain level of savings, has kept apart from the companionate circles of both the old and the new emigration. These people are often of at least middle class background, have higher education, and possess occupational skills. Many are young, financially ambitious, and rejecting of the life they see in the Polish American communities. How many will remain is hard to predict, as are their future relations with the other Polish Americans.

An important variable in all companionate circle interaction is, of course, the availability and convenience of contact. People who live far apart and who are not accustomed to using indirect forms of interaction may not be able to share much of their lives with others whom they consider their peers in Polonia. We will now examine the composition of several of Polonia's companionate circles.

The Intelligentsia

The intelligentsia forms probably the most geographically scattered companionate circle of Polish Americans. Some members (such as newspaper editors of the ethnic or national press) are located in the heart of the community, while others (those associated with various teaching, research, or artistic centers, and a variety of economic organizations) are apt to be living outside of the geographical confines of Polish American settlements. The circle consists of first generation emigrants (mostly post-World War II refugees, excombattants, or recent emigres) plus the artists and other intellectuals of succeeding generations. The intelligentsia prides itself in speaking literary Polish, but is necessarily bilingual if involved in American work organizations. It tends to have a cosmopolitan outlook, keeping in touch with international events but retaining a strong interest in Poland, and its members read publications of fellow Polish intellectuals in other parts of the world. The intelligentsia is geographically mobile and meets with fellow nationals at scientific gatherings or "cultural events" such as concerts or speeches. Members also keep in touch indirectly through correspondence and through each other's visible products of work.

The intelligentsia can include people whose occupational status is not usually associated with intellectual or artistic endeavor. This is due to two main factors: the meaning of the intelligentsia in Poland (as discussed in chapter 2), and the presence of people who were forced out of a particular occupational background in Poland and were unable to transfer it to the American society. The Polish class system defined the intelligentsia not in terms of occupation, or professional and technical proficiency, but in terms of the combination of demeanor, knowledge of literary and artistic culture, and association with others of the "cultured man" or "cultured woman" class. This package of personal traits separated, for example, the businessman from a member of the intelligentsia even if the former had many more economic resources with which to buy artistic goods. It also accounted for the lower social position given to doctors, lawyers, and engineers. By the same token, a lawyer or businessman could belong to the intelligentsia if his life style and demeanor were appropriate. Within the intelligentsia, the highest status was accorded to professors holding full academic "chairs" in the universities.

The right and ability to retain intelligentsia status even when holding an inferior occupational position developed in Poland and has been institutionalized in Polonia. Emigration or forced expulsion from Poland often occurred, especially when it was managed by foreign powers. The intelligentsia was the most likely of the social classes to be taking an active part in political revolts or to be defined by the occupying powers as dangerous. (This is why the Nazis and the Soviets tried to remove that layer of the Polish society permanently and why so many who survived have not returned to Poland.) Often their occupational skills could not be transferred to the country of settlement because they were dependent upon language skills or because the bearer did not have high enough cosmopolitan status to be offered equivalent positions by the dominant society. Polonia, in America and elsewhere, simply could not absorb into its own institutions the large numbers of newly emigrating Poles. Many had to obtain positions inferior to those traditionally identified with the intelligentsia (Mostwin, 1971). Such immigrants tried to maintain the life style and circle of association which would retain their class identification, and the community generally allowed such a status claim in spite of the occupational and often financial decrystallization.

In addition to the members described above, included in the intelligentsia are a few members of the clergy, but only if they share the "cultured" demeanor and life style. The Polish American clergy itself is highly decrystallized in status, not so much in terms of the hierarchy in the Roman Catholic church, but in terms of education and cosmopolitan versus local orientation.

The intelligentsia, although geographically dispersed, has been able to organize occasions for contact. Four major events recently brought together members of this companionate circle: the three Congresses of Polish American Scholars and Scientists, on the American continent and the Meeting of the Scholars of Polish Descent in Poland. The first Congress drew 470 participants and 150 guests, some of whom were not of Polish descent (Zeranska, 1971). Almost all, however, had been born in Poland. The tendency of the intelligentsia to cross ethnic lines in America (Gordon, 1964) was also evidenced by the presence of many Polish Jews who share Polish culture and scientific interest with Poles of other religions. The meeting of the Scholars of Polish Descent drew Poles from various parts of the world. All four congresses used both Polish and English as languages of communication, and three were devoted to research and intellectual activity in general rather than only to Polish or Polonian matters. Many are members of the Polish Institute of Arts and Sciences in America.

Some members of Polonia's intelligentsia meet at the annual convention of the Polish American Historical Association which is held in conjunction with the meetings of the American Historical Society. They also meet at other events sponsored by organizations devoted to their interests on less than national levels. Lectures, concerts, and art exhibits draw Polish Americans to the newly organized Center for Polish Studies and Culture at the Orchard Lake Schools and Seminary in Michigan (*Polish American Congress News Letter*, July 15, 1969:7).

Professional
and Business Elites

The second type of elite in Polonia which forms its own companionate circle is the professional. Doctors, lawyers, and dentists are not given as much prestige in Poland as are the "cultured" intelligentsia (Szczepanski, 1962) because their professions are considered technical rather than intellectual. However, they have acquired some of the prestige associated with such professions in America. In addition, some professionals claim intelligentsia status. The professional specialists in different activities, such as medicine and law have separate societies, and publish their own journals.

The business elites include a few millionaires, such as the president of Mrs. Paul's Kitchen who has been so active in organizing "Project: Pole" (see chapter 4); some manufacturers, specifically heads of sausage-making firms; people holding high positions in insurance, banking, and similar ventures; broadcast media personalities; and travel agents. Emmons (1971) studied the members of what he called the "Polish American Business and Professional Men's Association" in Chicago and found that most of the men were self-made (see also *Michigan's Challenge: The Polish Americans of Michigan*, 1972). Emmons found a "marked pattern of upward mobility" among economic elites although few had fathers who "graduated from high school compared to adult white males and even other Poles" (p. 205). Chicago's economic elite does not necessarily live in the ethnic community (where many have clients or customers). Although

96 percent of the members who responded to Emmons' questionnaire had been brought up in a neighborhood where the Poles were the largest ethnic group, only 47 percent are now living in areas of such ethnic preponderance (p. 113). This means that the companionate circle draws people territorially scattered in their home life. This distribution exists in spite of the fact that the "Business and Professional Men's Association" members tend to be foreign stock—17 percent were born in Poland, 65 percent were born in America of foreign or mixed parents, and only 19 percent were born in America of native parentage. Emmons concludes that:

> normal class factors are operating to pull the elite in higher status ethnic roles away from the old neighborhood. This interpretation is consistent with eth-class theory, supports my contention that higher-status ethnic leadership roles contribute to mobility in the wider society, but contradicts my contention that upwardly mobile ethnic leaders show greater commitment to the ethnic group than do the general ethnic population (p. 115).

The last comment is based on the assumption that ethnic commitment would encourage the elite to remain in the ethnic neighborhood.

According to Emmons, the elite shared conservative attitudes toward the black civil rights movement; toward intellectuals (they tended to agree with former Vice President Agnew's "impudent snobs" comment); and toward "rebellious youth" (they felt that the U.S. "is leaning too much toward socialism)" (pp. 124–28). These attitudes were judged much more conservative than those of a matched sample of non-Polish professional, technical, and managerial white males. Such attitudes are apt to both encourage and result from interaction and intercommunication.

Political and Organizational Elites

For the most part, Polish Americans have not been very influential in American politics until recent years. However, there are sufficient numbers of persons who now hold or have held held political office to form a political elite. This group's members are often associated with the business, professional, or organizational elites because that was their initial status location before they got into politics. Members of this elite have had the sponsorship of the major organizations of their community, or they would not have won office or been appointed. They spend a great deal of time interacting with people upon whose vote they are directly or indirectly dependent.

The organizational leaders form several levels of interactional circles. The top circle is composed of the presidents and main officers of the major organizations. In these top circles a person often retains his status even after he has left the office. Most of the officers of Polonia's major organizations are in their positions for many years. The first president of the Polish American Congress, for example, held that office for 24 years. Each organization and each locality has its own elite.

Other Companionate Circles

The middle range of Polonia's companionate circles includes religious personnel and excombatants. The excombatants form one of the most active and mutually interactive groups who, particularly if they served during World War II and in the Polish Armed Services, tend to retain sufficient contact to form a companionate circle. The clergy, on the other hand, is internally very differentiated, mostly by age and education. Thus, for example, the highly educated heads of major schools or specialists in scientific fields form part of the intelligentsia, as mentioned before or are involved with organizational elites. The parish priests are often the leaders of their communities, especially in the absence of competing elites. The companionate circle of the parish priest depends not only on his personal status, but on the match between his status and that of his parish members. Some nuns have acquired higher status than their orders are assigned in the community, because of their leadership positions, because they act as representatives of the religious circle, or because of individually acquired education or skills.

Emmons (1971) found another elite and companionate circle, made up of the top of the blue-collar classes in "the Polka world." The circle contains "personalities" connected with the playing, recording, or mass broadcasting of Polka music, the bands, and their fans. Although most of the bands perform only as a second vocation, the "Polka world" involves a whole ideological and economic substructure. The performers are paid, belong in some cases to unions, play in lounges, at weddings, and, particularly during summer months, at numerous "pikniks" and other occasions drawing working class Polish Americans together. The circle includes the fans, brought together not only by contact but by sharing a "working-class leisure culture with community values of happiness, merrymaking, nonviolence and ethnic-kin-peer loyalty" (Emmons, 1971: 173). The members of the Polka Federation communicate news of events in different localities through two periodicals and get together annually in Chicago for three days of festivities and competition. The members of the Chicago branch whom Emmons (1971) studied are much more apt to be

third generation Polish Americans than were members of the Polish Business and Professional Men's Association. Most of them were born in Polish
neighborhoods and most of them still live in such areas, partly because
their fans and clients are still so located, as are the lounges where they
play or hear Polka music (Emmons, 1971:116). Most of the members have
not gone beyond high school. They are the second and third generation
Polish Americans who have risen to the top of the working class community to become leaders in one of the few nonparish circles which is tied
to folk ethnic culture. Interestingly, the Polka world elite is not restricted
to Polonia in organizational membership: the respondents to Emmons'
(1971) questionnaire list a median of three nonethnic groups. (These
memberships were not specified so we do not know if the groups were
or were not composed mainly of fellow ethnics.)

INTERACTION AMONG
COMPANIONATE CIRCLES

Generally speaking, the Polish American intelligentsia does not get
along comfortably with the political, economic, or organizational elites.
One organization which brings the four types of elites together, and even
contains some members of the less prestigious classes in some member
clubs, is the American Council of Polish Cultural Clubs. The member
clubs arrange artistic events which draw both Polish and non-Polish
audiences. Their activities vary considerably according to the composition of the club. For example in 1969 the Musicians Club of Phoenix presented a salute to Poland featuring women composers of that country. In
1972 the Polish Heritage Club of Grand Rapids, Michigan, arranged a
month-long exhibit of Polish Christmas customs (*The Quarterly Review*,
January-March, 1972:8), while the Washington, D.C. Polish American
Arts Association in 1973 organized a puppet nativity scene based on Polish customs, speeches on Copernicus, an essay contest in conjunction with
the United States projected celebration of its 200 year anniversary of
independence, etc.

The various Polonian elites, (mainly the white collar ones) get together for special occasions which draw from many organizational and
even community sources. For example, the president of the Museum of
Science and Industry in Chicago, who is not a Polish American, invited
a number of university professors, members of the Polish Institute of
Arts and Sciences in America, and organizational and mass communication leaders to the opening of a Copernican Exhibition at the museum.
The Copernican celebrations all over the country drew local elites and
the main banquet in New York drew them from all over Polonia.

The elites of the national scene and in the major settlements attend special social events, most of which are organized at regular intervals, such as the debutante or charity "balls" or dinner dances. The daily newspapers which service organizational members scattered throughout the United States announce and describe such events and the names of participants become known superterritorially. The professional elites, the associations of excombatants, women's clubs and many of the other more prestigious associations have regular social events, inviting the members of other professions and companionate peers in other elites. The elite circles, and many peripheral members, including the recent second generation youth of the new emigration, attend performances of Polish and Polonian artists, such as the Warsaw Philharmonic, the Mazowsze dancers, various theater groups, and concerts of individual pianists, violinists, and singers. Chicago used to have a permanent Polish theater, but even now it still musters together a cast for a special Polish play or operetta. The "Student Beggar," a play based on an important event in Polish history, was performed in both Polish and English in Milwaukee in 1973; a Polish language comedy toured Polonia's local communities the next year. In New York, where a proportionately large number of new emigration intelligentsia is living and developing a cultural life with the help of other elites, the Polish Artists Association (named after a very prestigious group in Poland) is currently attempting to organize a permanent professional theater (*The Quarterly Review*, April-June, 1973). Its aim is to become "a true center of Polish culture, presenting the great achievements of Polish drama, literature, music, dance, and film to the American public, and especially to Polish American youth which knows so little of its ancestry but wants so much to be proud of it (p. 11)."

Inter-elite events which draw Polish Americans from many classes include the traditional May Third celebrations of Polish Constitution Day (which usually consists of a parade with folk costumes and bands, and speeches by Polish American and American political leaders), and, in New York, Pulaski Day (with a parade estimated in 1973 to include 200,-000 persons).

Associations organize social events to bring together not only their members but peers in "sister" groups and other elites at the same status level. Those events are part of Polonia's life throughout the social structure. Invitations to such parties range from formal engraved invitations (typical of Copernican dinners) to the broad "all our friends in Polonia" newspaper announcements. Often, the middle and lower range groups list the names of officers of the higher levels of organizational structure and community leaders who are expected to attend a social event. As mentioned before, the social status of the hosting group is measured by the importance of the persons in attendance and there is strong feeling over the slight implied by the failure of the appropriate companionate circle members to attend. Local groups also compete for status as measured by the excellence of the band, the size of attendance, the extra activities, and the meeting of goals.

The associational style of events among the different companionate circles drawing upon their own members differs not only in the manner of invitation, but in the appearance of the guests and the hosts, the content of the activity and flow of action, the foods and beverages served, the manner of serving, and the closing ceremonies. The language spoken, the forms of humor, and the manner of deference and demeanor also vary considerably. The elites meet in country clubs, fashionable hotels and independent restaurants. They wear formal clothing at major events, and dinner is preceded by a "cocktail hour" (adopted from American culture). Waiters serve French or American style foods at tables laid with a variety of crystal, china, and silverware. The working class social events, on the other hand, are likely to take place in meeting halls with folding chairs, tables decorated by paper covers, mugs without saucers, liquor or "pop" bottles standing on the tables and plain silverware. The serving is "family style"—the dishes are brought from the kitchen by women in cooking clothes and passed from person to person. The working class menu contains the standard peasant fare of potatoes, sauerkraut, Polish sausage, "pierogi" or dumplings filled with plums, cheese, cabbage or meat, and other dishes identified as typically Polish (see menus in most lower or even middle class Polish restaurants and recipes in such books as *Michigan's Challenge: the Polish Americans of Michigan*, (1972:26–27).

While the Advocates Society, composed of Polish-American lawyers in the Chicago area, meet in places like French Lick, Indiana, for a golf outing with formal evening events designed to please the wives, the summer schedule for working class families includes excursions to youth camps or religious shrines, and the Polish-American version of the American "piknik." The "piknik" is usually held at a forest preserve or in a specially equipped commercial "grove" containing a place for the band, a dance floor, a bar, and lights for evening hours. If it is a major event in the local community, it is apt to have been described in the local press, with details as to special attractions, including expected guests. The attractions most often mentioned are music from one or more alternating Polka bands, door and other prizes, sports or product contests, a cash bar, foods such as sausage available for purchase, or the right to bring one's food, and the company of others. The event is likely to last all day and involve people who have met for years in this style although they may belong to a variety of different clubs.

In the northern and older settlements of Polonia, life's ebb and flow varies considerably by season. Summer is a time for travel, ranging from visits to the "fatherland" to bus riding excursions to seminaries. Outings in country clubs, drawing elites from all over the country are duplicated in "piknik" groves by other companionate circles. The fall reintroduces the "business" or function-oriented activity of associations, and clubs all over Polonia announce them regularly in the periodicals. Fund raising events are carried out, representatives sent to federated governing bodies or congresses, and long-range plans formulated for the social events preceding and following Christmas and New Year's Eve. Christmas is a very important period in Polonia, one during which many Polish Americans act out the few remaining folk rituals or religious ceremonials. Even nonreligious members of the community, or "Americans of Polish heritage" who really do not identify with Polonia will revive their remaining ties by putting hay under the table cloth, setting an extra seat for the hungry stranger, serving the dinner with the traditional thirteen courses when the first star appears in the sky on Christmas Eve and going to midnight mass in a Polish church. Christmas carols will be sung in Polish, with even the youth formulating a few familiar words in response to the piano or the record from Poland.

Parties and organizational life continue until Lent when, for forty days, even nonreligious Polish Americans try to "give up something" as a symbol of sacrifice. Easter is also an important holiday in Polonia, although some of the traditional rituals are less often reported than in the past (Zand, 1957). Spring increases outdoor activities and those "balls" and dinners which are semi-annual or not staged during the winter season. Organizations usually have end-of-the year events. Of course, throughout the year the flow of interactional activity is punctuated by Polish and American holidays, political action such as protest meetings, and so forth.

Naturally all of Polonia's life does not focus on organizational activity, although that is the structure holding the community together. People get together informally, with friends or relatives at times of leisure. Lunches are shared, parties planned, and central meeting places draw members of the various companionate circles. Until recently, for example, the elites of Chicago's northwest Polonia were bound to meet in a central restaurant, coming there before or after events such as dances or mass, or arranging to see each other more formally. Restaurants still provide meeting places, as do the "Polish homes" built in various communities. The church is less of a community center than in the early years when it was studied by Thomas and Znaniecki (1918–1920), but there are still parishes which retain a Polish flavor and which even pull people who are geographically scattered, at least on special occasions (see Radzialowski, 1974: "A View from a Polish Ghetto").

As in all ethnic communities, weddings, christenings, and funerals provide a guarantee of special events affording contact with intimates and acquaintances (Zand, 1959a: "Polish American Weddings and Christenings"). The Polish American wedding in stereotype is a prolonged and heavy drinking affair, but the actual weddings vary considerably among the different companionate circles. Many are quite indistinguishable from weddings of similar companionate circles in other communities. In fact, as in much of ethnic culture, the lower the social class, the more common are cultural variations in religious and social events.

Functions of Cooperative Companionate Circle Events

In addition to offering opportunities for social interaction, the function of most events is to acquire funds for "charitable" or other projects. This is usually done by collecting "donations" instead of charging for tickets, a procedure enabling the event to be classified as tax free. Since groups compete not only in the format of their events but in the size of the contribution they make to the organizational or interorganizational goals, the money raised at the events is significant in many latent ways. For example, there was an obvious competition among associations in Chicago in 1973 in the amount each gave for the Copernican statue. Each major contribution was highlighted by press photographs, and the smaller or individual ones were listed in special columns of the daily or organizational press.

According to Puacz (1972), the funds raised in Polonia are maintaining thirty-four major special or on-going activities in the community including colleges, hospitals, a museum, a religious shrine, the interorganizational political association and its activities, and the building of a variety of centers and statues. In addition, this money is continuing to help Poland in the rebuilding of its cultural symbols. Of course, the Polish Americans are still sending extensive financial aid to families in Poland. There are from two to three million packages and nearly $15,000,-000 in cash sent to Poland yearly. Puacz also stated that $3,000,000 to $5,000,000 "flows yearly in letters and is given to Polish family members during visits. This does not count money taken by returnees or business transactions" (p. 105).

Puacz (1972), expressed strong concern that Polonia's fund-raising efforts are economically inefficient because of the procedures by which the funds collected by the groups are being distributed. According to Puacz, each of the fraternal societies and federated groups collects dues and sends them to the national headquarters along with a certain percentile assessment for national activities. However, the monies collected from the parties, bazaars, picnics and other fund-raising activities are kept by the local groups, usually "sleeping" in bank accounts. Thus, there are really "5,000 independent dispersers of finances" (p. 105). The author obtains the figure of 5,000 by adding the official membership claims by the Polish National Alliance of 320,000 members in 2,000 local groups with 40 district offices, to an estimated number of local groups of the other associations. Control over the funds of each local group lies in the hands of its local officers, who, according to Puacz, use "old fashioned methods of dispersal," responding with small contributions to each bequest deemed deserving. Puacz suggests that these funds be merged and professionally distributed in ways which could more efficiently benefit Polonia.

What Puacz fails to consider is that the fund-raising activities and the monies collected perform more than just economic functions. The very method of raising and distributing the money is highly functional for the status competition so important in Polonia's life. One of the advantages of being an active member and especially an officer in any of the 5,000 groups (if Puacz's estimation is correct) is the right to organize fund-raising efforts in competition with other groups and then to sit in judgment over requests for contributions. Each bequest is then officially documented in organizational records and the contribution, when decided upon, is given a great deal of publicity. Thus, Puacz's efficiency increasing plan would deprive all the leaders of all the small groups of the pleasures of the competition and the power of deciding which of Polonia's or Poland's special projects deserves some of the rewards of their efforts.

COMPANIONATE CIRCLES
AND LOCAL COMMUNITY LIFE

It is not the function of this book to deal with all the local variations of the Polonian themes. It is important, however, to show how the history, manner of settlement, and composition of the immigrant stream have differentiated life in local ethnic communities.[3] The communities discussed below (Hamtramck, Michigan; Buffalo, New York; Los Angeles, California) have been the subjects of studies. We hope to obtain more data on the social structure and life of Polonian communities from the projected study by sociologists of the Polish Institute of Arts and Sciences in America.

[3] It does not make much sense to present data from locations such as *Yankee City* since there were so few Poles there and since the analyses of the community is so badly outdated. There are other studies of local communities, mainly in the form of M.A. theses or dissertations but their usual emphasis is on the Polish Americans as assimilating persons rather than on the structure and life of the community. The three communities selected here for discussion are described with sufficient detail and are so different from each other that they bear closer attention.

Hamtramck

Hamtramck, Michigan (Wood, 1955) has been a separate city—a political enclave surrounded by Detroit—which has been inhabited mainly by Poles and Polish Americans until very recent years. The fact that it has been politically independent and able to elect or appoint its own officials has been an important factor in its life. This political independence is not complete, since there are many overlapping jurisdictions and interests of police, courts, and welfare; but it is closer to having institutional completeness and social isolation than any other local Polonian community. Hamtramck was an area of secondary settlement by the Poles who came in the first two decades of the twentieth century when, with the opening of automobile plants, unskilled labor was needed. They have continued, as late as the 1950s, to work in jobs similar to the ones they first entered (Wood, 1955). Hamtramck exploded in population before the 1930s. Then, during the depression, many Polish families moved out of the industrial area to Polish farming communities in the "Thumb" section of Michigan (Wood, 1955:19). The population dropped from a high of 56,-268 in 1930 to 49,838 in 1940. Movement of the younger native born children of the immigrants in the 1940s again dropped the total population to 43,455 in 1950 (Wood, 1955:10). Agocs' (1971) analysis of the 1960 census data led her to conclude that ". . . the center of Italian, Polish, German and Jewish concentration, for example, have shifted outward in a 'corridor' pattern, to some of the northern and northeastern suburbs" (p. 84).

The Poles remaining in Hamtramck as the blacks move in are older and they are home owners. Most of the wooden houses closely lining the streets which cross the central business artery would not draw a fortune on the modern real estate market; but they are solid, carefully tended, and fairly substantial in size. The main street does not have many buildings over two stories high. Store fronts display bakery goods, sausage, and related meat products; there is an unusual number of shoe stores and podiatric and chiropratic offices (standing for long hours in automobile assembly plants created feet and back problems). Some of the store fronts are vacant, others cater to young black adults.

As of 1960, 63 percent of the Polish stock people were still living in the metropolitan area of Detroit and the enclaves; the remaining 37 percent had already become the city's suburbanites (Agocs, 1971:85). Few Michigan Polish Americans (Agocs, 1971:91–92) had turned to higher education as a means of upward mobility. The 1960 median school years completed was 7.0 for the first generation and 10.3 for the second generation. Their overall image is still one of lower or working class. As late as 1971, Musick records a negative attitude toward higher education and there is no evidence of more intelligentsia among the new emigrants in Hamtramck although there are some members in the Detroit area.

Musick (1971), interviewing in Hamtramck, found respondents very much still oriented toward "hard work," opposed to public welfare programs which would decrease the value of money earned in the traditional way, and rejective of managerial positions and of having wives work. "In Hamtramck, wealth and consumption of material goods are of much less importance than pride in one's property, and concern for neighbor's property" (p. 6). The Polish residents define themselves as individualistic and have a "sense of personal identity which is drawn not from the larger society but from the Polish sub-culture of Hamtramck" (p. 6). They have a sense of being apart, of being unique and individual which results from their relationship to the values, norms and criteria of prestige which are unique to the Polish subculture of Hamtramck and remarkably different from those of the larger society" (p. 6). Of course, the Polish Americans Musick is describing are those who have been left behind as the younger generations moved away. The consequences of being left behind are evident in the daily life of Hamtramck's older Polish Americans. Most residents of Hamtramck have lived in the town most of their lives. The men hold blue collar jobs, identify with the Roman Catholic church, and hold peasant style attitudes toward health and other subjects of daily interest. Most live with their mates in their own homes, some still housing boarders. Their offspring, located elsewhere and enjoying more middle class lives, are not deeply involved in the life of the community.

It is somewhat surprising, in view of the current social structure of the community, to find the reported extensiveness and complexity of Hamtramck's interlocking social activity at the height of its life.[4] Although reported in Detroit newspapers mostly in terms of its scandals, criminal and juvenile delinquency rates, and internal conflict, this working man's community retained a highly developed organizational system enabling a viable status competition. In the absence of higher education as a basic source of prestige, this competition used land possession, membership in organizations, and personal reputations to build status packages. The geographical barriers separating Hamtramck from the rest of

---

[4] The composition of Hamtramck's population seems to have been relatively flat in socioeconomic terms, when compared to that of Chicago or New York. In fact, Wood (1955) found the number of professionals very low in 1950, one-fourth of that of neighboring Highland Park which had few Polish Americans. There were only half as many proprietors as in Highland Park, which also had a higher educational and combined socioeconomic median achievement.

Detroit's population and the stability of the Poles' residential settlement resulted in the development of a common life style and a large-scale reproduction of village life. Political life afforded many opportunities for leadership roles. Although priests and nuns, small shop keepers, and a few professional men formed the elite, this social and political life gave other community residents many occasions for establishing individual records.

Buffalo

The Polonian community of Buffalo, New York, has been the subject of several studies (Carpenter and Katz, 1927; 1929; Obidinski, 1968) and appears to have some distinctive features. Obidinski (1968) found that the Polish American community of Buffalo is clustered in several neighborhoods out of its initial concentration in the "East End" (p. 23). The areas of current settlement are varied by social class so that upward mobility is possible within the confines of the city. The initial settlers were part of the immigrant flow which "passed through Buffalo en route to midwest cities such as Chicago, Detroit, Milwaukee and Cleveland . . ." (p. 33). Some decided to remain there but "for some of the arrivals, . . . Buffalo was not merely a stop-over point but literally the end of the line—as the western terminus of some railroads out of New York City—and accessible to those who could pay the $7.50 fare" (p. 33).

The initial homogeneity of the community (mainly former peasants) was broken only by the presence of priests and nuns who formed the leadership elite. They organized not only churches and parishes, but parochial schools, organizations outside of religious confines, and the press. For example, a priest was the owner and editor of the first Polish language newspaper in Buffalo and was the cofounder (with another priest) of the Polish Union of America. In fact, Obidinski (1968) attributes the "consolidation of the subcommunity" to Catholicism, the religious leaders, the churches, and their organizations.

> In 1966, when the Buffalo subcommunity was almost 100 years old, many persons and committees planned events and publications in observance of the Polish Millennium commemorating 1,000 years of Christianity among the Polish people. Polish-American clergymen and nuns organized local Millennial events and provided a historical record of the subcommunity. In a literal sense, the Buffalo subcommunity retains its close ties with the church (pp. 62–63).

Although it has recently expanded into several neighborhoods and is less homogeneous, Obidinski (1968) finds a definite ethnic subcommunity in Buffalo, persisting over four generations. According to him, "familial and religious institutional patterns are more crucial to subcommunity persistence than are economic or political institutional patterns" (p. 16). Also,

> the acceptance of traditional ethnic patterns and participation in ethnic associations vary with social class levels within the subcommunity. The Polish-American subcommunity in Buffalo continues to exist despite increased differences among members. Its continued survival, however, is a function of specific institutional practices of persons found at certain class levels (p. 16).

This refers to the fact that the upper classes tend to live outside the community's territorial boundaries, to participate in organizations of other identity, and to agree less with traditional attitudes than do the lower classes. Their ethnicity is expressed more in familial and religious ties than in total community involvement.

Another significant characteristic of Buffalo's Polonia is the size of the Polish American segment in proportion to the total population of Buffalo. The Polish Americans of Buffalo are relatively few in number when compared to Chicago or their own past, having dropped from 200,000 foreign stock in 1940 to 82,249 in 1960 (Obidinski, 1968:50), but they comprise a high 15 percent of the total Buffalo population which stood at 533,000 in 1960. Furthermore, the succeeding generations of Polish Americans seem to have influenced the whole city's life on the political and social level.

Although Obidinski (1968) concludes that it has been mainly the family and religious interaction which has kept the ethnic community together in the face of increasing internal differences, there seems to be a semblance of a superstructure which may be assisting the process. In the past, a major focal point of Buffalo's social life had been its Dom Polski (Polish Home) which was similar in function to community centers:

> The Dom Polski (Polish Home) in Buffalo was fortunate in having a branch of the municipal public library housed on its first floor; this not only enhanced the character of a community center, but added to its income, which was augmented further by the rental of space to two dignified businesses—a men's clothing store and a drugstore—enabling it to exist without too much financial stress. In most other cities, however, the Dom Narodowy had to bolster its existence with a saloon and so did not enjoy the patronage of the "better societies" (Zand, as quoted by Obidinski, 1968:47).

Although Obidinski (1968) does not refer to an organizational superstructure which could contribute to the preservation of Buffalo's Polonia over the four generations, he found his sample from a list of eighty-four voluntary organizations. Thus, the community is organizationally active beyond the Dom Polski, benefiting also from geographical concentration of its population. Most of Obidinski's respondents of even the third generation live in neighborhoods which they consider as either "Mostly Polish or Polish-American" (41 percent) or at least "half Polish, half American" (38 percent). Only 29 percent are now living in areas they define as "neither Polish nor Polish American" (p. 92).

Buffalo's Polonia, therefore, is sociologically interesting because within it exist the heterogeneous upwardly mobile second, third, and later generations of Polish Americans. As Obidinski (1968) points out, this coexistence is made possible by continued religious and family centered interaction which bridges class differences. An interesting subject of future study is the extent to which voluntary organizations serve as the source of anticipatory and in-role socialization of the descendants of the Polish peasant immigrants who are moving up the socioeconomic ladder. An additional question is the extent to which the ethnic community can provide some of this anticipatory and in-group socialization, and the problems it has of doing so in view of its traditional link with the peasant folk culture. The problems seem less apt to arise in more complex ethnic communities (such as the Polonia of Chicago) because the overlap and openness of boundaries of companionate circles would make movement possible, if not always pleasant.

Los Angeles

The Los Angeles Polonian community is the most loosely structured and least demanding of its members of all those which have been studied to date.[5] Sandberg (1974) feels that the people drawn to "the West, many of whom live in Southern California, represent a group of higher socioeconomic status than the national population of Polonia, which is largely working class" (p. 19). He draws this conclusion from the assumption that "those who are better educated are more mobile" (p. 19). The Los Angeles area Polish American residents moved there from other parts of America; the city was certainly not the port of entry of most immigrants from Poland or other European countries.

The Polish American community of Los Angeles is a perfect illustration of Etzioni's (1959) statement that the web of social relations can

---

[5] According to Sandberg (1974) the Los Angeles Polonia contains 73,959 Polish foreign stock residents of whom "31,877 were foreign born and 42,082 were native white of foreign or mixed parentage" (p. 19–20). This is a high ratio of first generation Polish Americans, most of whom are of the new emigration.

exist in spite of residential dispersal even into suburban locations.[6] The dispersal is not just into several settlements or local neighborhoods as in Buffalo. Rather, the families have dispersed and there are only a few clusters of group settlement. The Polish stock first and second generation residents of Los Angeles reside in 632 of the 710 Census tracts and are "represented in all of the separately incorporated communities within the SMSA" (Sandberg, 1974:19). There are only ten tracts in Los Angeles and one outside the city limits which contain 500 or more people of Polish foreign stock each. In spite of the dispersal, the community is able to maintain both a Roman Catholic parish and a Polish National Catholic church. As of 1950 "a directory indicated that there were 30 Polish American groups in the Los Angeles area, including branches of the major fraternal associations, groups of veterans, labor, business and professional people, the Polish Literary and Dramatic Circle and the Polish University Club" (p. 21).

Because of the initial settlement patterns and the background of the Polish American settlers of the Los Angeles area, it is not surprising that Sandberg (1974) found a much greater weakening of extended family ties than did Obidinski (1968) in Buffalo. Also, as the Los Angeles Polish Americans have become more prosperous and middle-class in their life styles, in a community with very flexible and non-traditional social structures, the pervasiveness of their ethnicity has

> diminished considerably but continues to be a factor in the lives of many people. The bond of identity is expressed through formal and informal structural associations and maintained by a common history and tradition. It may also be supported by the currently fashionable voicing of ethnic identification and pride, as well as by the emergence of a new militancy resulting from the abrasiveness of intergroup contacts and perceptions (Sandberg, 1974:73).

This continued ethnic identification does not cover all members of the third and fourth generation youth, many of whom seem to be denying identification as Polish Americans in the face of a "comparatively hostile climate" (p. 74). However, the interesting conclusion of this study is that there can be an "emergence of new forms of ethnic identification and communication, which enable the growing numbers of ethnics residing in suburban settings to maintain group continuity" (p. 74). If the shift to higher education as a method of status competition achievement in the broader society is developing, as we hypothesize in this book, then the

---

[6] Specifically, Etzioni (1959:258) states "that a group can maintain its cultural and social integration and identity, without having an ecological basis.

shift of identification and association from the traditional culture and companionate circles will have to take place all over American Polonia. The Los Angeles model may be one which other local communities will be developing.

Other Polonian
Local Communities

The local Polonian communities range from small towns such as Panna Maria, Texas, to large cities such as New York. Panna Maria is known in Polonia as the first town settled entirely by Polish immigrants. Founded in 1854 by 100 Polish families who traveled west, it was named after the mother saint so important to Polish Catholicism.

Abramson (1971) chose four cities in the Connecticut Valley and analyzed their demographic characteristics. He found that 82 percent of the Poles were Catholic, 5 percent were Protestant, and 13 percent were Jewish (p. 19). The socioeconomic resources available to the Polish Americans again reflected the burden of a past lack of education. Only 22 percent of the Polish Catholics were in white collar occupations, and these people were the least likely of all groups to have attended college, their 18 percent being followed by 20 percent for other east Europeans. The Protestants had a 53 percent college attendance record among the white collar workers and the Jews had a 49 percent record. Among the blue collar workers, the French Canadians, the Italians, the blacks, and the Protestants had fewer college attenders than had the Polish Catholics, but even here the Polish total was 13 percent. This would indicate a trend toward status decrystallization, with educational achievement preceding occupational mobility out of the blue collar world. This conclusion is supported by income figures, in that few Polish Americans in white collar jobs are as yet living on annual family incomes of $10,000 or more, while almost the same proportion of their blue collar workers have equivalent incomes (12 percent).

The Connecticut Valley Polish Americans are moving away from total Democratic party affiliation found typical by Abel (1912) in the 1920s—only 64 percent being so identified while 15 percent are Republican and 21 percent independent. (The last figure is high in comparison with other groups and the distribution does not vary by blue-white collar differences.) Although only 20 percent of the respondents thought that race relations in the United States were getting better, 41 percent saw them as the same and only 35 percent as worse. Interestingly enough, only 8 percent of the blacks saw them as getting worse. Unfortunately, the article describing the Connecticut Valley Polish Americans did not deal with the social structure of their communities. The Polish American Congress has a division in the state and most of its individual members live in Connecticut or Texas (Zmurkiewicz, 1972:53).

The Polish Americans of Washington, D.C. tend to be of a different background; many came with the new emigration and found jobs with the federal government. A few are elected representatives of their ethnics in other parts of the country. They tend to be active in the cultural and political clubs and companionate circles. There is sufficient cohesion in the community to organize a Polish American Day on the mall at the Washington Monument with the cooperation of the United States Park Service. Washington's Polonia is in touch with other communities—visiting groups from other Polish American communities usually get in touch with local organizations. The presence of the Washington office of the Polish American Congress tends to focus political activity there, and the Copernican Year festivities brought together scholars and politicians of many nationalities.

New York contains a great variety of different companionate circles, all trying to work out compromises in their relations with surrounding ethnic groups. John Lindsay (1972) when mayor of New York, reported that in a "section of Brooklyn, Polish-Americans and Puerto Ricans have joined together to start a multi-service community center and plan to push for a day care center as well." In other areas, as reported by Novak (1971), the Polish Americans and the other blue-collar ethnics are hostile toward the blacks, while themselves developing a "new ethnicity." Both Lindsay (1972) and Novak (1972) report on a new group of Polish Americans, the children of "white ethnic" families who have flooded into "the city's Open Enrollment Program, which guarantees a place in the City University system to every New York high school graduate" (Lindsay, 1972:147).

Simultaneously, New York has a highly developed intelligentsia companionate circle centered around the Polish Institute of Arts and Sciences in America. Thus, New York and its environs seem to have a pyramidal social structure, more so than is evident in other local communities such as Cleveland which reports middle range companionate activities.

SUMMARY

Life in Polonia is organized into the activities of various (sometimes overlapping) companionate relationship circles, ranked by social status, size, and flexibility of boundaries. The companionate circles contain different personnel and ranges of activities of interaction. Status crystallization and intercircle differentiation are evident in the demeanor and content of interaction within each companionate circle when viewed from the outside, but status decrystallization and flexibility form an internally important part of the life of Polonia and enable the existence of the circles and status competition.

Local neighborhoods, settlements or communities and Polonia as a whole can bring together the various circles, or their representatives, for special events but generally most of the circles do not have much in common. The elites are split among the intelligentsia, the professional and business, and the political and organizational circles among the white-collar segment of the population, and among "the Polka World," the local parish clergy, and organizational leaders and officials in other groups in the blue-collar segment. The flow of activity is influenced by seasonal changes, national Polish or American holidays, or local special events. Of recent years some of the special events have been systematized throughout Polonia through the efforts of superterritorial leaders as part of the campaign to change the image of Polish Americans in American society. Thus, special events have clustered around the Copernican Year, and will be centered on the Conrad Year and the ethnic celebration of America's bicentennial.

This book has been devoted to an analysis of the ethnic community, locally and super-territorially structured through companionate circles, organizations, and the press; developed in America by the emigrating Poles and their descendants with the help of transient Polish nationals, and influenced by its relations with both Poland and America. We have not followed the usual approach to ethnic Americans of tracing the changes in their demographic characteristics, the effects of acculturation, and the problems of assimilation. Rather, our major focus has been Polonia's social structure and the companionate circles of its internal life—the community as created, maintained, and modified over a century of organizational existence.

The Poles who emigrated to America were mainly of two social classes. The upper class immigrants or exiles included political party leaders, former members of Poland's governments or armed services, the intelligentsia, and some members of the new emigration who had been displaced by World War II and its aftermath. The second group was made up of the peasants in all their subclass,

The Long View

folk, and regional variations. Most came not to stay but to weather out the political storms in Poland or to accumulate the means for increasing their status back home. They brought with them two different views of their own "national character" the *szlachta* and the peasant, with overlapping images of individualism and concern with social status. They also brought many different packages of cultural baggage and identity (ranging from cosmopolitan, to nationalistic, to politically patriotic to folk). Most came as part of a large wave of immigration and settled in relatively concentrated communities that were physically or socially segregated from other national or ethnic groups.

Although they were planning on returning to Poland, they dug in to gather as fast as possible the means of insuring or improving status back home—money with which to buy land and durable property. The peasants turned first to the Roman Catholic Church, with the help of a few Polish priests and nuns, to build a complex and status competition satisfying parish system; they formed mutual aid societies providing not only security but opportunities for interaction. The upper strata formed nationalistic groups, literary magazines, and newspapers. Gradually the two major status groups, the *szlachta* and the peasants (socially isolated in Poland's past) began forming a common community with the help of newly emerging intermediary levels who gradually filled in the previously empty rungs of the social status ladder. The filling-in process occurred through status decrystallization and mobility of both groups, and with the help of repeated waves of newcomers entering with different backgrounds. The emerging ethnic community depended heavily on increased mobility and an expanded status competition as it created new companionate circles and a life style which could draw second and third generation Polish Americans and, gradually, even the new emigration.

As they built their local and superterritorial structures, the Polonians were influenced by the fact that Poland wished to regain its independence from foreign occupiers. Polish political leaders turned to the increasingly affluent Polish Americans in an effort to obtain their financial, and later military, cooperation. However, they were unable to convert the majority of the Polish Americans from folk people (who lacked formal education and held anti-intellectual attitudes) into members of the national culture society. Eventually, efforts to ignite patriotism combined with promises, direct or implied, of status gain and humanitarian interests in the welfare of friends and relations in Poland drew Polonia's attention to events in Europe, and especially in Poland, to such an extent that Polonia began to identify itself as the "fourth province of Poland." It turned this identification into millions of dollars of official and informal help both before and after World War I.

Gradually the fervor of war-related activity died down. The Polish Americans became disillusioned with their relations with Poland and the local scene gained their attention. Most realized that they would not return to Poland, being comfortably settled on this side of the ocean. Polonia's leaders became concerned with building a new ideology justifying the continued existence of the community and its organizations, providing an alternative identity to being "the fourth province of Poland." This they succeeded in doing as early as the 1920s and 1930s by defining American society as pluralistic and Polonia as a necessary component of the mosaic. They thus rejected the melting pot view of this country.

While these ideological changes were taking place, the vitality and complexity of the status competition, using internally developed criteria and hierarchies, and institutionalizing both cooperation and conflict, continued. The competition allowed for the use of external social control agencies to win the personal, family, or organizational struggle. The ideology simply supplied new hierarchies of status symbols and new activities in which success could be measured. One of the components of the ideology defining identity was the belief in a unique national character which prevented community cooperation and almost guaranteed internal conflict and competition. Armed with this ideology, Polish Americans felt justified in retaining the right to control their own destiny by remaining in the status competition and preventing others from gaining control. Few people have willingly withdrawn from the competition and acquiesced to leadership by someone else who was, after all, no better. Individualistic behavior may have prevented cooperation in the community and may have made public any conflict, but it has definitely prevented life from being dull or passive throughout Polonia's history.

The community developed not just a web of primary relations, but a whole system of patterned, established social relations, social roles, and groups. The activities of these social units created occasions for repeated contact performing multiple manifest and latent functions. They helped to crystallize, maintain, and then modify the ideology and community identity; they provided the arena for the status competition and sources of prestige; they contributed to the creation of new groups, as schisms occurred in the established ones; and they offered a very active social life. It is this web of formal and informal interaction which prevented the community from reaching the complete disorganization, and personal or family demoralization predicted by many of its observers (Thomas and Znaniecki, 1918–1920). If the hypotheses in this book are correct, the very characteristic which contributed to predictions of community failure was part of the web holding the community together and drawing members' interest inward rather than encouraging a passive adjustment to an acculturated minority status position. The complex competitive social structure of the community served to cushion, dissipate, and even deflect some of the consequences of the intensive change brought about by immigration, and provided the bond needed to create a new social system.

One of the reasons Thomas and Znaniecki (1918–1920) predicted strong social disorganization among the Polish Americans was their view of human culture as a total fabric. They assumed the peasant culture contained a stable set of norms, which was being subjected to constant attacks from deviation or at least nonconformity, ending in a complete collapse. The history of Polonia over the years, locally or as a superterritorial community, indicates that its cultural fabric was much more flexible and viable, based on the social structure and gradually changing, bending, and modifying as new norms were introduced purposely or through unconscious diffusion by its members. Individuals learned or invented new ways of behaving which they evaluated as meaningful or useful, and they then tried to convince others in their companionate circles to modify their behavior. Change occurred as part of an ongoing social process so that many individuals did not have to face it alone, with "demoralizing" consequences that would have been totally disruptive.

It would be interesting to trace the changes in a community's cultural content during the acculturation process—the items retained and dropped by the different companionate circles and the rhythm of life produced by these changes. Such a study is the proper province of acculturation theorists. Polonia itself has been very conscious of these changes. Its intelligentsia has expressed frequent irritation both over the Polish American tendency to cling to folk culture items, and over the trend toward Americanization while there remains an easily available national literary Polish culture. Most of the companionate circles within Polonia, and some of the more settled intelligentsia itself, have gradually left the folk or national Polish cultures for those of an ethnic community, diversified by the ethclass exclusiveness. Although the Polonian life styles have changed over the decades, there still remains a heavy peasant and blue collar influence (as sadly commented upon by the intelligentsia, the other elites, or those who are rapidly upwardly mobile).

Although family status is important at birth, mobility has been possible within "decent" boundaries. Members of the community have marshalled resources, including family members, to solidify upward steps and to drop status-demeaning habits or members, watching simultaneously what was happening to neighbors and companionate circle peers, using gossip to establish their own status points and to crystallize their own reputations. Ventures into new means of seeking status (which were not part of the traditional peasant folk culture or part of the evolving Polonian life) were not frequent because too much was at stake. Sending children to school beyond the required minimum, for example, deprived the family of money which could be immediately converted to status points. Further, education could cause the younger generations to reject the folk culture. Higher education in "foreign" schools that were unconcerned with morality might have unpredictable effects and was generally to be avoided. For girls it was a waste of time; for boys it was a source of trouble (unless it was in Catholic seminaries in preparation for religious roles.)

Daily work for the males, homemaking for the females, and parish schools until "adulthood" for the children continued during the days of Polonia's history. But life had a different flavor in the after-work hours. Meetings were held; elections of officials afforded opportunities for gaining leadership roles which were reflected in status gains for years. Obligations to Poland and the Polish government in exile were met. Polite companionship interaction took place at central congregating places such as restaurants. All this activity was available not only to the elites but also to the former peasants. Seasonal variations in activity added spice to life, and all levels of formality and informality supplied a rich choice for those wishing, and being accepted into, companionship relations. In the meantime, of course, some people who were eligible to form part of this network never became involved. Many dropped out of Polonia, often to the extent of changing their names and concealing other visible traces of Polishness.

The community acquired and retained a negative image in America, and a very low social status in relation to other groups. This situation personally affected the members who left Polonia to enter into status competition with outsiders. In recent years, the college-attending youth, finally freed from prior constraints, gingerly entered technical occupations, feeling heavily the inferiority of being branded a "Polak." However, the intelligentsia, swollen in number by new emigrants, kept reminding the rest of Polonia of the importance of shifting into a cultural identification more in keeping with the middle-class habits and ideologies of an increasingly affluent, "leisure," and "culture" oriented society. These trends seem to have combined with Polish jokes to change dramatically Polonia's orientation to its own life, functions, and the broader society. It is doubtful that the Polish jokes could have brought about the change this dramatically and this rapidly by themselves; in fact, they are phasing out by now so that many readers may not even be familiar with them. However, they were sufficiently negative, sufficiently status depreciating, and sufficiently timely to produce a strong reaction and a mobilization of Polonia's resources into an antidefamation campaign. The main weapons of this campaign are the very aspects of Polish national culture which the intelligentsia, the Polish visitors, and the new emigrants have consistently pushed in the past: the literary, scientific, artistic national culture, especially those items which are known, or can be made known, to the American society.

It is hard to determine how successful Polonia's leadership and elites will be in changing Polish American identity from folk patterns to identification with Polish culture foreign to many of the people. The community claims that the youth will turn in this direction, demanding formal schooling into this Polish culture rather than depending upon the memories and cultural food-dance-costume-religious items of their parents or grandparents. Of course, the usual method of dealing with stigmatized identity is to remove the source of stigma by removing the identity and, in the case of Polish Americans in contrast to the visible blacks—this is possible.

Polonia as a social structure has been revitalized by the antidefamation campaign. The fraternals still continue their existence safe in their financial base and their continued ability to draw new people because of the obvious benefits. The opportunities to gain social status through office holding or even membership in the numerous groups continue to draw those interested in internal status competition (even if they are simultaneously involved in external status competition). As the old emigration dies off, many features of peasant, uneducated, blue-collar life will vanish. We cannot predict how long the community will last in its present form and how it will change as its composition and American society change. It cannot become a minority status community of the type described by Kramer (1970) unless all national or ethnic flavor vanishes. It could dissolve through the assimilation of individual or family members, or each ethclass could break into appropriate class companionship outside of its boundaries. The pervasiveness of ethnic identity on the part of individuals is likely to decrease and change content. But the community's life is dependent upon the willingness of sufficient numbers of people to maintain some level of involvement in the web of social relations through the formal groups which it can financially support. This the people could do from suburbs and scattered residences all over the country (Etzioni, 1959; Sandberg, 1974) while simultaneously leading nonethnic or non-Polish lives in other social relations. An ethnic communty need not be a total community, nor does it require that all of its members participate in all of its institutions in order to have institutional complexity. Its binding ties of the past could continue in the future through involvement in the status competition, but the cultural folk base is not likely to be retained nor to be sufficiently meaningful to result in a revival of interest by younger generations. The question remaining is whether it can be replaced by a Polish national culture base of sufficient viability to retain its social structure while replacing the organizations and institutions based on the limited culture of the Polish peasant in America.

Appendices

RECORDED DATA ON POLISH ORGANIZATIONS IN AMERICA, SELECTED YEARS

Association	Year Founded	Head-quarters	1924 Members	1924 Lodges	1935 Members	1935 Lodges
Polish Roman Catholic Union	1873	Ill.	83,326	930	161,769	1,147
Polish National Alliance	1880	Ill.	139,137	1,648	272,750	1,869
Polish Union of the United States	1890	Pa.	18,520	163	18,153	149
Alliance of Poles of America	1895	Ohio	7,015	86	———	———
Polish Association of America	1895	Wis.	10,272	179	8,740	147
Polish Women's Alliance of America	1898	Ill.	21,546	235	59,964	618
Union of Poles in America	1898	Ohio	5,850	52	———	———
Polish Benefit Association	1900	Pa.	———	———	———	———
Association of Sons of Poland	1903	N.J.	———	———	14,879	104
Polish National Alliance of Brooklyn	1905	N.Y.	9,000	131	———	———
American Federation of Polish Jews	1908	N.Y.	———	———	———	———
Polish National Union of America	1908	Pa.	6,192	122	15,211	192
Polish Alma Mater of America	1910	Ill.	6,544	125	6,799	106
United Polish Women of America	1912	Ill.	———	———	———	———
Association of Polish Women of the United States	1913	Ohio	———	———	———	———
Union of Polish Women in America	1920	Ohio	———	———	———	———
Polish Union of America	1917	N.Y.	21,546	235	35,183	257
Polish Falcons of America	1928	Pa.	12,500	285	———	———
Mutual Aid Assoc. of the New Polish Emigration	1949	Ill.	———	———	———	———
TOTALS			341,448	4,191	593,448	4,589

Sources: 1924: Szawleski (1924).
1935: The Fraternal Monitor (1937).
1950: The Fraternal Field (1950).
1959, 1968, 1973: Gale Research Company (1959, 1968, 1973).

1950		1959		1968		1973	
Members	Lodges	Members	Lodges	Members	Lodges	Members	Lodges
175,397	1,095	177,000	——	——	——	——	——
316,422	1,720	339,295	1,891	326,332	332	332,962	1,405
18,742	159	——	——	17,330	343	16,226	324
13,357	100	——	——	16,000	90	20,000	89
7,614	172	——	——	6,543	——	6,543	——
76,215	1,157	90,000	——	91,000	767	91,000	767
11,119	100	——	——	——	——	——	——
23,751	132	——	——	24,654	132	24,654	132
16,763	119	18,000	12	18,000	120	18,000	120
18,700	141	——	——	——	——	——	——
——	——	——	——	3,000	30	——	——
28,065	236	——	——	32,142	237	32,550	231
7,062	103	——	——	5,300	81	5,300	81
4,219	56	——	——	——	——	——	——
2,517	42	——	——	——	——	——	——
——	——	——	——	9,379	77	9,379	77
24,805	241	——	——	——	——	——	——
17,890	201	——	——	28,100	——	28,100	——
——	——	——	——	750	——	750	——
762,638	5,774	624,295	1,903	578,530	2,209	585,464	3,226

APPENDIX B

NONFRATERNAL POLISH AMERICAN VOLUNTARY ASSOCIATIONS

Category and Name	Year Founded	Head-quarters	1959		1968		1973	
			Members	Lodges	Members	Lodges	Members	Lodges
Cultural								
Polish Singers Alliance	1889	N.Y.	5,000	115	100	15	—	115
Josef Pilsudzki Institute of America for Research in the Modern History of Poland	1943	N.Y.	—	—	—	—	—	—
American Council of Polish Cultural Clubs	—	Rotates	—	—	1,300	25	1,300	25
General Pulaski Heritage Foundation	—	N.Y.	—	—	—	—	2,600	—
Kosciuszko Foundation	1925	N.Y.	1,650	—	2,000	—	2,000	—
Paderewski Foundation	1948		—	—	—	—	—	—
Polish Institute of Arts and Sciences of America	1942		250	—	480	—	641	—
Welfare and Public Aid								
American Relief for Poland	1939	Ill.	—	—	—	—	—	—
Black-Polish Conference of Greater Detroit	1968	Mich.	—	—	—	—	213	—
Catholic League for Religious Assistance to Poland	1943	Ill.	—	—	—	—	800	—
Polish American Immigration and Relief Committee	1947	N.Y.	—	—	400	—	—	—
Polish American Congress	1944		—	—	—	—	—	—

Veterans

	Founded	Location						
Polish Army Veterans Association of America	1921	N.Y.	10,150	137	4,750	139	4,750	137
Polish Legion of American Veterans	1921	Ill.	—	—	10,000	113	15,000	127
Polish Legion of American Veterans, Ladies Auxiliary	1921	Ill.	—	—	—	—	8,000	102
Occupational and Professional								
National Advocates Society	—	Ill.	500	—	1,000	—	1,000	—
National Medical and Dental Association	1900	Mich.	1,000	—	1,000	—	1,000	—
TOTALS			18,550	252	21,030	299	37,304	513

Source: Compiled from Gale Research Company, *Encyclopedia of Associations*. Gale Research, Detroit, Michigan. 2nd, 5th, and 8th Editions (1959, 1968, 1973).

153

EMPLOYMENT STATUS AND MAJOR OCCUPATION GROUP OF THE MALE POPULATION 16 YEARS OLD AND OVER, BY ETHNIC ORIGIN 1969 (000 omitted)

	Total	English	German	Irish	Russian	Spanish	Polish 1969[a]	Polish 1971[b]	Polish 1972[c]	NORC[d]
Male, 16 years old and over	63,303	6,615	7,595	4,697	2,710	2,491	—	1,549	1,837	—
Civilian labor force	50,293	5,197	6,203	3,712	2,149	2,022	—	1,284	1,426	—
Percent in labor force	79.4	78.6	81.7	79.3	82.9	81.2	—	82.9	77.6	—
Percent unemployed	2.8	2.1	1.6	2.3	1.7	5.1	—	2.3	5.1	—
Male employed	48,892	5,088	6,102	3,630	2,112	1,252	—	1,252	1,354	—
Percent, total	100.0	100.0	100.0	100.0	100.0	100.0	—	100.0	100.0	—
Prof., tech., and kindred wkrs.	14.0	16.7	14.8	14.1	13.5	7.9	17.7	14.5	18.1	9.5
Farmers and farm managers	3.4	4.4	6.7	3.6	0.4	0.6		1.6	0.9	0.8
Mgrs., offs., and propsl, exc farm	14.2	16.9	15.4	15.5	14.9	7.4	14.5	15.2	12.9	7.1
Clerical and kindred wkrs.	7.0	7.3	5.8	8.5	9.1	6.7	9.1	8.8	7.9	11.9
Sales workers	5.6	6.0	6.1	6.3	5.2	3.3	6.5	6.2	6.3	6.6
Craftsman, foreman, and kindred workers	20.4	19.9	21.7	20.8	22.7	18.5	22.8	24.4	23.3	28.6
Operatives and kindred wkrs.	20.0	17.8	18.2	17.9	20.0	28.6	18.1	19.6	18.3	27.0
Private household workers	0.1	0.1					4.8			
Service workers, exc. private household	6.5	5.0	4.7	6.0	7.5	10.5		3.0	7.7	7.1
Farm laborers and foreman	1.7	1.2	1.6	1.0	0.2	4.8	5.2	0.6	0.4	0.0
Laborers, exc. farm and mine	7.1	4.9	4.9	6.1	6.4	11.8	1.2	6.1	4.3	2.4

Sources: [a] U.S. Bureau of the Census, *"Current Population Reports*, Series P-20, No. 221, November 1969, T-15, "Characteristics of the Population by Ethnic Origin." Washington, D.C.: Government Printing Office, 1971.
[b] U.S. Bureau of the Census, *Current Population Reports*, Series P-20, No. 249, March 1972, "Characteristics of the Population by Ethnic Origin." Washington, D.C.: Government Printing Office, 1972.
[c] U.S. Bureau of the Census, *Current Population Reports*, Series P-20, No. 249, April 1973, T-7, "Characteristics of the Population by Ethnic Origin." Washington, D.C.: Government Printing Office, 1973.
[d] Andrew Greeley, *Ethnicity in the United States*. New York: John Wiley, 1974.

EMPLOYMENT STATUS AND MAJOR OCCUPATION GROUP OF THE FEMALE POPULATION
16 YEARS OLD AND OVER, BY ETHNIC ORIGIN (000 omitted)

Subject	Total	Origin								
		English	German	Irish	Italian	Polish	Russian	Spanish	Other	Not Reported
Female, 16 years old and over, total	71,936a	7,841	7,753	5,586	2,882	1,676	923	2,822	35,545	6,902
Civilian labor force	31,716	3,170	3,301	2,324	1,213	740	350	1,146	16,444	3,026
Per cent in labor force	44.1	40.4	41.6	42.1	44.2	37.9	37.9	40.6	46.3	43.9
Per cent unemployed	4.8	2.9	3.7	4.1	4.5	4.1	4.9	7.5	5.5	4.4
Female employed of total	30,176	3,076	3,175	2,224	1,155	710	330	1,060	15,538	2,872
Per cent distributions	100.0	100.0	100.0	100.0	100.0	100.0	100.0	100.0	100.0	100.0
Prof., tech., kindred workers	14.4	16.6	16.6	14.9	9.7	13.1	23.0	8.6	14.5	11.9
Farmers, farm managers	0.2	0.4	0.4	0.2					0.2	0.2
Mgrs., offs., props., exc. farm	4.3	6.1	4.1	6.0	4.5	3.4	10.6	1.7	3.8	4.6
Clerical, kindred workers	34.1	34.9	33.6	35.6	39.4	35.6	43.6	25.6	33.9	33.4
Sales workers	7.2	8.4	7.6	7.0	7.4	8.5	8.8	6.0	7.8	7.6
Craftsmen, foremen, kindred workers	1.1	1.3	0.9	0.9	2.2	1.1	2.1	1.1	0.9	1.1
Operatives, kindred workers	15.3	13.4	13.0	13.1	25.3	19.2	6.7	32.8	13.5	20.5
Private household workers	5.8	3.9	4.5	3.6	0.9	2.1	0.9	6.4	7.8	3.5
Service workers, exc. private household	15.8	13.5	15.9	16.9	10.4	15.5	3.9	17.1	16.7	16.1
Farm laborers, foremen	1.4	1.3	2.9	1.2	0.2	1.3	0.3	0.8	1.3	1.6
Laborers, exc. farm-mine	0.5	0.2	0.3	0.6	0.2	0.3	—	0.8	0.5	0.6

a Represents zero or rounds to zero.
Source: U.S. Bureau of Census, Current Population Reports, Series P-20, No. 221, "Characteristics of the Population by Ethnic Origin." November 1969, Washington D.C.: Government Printing Office, 1971.

APPENDIX E

HIGHEST GRADE OF SCHOOL COMPLETED BY PERSONS 25 YEARS OLD AND OVER, BY ETHNIC ORIGIN

Origin	Total (thousands)	Percent distribution by years of school completed							Median school years completed
		Total	Elementary		High school		College		
			0 to 7 years	8 years	1 to 3 years	4 years	1 to 3 years	4 years or more	
Total, 25 years old and over	106,284	100.0	13.8	13.4	17.6	33.9	10.3	11.0	12.2
25 to 34 years old	23,884	100.0	4.5	4.8	17.4	43.5	14.7	15.2	12.5
English	2,301	100.0	4.3	4.6	15.5	41.2	16.8	17.6	12.6
German	2,848	100.0	1.6	4.1	14.8	47.4	14.6	17.5	12.6
Irish	1,670	100.0	2.6	3.7	18.8	45.1	15.9	13.9	12.6
Italian	902	100.0	5.3	3.3	16.3	50.4	12.7	11.9	12.5
Polish	503	100.0	1.3	3.0	10.6	53.8	15.1	16.2	12.7
Russian	209	100.0	0.7	0.7	3.7	24.7	17.7	52.5	16+
Spanish	1,239	100.0	19.2	10.0	23.5	32.2	9.8	5.3	11.7
Other	11,625	100.0	3.6	4.4	17.5	43.3	15.6	15.6	12.6
Not reported	2,585	100.0	6.2	7.2	20.3	43.6	10.9	11.8	12.4
35 years old and over	82,400	100.0	16.5	15.9	17.6	31.1	9.1	9.8	12.0
English	9,698	100.0	11.9	13.7	17.8	31.7	11.1	13.6	12.2
German	9,977	100.0	10.6	22.0	16.1	34.2	8.6	8.5	12.0
Irish	6,960	100.0	14.3	16.3	18.8	32.9	8.4	9.3	12.0
Italian	3,780	100.0	23.5	17.7	20.0	27.6	5.2	5.9	10.3
Polish	2,266	100.0	18.5	19.0	19.2	30.9	5.2	7.2	10.9
Russian	1,375	100.0	10.8	12.1	11.9	35.1	11.7	18.4	12.4
Spanish	2,576	100.0	43.0	14.4	14.9	17.5	5.7	4.5	8.5
Other	37,661	100.0	16.5	14.3	17.8	31.1	9.9	10.4	12.0
Not reported	8,106	100.0	20.4	17.3	17.6	30.0	7.4	7.4	11.1

Source: U.S. Bureau of the Census, *Current Population Reports,* Series P-20, No. 221, "Characteristics of the Population by Ethnic Origin," November 1969. Washington, D.C.: Government Printing Office, 1971.

Bibliography

American Council of Polish Cultural Clubs, *The Quarterly Review*. Falls Church, Va. 1972–1974.

Abel, Theodore. "Sundeland: A Study of Changes in the Group-Life of Poles in New England Farming Community." In Edmund De.S. Brunner (Ed.), *Immigrant Farmers and Their Children*. Garden City, N.Y.: Doubleday, 1929: 213–43.

Abramson, Harold J. "Ethnic Pluralism in the Central City." In Otto Feinstein (Ed.), *Ethnic Groups in the City*. Lexington, Mass.: Heath Lexington Books, 1971:17–28.

———. *Ethnic Diversity in Catholic America*. New York: John Wiley, 1973.

Agocs, Carol. "Ethnicity in Detroit." In Otto Feinstein (Ed.), *Ethnic Groups in the City*. Lexington, Mass.: D. C. Heath, 1971:81–106.

"Anti-Defamation off to a Good Start." *Polish American Congress News Letter*, Chicago, 19, No. 2 (July 15, 1969).

Barc, Franciszek (Ed.), *65 Lat Zjednoczenia Polskiego Rzymsko-Katolickiego w Ameryce*. Chicago: Polish Roman Catholic Union, 1938.

Baretski, Charles Allan. "How Polonia Reacts to Inadequate Recognition in the Political Arena." *Polish American Studies*, 28, 1 (Spring 1971):43–53.

Barth, Fredrik (Ed.), *Ethnic Groups and Boundaries*. Boston: Little, Brown, 1969.

Benet, Sula. *Song, Dance and Customs of Peasant Poland*. New York: Roy, 1951.

Bethell, Nicholas. *Gomulka: His Poland and His Communism*. Middlesex, England: Penguin Books, 1972.

The Black-Polish Conference Newsletter. "Neighbors Unite to Stay Integrated." June 1973:2.

Blumer, Herbert. *Critiques of Research in the Social Sciences: An Appraisal of Thomas and Znaniecki's "The Polish Peasant in Europe and America*. New York: Social Science Research Council, 1939.

Bogue, Donald J. *The Population of the United States*. Glencoe, Ill.: The Free Press, 1969.

Bolek, Francis. *Who's Who in Polish America*. 3rd ed. New York: Harbinger House, 1943.

———. *The Polish-American School System*. New York: Columbia Press Corporation, 1948.

Borkowski, Thomas. "Some Patterns in Polish Surname Changes." *Polish American Studies*, 20, 1 (January-June 1963):14–16.

Borun, Thaddeus (Comp.). *We, The Milwaukee Poles*. Milwaukee: Mowiny Publishing Company, 1946.

Boswell, A. Bruce. "Territorial Division and the Mongol Invasions, 1202–1300." W. F. Reddaway, J. H. Penson, O. Halekci, and R. Dyboski (Eds.), *The*

Cambridge History of Poland. Cambridge, England: University Press, 1950: V. 1:85–107.

Bott, Elizabeth J. *Family and Social Network*. London: Tavistock, 1957.

Bowler, Alida C. "Recent Statistics on Crime and the Foreign Born." Part II, National Commission on Law Observance and Enforcement, *Report on Crime and the Foreign Born*. Washington, D.C.: Government Printing Office, 1931:83–193.

Breton, Raymond. "Institutional Completeness of Ethnic Communities and the Personal Relations of Immigrants." *American Journal of Sociology*, LXX, 2, (September, 1964):193–205.

Bruckner, A. "Polish Cultural Life in the Seventeenth Century," in Reddaway, 1951.

Brunner, Edmund De.S. *Immigrant Farmers and Their Children*. Garden City, N.Y.: Doubleday, 1929.

Bugelski, B. R. "Assimilation Through Intermarriage." *Social Forces* 40, 2 (December 1961):148–53.

Burton, Ronald. "Status Consistency and Secondary Stratification Characteristics in an Urban Metropolis." Unpublished Ph.D. dissertation, Department of Sociology, Michigan State University, 1972.

Carpenter, Niles and Daniel Katz. "The Cultural Adjustment of the Polish Group in the City of Buffalo: An Experiment in the Technique of Social Investigation." *Social Forces*, 6 (September 1927):76–90.

———. "A Study of Acculturation the Polish Group of Buffalo, 1926–1928." *The University of Buffalo Studies*, 7 (June 1929):103–31.

Chicago Sun-Times Magazine, *Midwest*. "Poland: Reaching for the Good Life." September 23, 1983.

Chicago Tribune. "Seven Centuries Ago a Polish King Knew That Men Could Differ, Yet Live Together Productively. He Did Something About It." (Advertisement). December 5, 1973:Section 1, p. 8.

Chrobot, Leonard. "The Effectiveness of the Polish Program at St. Mary's College, 1958–1968," *Polish American Studies*, 26, 2 (Autumn 1969):31–33.

Claghorn, Kate Holladay. *The Immigrant's Day in Court*. Originally published in 1923; republished in W. S. Bernard, (Ed.), *Americanization Series*. Montclair, N.J.: Patterson, Smith, 1971.

Conderacci, Greg. "Polish Americans Hit Ethnic Slurs, Praise Their Culture in Ads," *Wall Street Journal*, October 12, 1971:1.

Cross, Robert D. "How Historians Have Looked at Immigrants to the United States," *International Migration Review*, 7, 1 (Spring 1973):4–22.

Curti, Merle and Kendall Birr. "The Immigrant and the American Image in Europe, 1860–1914," *Mississippi Valley Historical Review*, 37, 2 (September 1950):203–30.

Davis, Allison, Burleigh B. Gardner, and Mary R. Gardner. *Deep South*. Chicago: University of Chicago Press, 1941.

Davis, Michael M. J. *Immigrant Health and the Community*. Originally published in 1921; republished in W. S. Bernard (Ed.), *Americanization Series*. Montclair, N.J.: Patterson, Smith, 1971.

deVise, Pierre. "Ethnic Shifts in Chicago." Working Paper 5.5, Chicago Regional Hospital Study, 1973.

Diamont, Stanley. "Kibbutz and Shtetl: The History and Idea." *Social Problems*, 2 (Fall 1957):71–99.

Diaz, May M. and Jack M. Potter. "The Social Life of Peasants." In Jack M.

Potter, May M. Diaz, and George M. Foster (Eds.), *Peasant Society*. Boston: Little, Brown, 1967.

Dingell, John. "Blast State Department on Polish Visas Policy," *Polish American Journal*, 63, 1 (January 1974):1.

Drachsler, Julian. *Democracy and Assimilation*. New York: Macmillan, 1920.

Duncan, Beverly and Otis Dudley Duncan. "Minorities and the Process of Stratification." *American Sociological Review*, 33, 3 (June 1968):356–64.

Dunin-Markiewicz, Alexsandra Maria. "Occupational and Educational Aspirations of Minority Group Adolescents in Face of an Unfavorable Ethnic Stereotype." Unpublished Ph.D. dissertation, Department of Psychology, Wayne State University, 1972.

Dziennik Zwiazkowy. "Poszukiwanie Danych o Stosunkach Polsko-Zydowskich," October 13–14, 1973:12. Chicago: The Alliance Printers. The complete years of 1952–1954 and 1973.

Ehrenpreis, Viktor J. in cooperation with Manfred Kridl. "Poland up to 1918," and "Poland, 1918–1945." In Joseph S. Roucek (Ed.), *Central Eastern Europe: Crucible of World Wars*. Englewood Cliffs, N.J.: Prentice-Hall, 1946.

Emmons, Charles F. "Economics and Political Leadership in Chicago's Polonia: Some Sources of Ethnic Persistence and Mobility." Unpublished Ph.D. dissertation, Department of Sociology, University of Illinois Circle Campus, 1971.

Etzioni, Amitai. "The Ghetto." *Social Forces*, 37, 3 (March 1959):258–62.

Fallers, L. A. (Ed.). *Immigrants and Associations*. The Hague: Mouton, 1967.

Feinstein, Otto (Ed.). *Ethnic Groups in the City*. Lexington, Mass.: Heath Lexington Books, 1971.

Finestone, Harold. "A Comparative Study of Reformation and Recidivism Among Italians and Polish Adult Male Criminal Offenders." Unpublished Ph.D. dissertation, Department of Sociology, University of Chicago, 1964.

————. "Reformation and Recidivism Among Italian and Polish Criminal Offenders," *American Journal of Sociology*, 72, 6 (May 1967):575–88.

Fishman, Joshua and John E. Hofman. "Mother Tongue and Nativity in the American Population." In Joshua Fishman, Vladimir C. Nahirny, John E. Hofman, and Robert G. Hayden (Eds.), *In Language Loyalty in the United States*. The Hague: Mouton, 1966.

Fleis-Fava, Sylvia. "The Relationship of Northwestern University Settlement to the Community." Unpublished Master's thesis, Department of Sociology, Northwestern University, 1950.

Form, William H. and Gregory P. Stone. "Urbanism, Anonymity and Status Symbolism." In Robert Gutman and David Papenoe (Eds.), *Neighborhood, City and Metropolis*. New York: Random House, 1970.

Fox, Paul. *The Polish National Catholic Church*. Scranton, Pa.: School of Christian Living, 1957.

The Fraternal Field, *The Fraternal Compend Digest*, 1950.

The Fraternal Monitor. *The Consolidated Chart of Insurance Organizations*, 63, 10 (May 1953). Rochester, N.Y.

The Fraternal Monitor, *Statistics Fraternal Societies*, 1937.

Gale Research Company. *Encyclopedia of Associations*. Editions 2 through 8. Detroit: Gale Research Company, 1959–1973.

Gans, Herbert. *The Urban Villagers: Group and Class in the Life of Italian-Americans*. New York: Free Press, 1962.

Gavin, Palmer John. *Americans by Choice*. Originally published in 1922; republished in W. S. Bernard (Ed.), *Americanization Series*. Montclair, N.J.: Patterson, Smith, 1971.

Gerson, Louis. *Woodrow Wilson and the Rebirth of Poland, 1914–1920*. Hamden, Conn.: The Shoe-String Press, 1972. (Originally published in 1953 by Yale University Press.)

Glazer, Nathan and Daniel P. Moynihan. *Beyond the Melting Pot: The Negroes, Puerto Ricans, Jews, Italians, and Irish of New York City*. 2nd ed. Cambridge, Mass.: M.I.T. Press, 1970.

Goffman, Irving. "Role Distance." In Irving Goffman, *Encounters*. Indianapolis: Bobbs-Merrill, 1961.

――――. "The Nature of Deference and Demeanor." In Irving Goffman, *Interaction Ritual*. Garden City, N.Y.: Doubleday, 1967.

――――. *Relations in Public*. New York: Basic Books, 1971.

Gordon, Milton M. *Assimilation in American Life*. New York: Oxford University Press, 1964.

Gould, K. H. "Social Role Expectations of Polonians by Social Class, Ethnic Identification and Generational Positioning." Unpublished Ph.D. dissertation, Department of Social Work, University of Pittsburgh, 1966.

Greeley, Andrew. "The Alienation of White Ethnic Groups." Paper presented at the National Unity Conference held at Sterling Forest Gardens, New York, November 19–20, 1969. (a)

――――. *Why Can't They Be Like Us?* New York: Institute of Human Relations Press, 1969. (b)

――――. "Ethnicity as an Influence on Behavior." In Otto Feinstein (Ed.), *Ethnic Groups in the City*. Lexington, Mass.: Heath Lexington Books, 1971.

――――. "Making it in America: Ethnic Groups and Social Status." *Social Policy* (September-October 1973):21–29.

――――. "The Ethnic and Religious Origins of Young American Scientists and Engineers: A Research Note." *International Migration Review*, 6, 3 (Fall 1972):282–87. Republished in Andrew Greeley, *Ethnicity in the United States*. New York: John Wiley, 1974. (a)

――――. *Ethnicity in the United States*. New York: John Wiley, 1974. (b)

Greeley, Andrew M. and Peter H. Rossi. *The Education of Catholic Americans*. Garden City, N.Y.: Doubleday, 1968.

Greene, Victor R. *The Slavic Community on Strike: Immigrant Labor in Pennsylvania Anthracite*. South Bend, Ind.: University of Notre Dame Press, 1968.

Gromada, Thaddeus. "Annual Report of the Acting Director and Secretary General." *Information Bulletin*, 10, 1 (Summer 1973):2–5. New York: Polish Institute of Arts and Sciences in America.

Gross, Felix. "The American Poles." A research project submitted by the Polish Institute of Arts and Sciences in America. New York: City University of New York, n.d.

Gwiazda Polarna. Weekly published in Stevens Point, Wisconsin.

Haiman, Mieczyslaw. *Zjednoczenie Polskie Rzymsko-Katolickie*. (*Polish Roman Catholic Union 1873–1948*). Chicago: Polish Roman Catholic Union, 1948.

Hall, Richard H. *Occupations and the Social Structure*. 2nd ed. Englewood Cliffs, N.J.: Prentice-Hall, 1975.

Hauser, Philip M. and Evelyn M. Kitagawa (Eds.). *Local Community Fact Book for Chicago, 1950*. Chicago: Community Inventory, University of Chicago, 1953.

Heaps, Willard. *The Story of Ellis Island*. New York: Seabury Press, 1967.

Heberle, Rudolf. "Displaced Persons in the Deep South." *Rural Sociology*, 16, 4 (December 1951):362–77.

Heller, Celia Stopnicka. "Assimilation: A Deviant Pattern among Jews of Interwar Poland." *Jewish Journal of Sociology* (December 1973):213–17.

———. "Anti-Zionism and the Political Struggle within the Elite of Poland." *Jewish Journal of Sociology*, 11, 2 (December 1969):133–50.

Herberg, Will. *Protestant-Catholic-Jew*. New York: Doubleday, 1955.

Hertzler, J. O. *American Social Institutions*. Boston: Allyn & Bacon, 1961.

Hourwich, Isaac A. *Immigration and Labour*. New York: Putnam's, 1912.

Hughes, Everett C. *The Sociological Eye*. Chicago. Aldine-Atherton, 1971.

———. *French Canada in Transition*. Chicago: University of Chicago Press, 1934.

Hughes, Everett C. and Helen McGill Hughes, *Where Peoples Meet*. Glencoe, Ill.: The Free Press, 1952.

Hutchinson, Edward P. "Immigration Policy since World War I." *Annals of the American Association of Political and Social Science*, 262 (March 1949):15–21.

———. *Immigrants and Their Children, 1850–1950*. New York: John Wiley, 1956.

Janta, Alexander. "Barriers into Bridges: Notes on the Problem of Polish Culture in America." *The Polish Review*, 2 (Spring-Summer 1957):79–97.

Johnson, Ruth. *The Assimilation Myth: A Study of Second Generation Immigrants in Western Australia*. The Hague: Martinus Nijhoff, 1969.

———. *Immigrants' Assimilation: A Study of Polish People in Western Australia*. New York: Perth, Paterson and Brokensha, 1965.

Jones, Maldwyn Allen. *American Immigration*. Chicago: University of Chicago Press, 1960.

Jurczak, Chester Andrew. "Ethnicity, Status and Generational Positioning: A Study of Health Practices among Polonians in Five Ethnic Islands." Unpublished Ph.D. dissertation, Department of Sociology, University of Pittsburgh, 1964.

Karlowiczowa, Jadwiga. *Historia Związku Polek w Ameryce*. Chicago: Sziazek Polek w Ameryce, 1938.

Karski, Jan. *Story of a Secret State*. Boston: Houghton Mifflin, 1944.

Kennedy, John F. *A Nation of Immigrants*. New York: Popular Library, 1964.

Kennedy, Ruby Jo Reeves. "Single or Triple Melting Pot: Intermarriage in New Haven." *American Journal of Sociology*, 58, 1 (July 1952):55–66.

Kirkpatrick, Clifford. *Intelligence and Immigration*. Baltimore: Williams and Wilkins, 1926: Mental Measurement Monographs, Serial 2.

Kitagawa, Evelyn and Karl E. Taeuber (Eds.). *Local Community Fact Book of the Chicago Metropolitan Area, 1960*. Chicago: University of Chicago Community Inventory, 1963.

Kobelinski, Michael, Anthony J. Fornelli, and David G. Roth. "The Executive Suite." The American Jewish Committee. Mimeographed. Reported in various mass communication media, 1974.

Kolm, Richard. "The Change of Cultural Identity: An Analysis of Factors Conditioning the Cultural Integration of Immigration." Unpublished dissertation, Department of Sociology, Wayne State University, 1961.

———. "The Identity Crisis of Polish-Americans." *The Quarterly Review*, 21, 2 (April-June 1969):1, 4.

———. "Ethnicity in Society and Community." In Otto Feinstein (Ed.), *Ethnic Groups in the City*. Lexington, Mass.: Heath Lexington Books, 1971. (a)

———. "Ethnicity." *Perspectives*, 1, 3 (July-September 1971):1, 6–7. (b)

Kos, Rabcewicz-Aubkowski, Ludwig. *The Poles in Canada.* Toronto: Polish Alliance Press, 1968.

Kosinski, Jerzy. *The Painted Bird.* New York: Bentham Books, 1972.

———. *Steps.* New York: Random House, 1968.

Kostrzewski, T. "Polish Americans." *Polish Medical and Dental Bulletin* (November 1938).

Kotlarz, Robert J. "Writings about the Changing of Polish Names in America." *Polish American Studies*, 20, 1 (January-June 1963): 1–4.

Kowalski, Thaddeus. *Anti-Defamation Guide.* Chicago: Polish American Congress, n.d.

Krakowska, Constance. "The Polish American Associations and the Liberation of Poland." *Polish American Studies*, 12, 1–2 (January-June 1955):11–18.

Kramer, Judith R. *The American Minority Community.* New York: Thomas Y. Crowell, 1970.

Kuniczak, Wieslaw. *The Silent Emigration.* Chicago: Polish Arts Club, 1968.

Kusielewicz, Eugene. "Reflections on the Cultural Condition of the Polish American Community." In Frank Renkiewicz (Ed.), *The Poles in America, 1608–1972.* Dobbs Ferry, N.Y.: Oceana Publications, 1973:97–123.

Kuznets, Simon and Ernest Rubin. "Immigration and the Foreign Born." Occasional Paper no. 46. New York: National Bureau of Economic Research, 1954.

Lard, Ann Gdab. *The Polish American Community of Philadelphia 1870–1920.* Ann Arbor: University of Michigan Microfilm, 1971.

Laumann, Edward O. "The Social Structure of Religious and Ethno-religious Groups in a Metropolitan Community." *American Sociological Review*, 34 (April 1969):182–97.

Lenski, Gerhard. *The Religious Factor.* New York: Doubleday, 1961.

Lieberson, Stanley. *Ethnic Patterns in American Cities.* New York: Free Press, 1963.

Lindsay, John V. "New York's Ethnic Boom." In Michael Wenk, S. M. Tomasi, and Geno Baroni (Eds.), *Pieces of a Dream.* New York: Center for Migration Studies, 1972.

Linton, Ralph. *The Science of Man.* New York: Appleton-Century-Crofts, 1936.

Lopata, Helena Znaniecki, "The Function of Voluntary Associations in an Ethnic Community: Polonia." In Ernest W. Burgess and Donald J. Bogue (Eds.), *Contributions to Urban Sociology.* Chicago: University of Chicago Press, 1964.

———. "A Restatement of the Relations Between Role and Status." *Sociology and Social Research*, 49, 1 (October 1964):58–68.

———. Loneliness: Forms and Components." *Social Problems*, 17, 2 (Fall 1969): 248–62. (a)

———. "The Social Involvement of American Widows." *American Behavioral Scientist* (Fall 1969):41–57. (b)

———. *Occupation: Housewife.* New York: Oxford University Press, 1971. (a)

———. "Roles, Status and Acculturation: Dimensions of Ethnic Identity." Paper presented at the Southern Sociological Association Meeting, Miami, Florida, 1971. (b)

———. "The Effect of Schooling on Social Contacts of Urban Women." *American Journal of Sociology.* 59, 3 (November 1973):604–19. (a)

———. "Self-identity in Marriage and Widowhood." *Sociological Quarterly*, 14, 3 (Summer 1973):407–18. (b)

———. "Social Relations of Black and White Widowed Women in a Northern Metropolis." *American Journal of Sociology*, 78, 4 (January 1973):241–48. Also in Joan Huber (ed.), *Changing Women in a Changing Society*. Chicago: University of Chicago Press, 1973. (c)

———. *Widowhood in an American City*. Cambridge, Mass.: Schenkman Publishing Company, General Learning Press, 1973 (d)

———. "Life Styles of Elderly Urbanites: Chicago of the 1970's." *The Gerontologist*, 15, 1 (February 1975):35–41.

———. "Polish Immigration to the United States of America: Problems of Estimation and Parameters." *International Migration Review*, 1975.

Lynd, Helen Merrell. *On Shame and the Search for Identity*. New York: Science Editions, 1965.

McCready, William C. "The Persistence of Ethnic Variation in American Families." In Andrew Greeley (Ed.), *Ethnicity in the United States*. New York: John Wiley, 1974.

MacIver, R. M. *Society*. New York: Farrar and Rinehard, 1937.

Makowski, William Boleslaus. *History and Intergration of Poles in Canada*. Niagra Peninsula, Canada: The Canadian Polish Congress, 1967.

Manning, Caroline. *The Immigrant Woman and Her Job*. Washington, D.C.: Government Printing Office, 1930.

Mazewski, Alojzy. "Excellent Speech of President Mazewski." *Dziennik Zwiazkowy* (September 19, 1973). p. 2.

———. "The Poles—a National Group Full of Dynamism and Individualism." *Dziennik Zwiazkowy* (October 17, 1973): p. 5.

Miaso, Josef. "Z Dziejow Oswiaty Polskiej w Stanach Zjednoczonych," *Problemy Polonii Zagranicznej*, 4 (1971):19–42.

The Michigan State Chamber of Commerce. *Michigan's Challenge: The Polish Americans of Michigan*. Lansing, Michigan: April 1972.

Miller, Commissioner. *Monthly Review*. Immigration and Naturalization Service, 6, 3 (September 1948):48.

Mostwin, Danuta. "Post World War II Polish Immigrants in the United States." *Polish American Studies*, 26, 2 (Autumn 1969):5–14.

———. "The Transplanted Family: A Study of the Social Adjustment of the Polish Immigrant Family to the United States after the Second World War." Columbia University, School of Social Work, University Microfilms of dissertations, 1971.

Mullan, Eugene. *The Mentality of the Arriving Immigrant*. New York: Arno Press, 1917.

Musick, John. "Ethnicity and the Economic Squeeze." The University of Michigan School of Social Work (April 1971): mimeographed.

Nam, Charles B. "Nationality Groups and Social Stratification." *Social Forces*, 37, 4 (May 1959):328–33.

Napolska, Sister Mary Remigia. *"The Polish Immigrant in Detroit to 1914*, Chicago: Polish Roman Catholic Union Archives and Museum, 15 (1945–1946).

National Commission on Law Observance and Enforcement. *Report on Crime and the Foreign Born*. Washington, D.C.: Government Printing Office, 1931.

Novak, Michael. *The Rise of the Unmeltable Ethnics.* New York: Macmillan, 1971.

———. "New Ethnic Politics vs. Old Ethnic Politics." In Michael Wenk, S. M. Tomasi, and Geno Baroni (Eds.), *Pieces of a Dream.* New York: Center for Migration Studies, 1972.

Nowakowski, Stefan. "Tendencje Rozwojowe Polonii Americanskiej." Polska Academia Nank Problemy Polonii Zagranicznej. III Warszawa Wydawnistwo Polonia, 1964.

Obidinski, Eugene. "Ethnic to Status Group: A Study of Polish Americans in Buffalo." Unpublished Ph.D. dissertation, State University of New York, Department of Sociology, 1968.

Packard, Vance. *The Status Seekers.* New York: Cardinal Pocket Books, 1959.

———. *The Pyramid Climbers.* Greenwich, Conn.: Fawcett, 1962.

———. *A Nation of Strangers.* New York: McKay, 1972.

Park, Robert. *The Immigrant Press and its Control.* New York: Harper & Row, 1922. Republished in W. S. Bernard (Ed.), *Americanization Studies.* Montclair, N.J.: Patterson Smith, 1971.

———. "Human Migration and Marginal Man." *American Journal of Sociology,* 33 (May 1928):881–93.

Petras, John W. "Polish Americans in Sociology and Fiction." *Polish American Studies,* 21, 1 (January-June 1964):16–32.

Piwowarski, Stanislaw. "Conference Underscores the Difference Between Polish Nation and Communist Regime." *Polish American Congress News Letter,* 1, 2 (July 20, 1970):7–8.

The Polish American Congress. *Purposes and Achievements.* Chicago: Polish American Congress, 1971, 1972.

Polish American Congress Newsletter, Chicago, 1969–1973.

The Polish Institute of Arts and Sciences in America. *Information Bulletin,* 10, 1 (Summer 1973).

The Polish-Italian Conference. *Program of the Saint Joseph's Day Reception.* Chicago, March 19, 1973.

Polish Pageant. *The Poles of Chicago, 1837–1937: Their Contributions to a Century of Progress.* Chicago: Polish Day Association, 1937.

Polzin, Theresita. *The Polish Americans: Whence and Whither.* Pulaski, Wis.: Franciscan Publishers, 1973.

Puacz, Edward. "Uwagi o Ofiarnosci Polonii Amerikanskiej." *Kultura,* Nr., 10/301. Paris: Instytut Literacki (October 1972):103–12.

Radzialowski, Thaddeus. "A View from a Polish Ghetto. Some Observations on the First One Hundred Years in Detroit." *Ethnicity,* 1, 2 (July 1974):125–50.

The Random House Dictionary of the English Language. Unabridged Edition. New York: Random House, 1966.

Reddaway, W. J., J. H. Penson, O. Halecki, and R. Dyboski (Eds.). *The Cambridge History of Poland.* 2 vols. Cambridge, England: The University Press, 1951.

Renkiewicz, Frank. "Language, Loyalty and Ethnic Culture." *Polish American Studies,* 26, 2 (August 1969):57–61.

——— (Ed.). *The Poles in America 1608–1972.* Dobbs Ferry, N.Y.: Oceana Publications, 1973.

Reymont, Ladislas. *The Peasants: Fall, Winter, Spring, Summer.* 4 vols. New York: Knopf, 1925.

Rooney, Elizabeth. "Polish Americans and Family Disorganization." *The American Catholic Sociological Review*, 18 (March 1957):47–51.

Rosenblum, Gerald. *Immigrant Workers*. New York: Basic Books, 1973.

Roucek, Joseph S. *Poles in the United States of America*. Gdynia, Poland: Baltic Institute, 1937.

——— (Ed.). *Slavonic Encyclopaedia*. New York: Philosophical Library, 1949.

Ruggiero, Mary. "The Executive Suite Study." Chicago: Joint Civic Committee of Italian Americans, 1970. Mimeographed.

Sacrum Polonian Millennium, VI, "The Contributions of the Poles to the Growth of Catholicism in the United States." Rome, 1959.

Sandberg, Neil C. *Ethnic Identity and Assimilation: The Polish American Community*. New York: Praeger, 1974.

Schermerhorn, Richard A. *These Our People*. Boston: D. C. Heath, 1949.

Sennett, Richard. "Genteel Backlash: Chicago, 1886." In Helena Z. Lopata, (Ed.), *Marriages and Families*. New York: Van Nostrand, 1973.

Shanas, Ethel and Gordon Streib, (Eds.). *Social Structure and the Family*. Englewood Cliffs, N.J.: Prentice-Hall, 1965.

Shaw, Clifford R. and Henry D. McKay. *Juvenile Delinquency and Urban Areas*. Chicago: University of Chicago Press, 1942.

Shriver, R. Sargent. Speech to the 9th Conference of the Polish National Congress. Quoted by Wlodzimierz Zmurkiewicz. *Protokol Dziewiatej Krajowej Konwencji Kongresu Polonii Amerykanskiej*, 1972: pp. 66–81.

Smith, William Carlson. *Americans in the Making*. New York: Appleton-Century-Crofts, 1939.

Stonequist, E. V. *The Marginal Man*. New York: Scribner's, 1937.

Stypulkowski, Zbigniew. "Polish-American Relations with Poland." Orchard Lake, Mich.: Orchard Lake Center for Polish Studies and Culture (November 1970): Monograph No. 3.

Super, Paul. *The Polish Tradition*. London: Maxlove, 1939.

Suttles, Gerald. *The Social Order of the Slum*. Chicago: University of Chicago Press, 1968.

Symmons-Symonolewicz, Konstantin. "The Polish-American Community Half a Century after *The Polish Peasant*." *The Polish Review*, 40, 3 (1966)1–7.

———. "The Polish Peasant in Europe and America: Its First Half a Century of Intellectual History (1918–1968)." *The Polish Review*, 13, 2 (Spring 1968): 14–27.

———. "Polonia Amerykanska." *Kultura* (Paris), No. 7/255-8/226 (July-August 1969):105–35.

Szawleski, Mieczyslaw. *Wychodztwo Polskie w Stanach Zjednoczonych Ameryki*. Warszawa: Zaklad-Narodowego Im. Ossolinskiego, 1924.

Szczepanski, Jan. "The Polish Intelligentsia, Past and Present." *World Politics*, 16, 3 (April 1962):406–20.

———. *Polish Society*. New York: Random House, 1970.

Taeuber, Alma F. and Karl E. Taeuber. "Recent Immigration and Studies of Ethnic Assimilation." *Demography*, 4, 2 (1967):798–808.

Taft, Donald. "Nationality and Crime." *American Journal of Sociology*, 1, 4 August 1936):724–36.

Theoharis, Athan. "The Republican Party and Yalta: Partisan Exploitation of the Polish American Concern over the Conference, 1945–1960." *Polish American Studies*, 28, 1 (Spring 1971):5–19.

Thomas, John L. "Marriage Prediction in The Polish Peasant." *American Journal of Sociology*, 55 (May 1950):573.

Thomas, William I. with Robert E. Park and Herbert A. Miller. *Old World Traits Transplanted*. Originally published in 1921. Montclair, N.J.: Patterson, Smith, 1971.

————. Comment on Blumer's Analysis in Herbert Blumer *Critiques of Research in the Social Sciences: An Appraisal of Thomas and Znaniecki's The Polish Peasant in Europe and America*. New York: Social Science Research Council, 1949.

Thomas, William I. and Florian Znaniecki. *The Polish Peasant in Europe and America*. 5 vols. Originally published in Boston: Richard G. Badger, 1918–1920. New York: Dover Publications, Inc., 1958 edition.

Thrasher, Frederick M. *The Gang: The Study of 1,313 Gangs in Chicago*. Chicago: University of Chicago Press, 1927.

Thurner, Arthur W. "Polish Americans in Chicago Politics, 1890–1920." *Polish American Studies*, 28, 1 (Spring 1971):20–42.

Tomczak, Anthony C. "The Poles in Chicago." *The Poles in America: Their Contribution to a Century of Progress*. Chicago: Polish Day Association, 1933.

Townsend, Peter. *The Family Life of Old People*. London: Routledge and Kegan Paul, 1967.

Tryfan, Barbara. "The Role of Rural Women in the Family." Warsaw, W.D.N. 365/9/72. Paper presented at the 3rd World Congress of Rural Sociology, Baton Rouge, Louisiana, 1972.

————. "Polska i Polonia: Spotkanie." *Tygodnik Kulturalny*, 1 (July 8, 1973): 1, 9; and "Polonia i Polska: Potomkowie Emigrantow" 2 (July 22, 1973):3, 11.

————. "Draft of International Comparative Studies on Social Security Needs of a Farmer's Family." Unpublished paper, Polish Academy of Sciences.

Tschan, Francis J., Harold J. Grimm, and J. Duane Squires. *Western Civilization*. Philadelphia: Lippincott, 1942.

Tullia, Sister Mary. "Polish American Sisterhoods and their Contribution to the Catholic Church in the United States." *Sacrum Poloniae Millennium: The Contribution of the Poles to the Growth of Catholicism in the United States*, 5–6, Rome (1959):255–369.

U.S. Bureau of the Census: *Prisoners in State and Federal Prisons and Reformatories: 1933*. Washington, D.C.: Government Printing Office, 1935, p. 29, Table 25.

————. *Historical Statistics of United States Colonial Times to 1957*. Washington, D.C.: Government Printing Office, 1960.

————. "Census of the Population." *Detailed Characteristics*, Final Report P.C. (1)-01. *United States Summary*. Washington, D.C.: Government Printing Office, 1970. (a)

————. *Current Population Reports*. Series P-20, November, 1969. N. 221, Characteristics of the Population by Ethnic Origin." N. 220, "Ethnic Origin and Educational Attainment." N. 226, "Fertility Variations by Ethnic Origin" (November, 1971). N. 249, "Characteristics of the Population by Ethnic Origin." Washington, D. C.: Government Printing Office, 1971, 1972.

————. Marital Status. P.C. (2)-4C, Table 2, 1970.

————. *Special Reports: National Origin and Language*. P.C. (2)-1a. Washington, D.C.: Government Printing Office, 1970. (b)

————. *Statistical Abstracts of the United States*. 93rd ed. Washington, D.C.: Government Printing Office, 1972; 94th ed. Washington, D.C.: Government Printing Office, 1973.

United States Bureau of Justice, Immigration Commission. *Immigration and Crime*. Report 26. Washington, D.C.: Government Printing Office, 1910; Report 36, 1911.

United States Department of Justice. *Annual Report to the Commissioner of Immigration and Naturalization*. Washington, D.C.: Government Printing Office, 1902–1972.

United States National Commission on Law and Enforcement. *Report on Crime and Foreign Born*. Washington, D.C.: Government Printing Office, 1935, p. 29, Table 25.

Wachtl, Karol. *Polonia w Ameryce*. Published in Philadelphia by the author, 1944.

Wagner, Stanley P. "The Polish American Vote in 1960." *Polish American Studies*, 21, 1 (January-June 1964):1–9.

Ware, Caroline. "Ethnic Communities." In Edwin R. A. Seligman (Ed.), *Encyclopedia of Social Sciences*. Vol. 11. New York: Macmillan, 1931.

Webster's Seventh New Collegiate Dictionary. Springfield, Mass.: Merriam, 1965.

Weed, Perry L. *The White Ethnic Movement and Ethnic Politics*. New York: Praeger, 1973.

Wenk, B., Michael S. M. Tomasi, and Geno Baroni (Eds.). *Pieces of a Dream: The Ethnic Worker's Crisis with America*. New York: Center for Migration Studies, 1972.

Wespiec, Jan. *Polish American Serial Publications, 1842–1966*. Published by the author in Chicago, 1968.

Whyte, William Foote. *Street Corner Society: The Social Structure of an Italian Slum*. Chicago: University of Chicago Press, 1955.

Wicislo, Aloysiu. "New Americans of Polish Descent." *Polish American Studies*, 16, 3–4 (Fall 1967):147–561.

Wirth, Louis and Eleanor H. Bernert (Eds.), *Local Community Fact Book of Chicago, 1940*. Chicago: University of Chicago Press, 1949.

Wirth, Louis. *The Ghetto*. Chicago: University of Chicago Press, 1928.

————. "Morale and Minority Groups." *The American Journal of Sociology*, 47, 3 (1942):415–33.

————. "The Problem of Minority Groups." In R. Linton (Ed.), *The Science of Man in the World Crisis*. New York: Columbia University Press, 1945.

————. "Urbanism as a Way of Life." *American Journal of Sociology*, 44 (July 1938):1–24. Reprinted in Robert Gutman and David Popenoe (Eds)., *Neighborhood, City and Metropolis*. New York: Random House, 1970.

Wood, Arthur Evans. *Hamtramck: Then and Now*. New York: Bookman Associates, 1955.

Wytrwal, Joseph A. *Poles in America*. Minneapolis: Lerner Publications, 1969. (a)

————. *Poles in American History and Tradition*. Detroit: Endurance Press, 1969. (b)

Yaffe, James. *The American Jews*. New York: Paperback Library, 1969.

Zagraniczny, Stanley J. "Some Reasons of Polish Surname Changes." *Polish American Studies*, 20, 1 (January-June 1963):12–14.

Zand, Helen Sankiewicz. "Polish Family Folkways in the United States." *Polish Americans Studies*, 13, 3-4 (July-December 1956):77–88.

———. "Institutional Folkways in the United States." *Polish American Studies*, 14, 1-2 (January-June 1957):24–32.

———. "Polish American Weddings and Christenings." *Polish American Studies*, 16, 1-2 (January-June 1959):24–33.

Zawodny, J. K. *Death in the Forest*. Notre Dame, Ind.: University of Notre Dame Press, 1962.

Zborowski, Mark and Elizabeth Herzog. *Life is with People: The Culture of the Shtetl*. New York: Schocken Books, 1952.

Zeranska, Alina. "Goals and Purpose of the Polish Scholars Convention." *Perspectives*, 1, 4 (October-December 1971):6.

Zmurkiewicz, Wlodzimierz. *Protokol Dziewiatej Krajowej Knowencji Kongresu Polonii Amerykanskiej*. No Date, no publishing information, probably 1972.

Znaniecki, Florian. *Modern Nationalities*. Urbana, Ill.: University of Illinois Press, 1952.

———. *Social Relations and Social Roles*. San Francisco: Chandler, 1965.

Zorbaugh, Harvey W. *The Gold Coast and the Slum*. Chicago: University of Chicago Press, 1929.

Zubrzycki, Jerzy. *Polish Immigrants in Britain*. The Hague: Martinus Nijhoff, 1956.

Zwiazek Narodowy Polski. *60-ta Rocznica: Pamietnik Jubileuszowy, 1880–1940*. Chicago: Dziennik Zwiazkowy, 1940.

Index